UNEQUAL TREATY 1898–1997

Hoisting the British Flag at Tai Po, 16 April 1899
(*Mary Evans Picture Library*)

UNEQUAL TREATY 1898–1997

China, Great Britain and Hong Kong's New Territories

PETER WESLEY-SMITH

HONG KONG
OXFORD UNIVERSITY PRESS
OXFORD NEW YORK MELBOURNE

Oxford University Press

Oxford London
New York Toronto Melbourne Auckland
Kuala Lumpur Singapore Hong Kong Tokyo
Delhi Bombay Calcutta Madras Karachi
Nairobi Dar es Salaam Cape Town

and associated companies in
Beirut Berlin Ibadan Mexico City Nicosia

First published in 1980
Second impression 1981
First issued in paperback 1983
Second paperback impression 1984

© *Oxford University Press 1980, 1983*

ISBN 0 19 583727 4

Printed by Liang Yu Printing Fty. Ltd.
Published by Oxford University Press, Warwick House,
Quarry Bay, Hong Kong.

to
my parents

PREFACE TO THIS EDITION

THE subject-matter of this book, first published in 1980, has been frequently and urgently discussed: the New Territories treaty is due to expire, and with it into oblivion in 1997 goes the United Kingdom's claim to much of the colony.

A major theme of the book is the importance in fact of a treaty derisively dismissed as unequal by one party and regarded as camouflage by the other. This theme has lately been confirmed: since the book was first published the existence of the treaty, aided by what seems to be diplomatic miscalculation, has produced a situation jeopardizing the prosperity and stability of the thriving city-state of Hong Kong. How much can be salvaged depends on Sino-British negotiations currently (July 1983) being held in Peking. Whatever the outcome, Hong Kong's interests have already suffered — quite, it is contended, unnecessarily and according to the wishes of neither China nor Great Britain.

In 1981 or before it was thought in Whitehall that some arrangement was needed to secure the status quo, or something like it, in Hong Kong up to and after 1997. The strategy adopted was to seek, in a highly public manner, a new agreement with China. A series of contacts culminated, in September 1982, in a visit to Peking by Mrs Margaret Thatcher. The British prime minister, perhaps wanting to negotiate from a position of strength, stated firmly and uncompromisingly that the unequal treaties were valid and must be observed until varied by mutual consent. Chinese officials were thus forced to reassert, in as visible a fashion, the traditional line that the treaties were unequal and of no binding force. Two new aspects of the debate prevented observers from regarding China's pronouncements as mere ideological rhetoric affirming recognized policy. The first was the context of specific negotiations for settlement of 'the Hong Kong problem'. The second was the choice of terms used by many Chinese leaders.

In Chapter 10 of this book it is noted that China's position on the unequal treaties relating to Hong Kong has been ambiguous: some statements suggest the treaties are legally irrelevant, while others seem to assume that the treaties are valid until China decides to abrogate them. The importance of the ambiguity is that, if the former stance is taken, 1997 means nothing, whereas the latter version guarantees great significance to the expiry of the New Territories lease.

The ambiguity has continued. On the one hand, Macao compatriot Mr Ma Man-kei, a member of the Chinese People's Political Consultative Conference, stated in July 1982 that as far as China was concerned the New Territories lease did not exist. A month earlier Huang Hua, China's foreign minister, referred again to his statement to the United Nations in 1972. The *Beijing Review*, on 23 August 1982, also repeated this announcement, affirmed that settlement of the Hong Kong question was still 'entirely within China's sovereign right', and added: 'The Chinese Government holds that the issue should be peacefully resolved in an appropriate way when conditions are ripe, and that until then the status quo should be maintained.' And the New China News Agency proclaimed the traditional line after Mrs Thatcher's visit:

Hong Kong is part of Chinese territory. The treaties concerning the Hong Kong area signed between the British government and the government of the Qing Dynasty of China in the past are unequal treaties which have never been accepted by the Chinese people. The consistent position of the government of the People's Republic of China has been that China is not bound by these unequal treaties and that the whole Hong Kong area will be recovered when conditions are ripe.

The vagueness of the time element permits Chinese pragmatism to prevail and Hong Kong's capitalist optimism to flourish. Insecurity postponed indefinitely is good for business.

Unfortunately another line has been simultaneously promulgated and seems to have achieved pre-eminence. This is that China must *recover* or *regain* sovereignty and that 1997 cannot be ignored. Huang Hua, for example, said in November 1979: 'The lease is due to expire in 1997. So there is still time.' The late Liao Chengzhi, director of the Office of Chinese Overseas Affairs, frequently spoke of China's recovery of sovereignty in 1997; Deng Xiaoping and premier Zhao Ziyang have done the same. After Mrs Thatcher's press conference in Hong Kong on 24 September 1982 the New China News Agency said that 'The Chinese Government's position on the recovery of sovereignty of the whole region of Hong Kong is unequivocal and known to all' — not the recovery of Hong Kong, but the recovery of sovereignty. Zhao Ziyang confirmed in March 1983 that Hong Kong would go back to China in 1997. Much speculation on the future has therefore taken it for granted

that 1997 marks the end of the British presence in Hong Kong; attention has accordingly been directed to the form of new administrative
arrangements. There is widespread consensus that Hong Kong will
become a 'special administrative region' under the new article 31 of the
Chinese constitution.

The implication, of course, is that China does *not* now have
sovereignty over the New Territories or Hong Kong as a whole,
that the treaties have been effective in denying the traditional
sovereign's rights over the territory. When the unequal treaty for the
lease of the New Territories expires in 1997 sovereignty reverts to
China — this is the orthodox view espoused by the British government
— and since no one wants Hong Kong Island and Kowloon without the
hinterland there is no point in observing the other two unequal treaties.
Nineteen ninety-seven is thus enormously important, for how can
sovereignty meaningfully be resumed by China while the political
status quo remains intact? The British must go, and since Hong Kong
cannot be allowed to become independent, China must reassert governmental control. However light the touch, the hand of Peking on the day-
to-day life of the territory is a prospect few citizens of Hong Kong contemplate with equanimity. Insecurity looming on the horizon is bad for
business.

There seem to be at least three reasons for the position taken by the
British government. First, the prime minister has maintained Britain's
traditional interpretation of the New Territories lease. Previously there
were sound policy grounds for insisting that full sovereignty over the
New Territories, limited only by the 99-year term, was transferred from
China in 1898. Good government in the leasehold demanded nothing
less: the Hong Kong authorities could not be fettered in their powers
over territory which became administratively absorbed into the established colony. But what was desirable in the early years is not necessarily a
suitable policy as the 99-year term draws to a close. The traditional view
has, in any event, achieved its objective of excluding China's claims to
some kind of governmental role in the New Territories, and it is unlikely
that a relaxation of that attitude would lead in modern circumstances to a
resurrection by China of former pretensions.

Secondly, the British have upheld the ordinary doctrine of international law that unequal treaties, particularly those involving the transfer
of territory, are valid. Yet, as this book attempts to demonstrate, there is
no ordinary international law doctrine on the effect and meaning of
international lease agreements; it is a respectable theory that some sort
of 'sovereignty', of an ultimate or titular or reversionary kind, remains

with the lessor state. Should the analysis presented in Chapter 10 below be adopted, the United Kingdom could accept with ease the description of China as sovereign over the New Territories. 'Effective sovereignty', exercised through the Hong Kong government, would remain with Britain, and there is no obligation in international law to surrender 'jurisdictional right' on the expiry of the original agreement if the titular sovereign has no objection. It would be less easy to abandon British claims to sovereignty over Hong Kong Island and Kowloon, but no such concession is required; it has not for many years been doubted that the ceded parts of Hong Kong cannot exist as British territory without the leasehold, and Chinese demands for the return of the New Territories in 1997 or after must be met by the return of Hong Kong and Kowloon as well.

Thus, it is suggested, Her Majesty's Government has been hoist with its own petard: by past policies which in present conditions are inimical to at least the short-term interests of Hong Kong, and by a particular version of international law framed in accordance with those policies yet not the irresistible conclusion of legal reasoning. There is probably a third reason, however, why the crucial step of initiating discussions on the future of Hong Kong was taken by Britain. This reason depends on an erroneous analysis of municipal constitutional law.

On the assumption that both Britain and China could permit the status quo in Hong Kong to remain after 1997, an apparent problem is the legal basis for the Hong Kong government's continued jurisdiction in the New Territories. Authority is presently contained in the order in council of 20 October 1898 (Appendix 2). It seems to have been assumed that the order in council is the *sine qua non* of jurisdiction, and because that document refers to 'the term described in the said Convention' (that is, 99 years), the Hong Kong government cannot legally govern in the New Territories after 1997. Amendment of the order in council, or enactment of an Act of Parliament or perhaps of a local ordinance, would be required to provide legality to governmental acts once the treaty has expired (see pp.189–90 below), and these are thought politically unwise. A new treaty is the best solution.

The defect in this reasoning is that it is not the order in council which grants the authority but the original act which the order in council simply recognizes and confirms. The order in council makes everything look 'legal' and regular, but it is not indispensable. The only requirement is that the executive branch of government clearly indicate what decision it has come to regarding the exercise of jurisdiction. If Her Majesty's Government has determined to stay on in the New Territories after the end of the lease the fact will be obvious, and that fact must be accepted by the courts as a conclusive declaration of the true extent of the government's jurisdiction. This is called the 'act of state' doctrine. It is founded on the inconvenience of two separate branches of government proceeding on different lines regarding important matters of state; the executive branch has the responsibility, facilities and knowledge for making political decisions in the field of foreign relations, and the judicial branch, lacking those attributes, defers to their judgment. When there is a precise statement in an order in council the courts will rely on it, but if there is no order in council or other document emanating from the crown (which would be the case if Her Majesty's Government ignored 1997 and stayed on without new legislation) the courts will look to the actual practice of the government as a binding determination of the issue. (See note 36, p. 236, below.)

The soundness of this version of the constitutional position is suggested in note 4, p. 240, below, but I formerly doubted whether the courts would be persuaded or that Her Majesty's Government could risk reliance upon a theory for which there is no indisputably direct judicial authority. If the crown's legal advisers ever seriously considered it, they apparently thought it too uncertain to form the basis of policy.

Whatever it was that led Mrs Thatcher to discuss the future of Hong Kong when she visited Peking in 1982, her decision to do so greatly accelerated the dissipation of confidence among Hong Kong citizens. It seems probable, also, that subsequent Chinese pronouncements were primarily a reaction to her insistence on the legality of the Convention of Peking. China now asserts the desire to recover sovereignty — yet, on the argument presented in this book, China is already residual sovereign over the New Territories, and if the unequal treaties are void *ab initio* China is *de jure* sovereign over the whole of Hong Kong. It was in China's interests, and Hong Kong's, to maintain that hard-line interpretation of international law; conditions will not necessarily be ripe in 1997. China and the United Kingdom could have come to a *sotto voce* understanding that sovereignty lies with China, that the status quo in Hong Kong is a relic of the past, and that at some unspecified future date the actual administration (not the sovereignty) will revert to the residual sovereign. (Portugal and China have come to a similar agreement in respect of Macao.) Instead, it seems that all vestiges of British rule in Hong Kong will disappear in 1997, and Hong Kong's prosperity and stability in the face of such a massive alteration of the constitution are already in doubt.

It is difficult not to conclude that legal considerations have here played a vital role in determining international political conduct. The history of the treaty reveals that this is often the case — and quite properly so, for law has a rightful role in international relations. It would be unfortunate, however, if legalistic ideas were permitted, quite inappropriately, to control the future.

School of Law,   PETER WESLEY-SMITH
University of Hong Kong,
July 1983.

PREFACE

GREAT BRITAIN'S colony of Hong Kong was acquired from China, under the terms of cession, in two stages: the island, by the 1842 Treaty of Nanking, and British Kowloon and Stonecutters Island in 1860. The 1898 Convention of Peking, which is the subject of this book, leased to Great Britain for ninety-nine years that part of Kwangtung province now known as the New Territories. It purported to add to the colony of Hong Kong a land area of over 350 square miles, including numerous islands, and a large body of sea.

The acquisition and occupation of the New Territories is a topic largely ignored by scholars. Little is known of the background to the convention, the details of its negotiation, the problems which it circumvented, and the problems which it created. There has been no thorough analysis of the legal meaning of the treaty document. This is a surprising lapse, for the importance of the New Territories convention cannot be doubted: it secured and maintains the land upon which the post-war industrial economy of Hong Kong depends, and, if the leasehold territory is to revert to China upon expiry of the convention in 1997, Hong Kong as a British colony cannot be expected to survive.

The convention has in fact proved of more significance than the lack of scholarly interest indicates. Dismissed by China as an unequal treaty, it nevertheless seems to remain in force; apparently regarded by Great Britain in 1898 as a convenient legal disguise for the virtual annexation of Hong Kong's hinterland for ninety-nine years, it has nevertheless been the source of some delicate diplomatic manoeuvring in this century. It is not a mere scrap of paper, for some legal meaning can be given to it and both China and Great Britain have attempted to follow more or less consistent, if differing, interpretations. Practical policy has been influenced by the wording of the lease document.

The historian of Hong Kong and of Sino-British relations therefore cannot ignore the Convention of Peking and its consequences. The diplomat, the local official, and the businessman concerned about the future of Hong Kong would also be wise to consult this treaty and its history. Indeed, the convention's terms are still occasionally referred to in modern-day Hong Kong by those who seek to rely on them in defiance of government policy. In 1975, for example, an applicant for habeas corpus argued before the Full Court that, as an immigrant from China, she had a right under the convention to land near the Walled City of Kowloon. And the Heung Yee Kuk, the official body advising the Hong Kong government on New Territories affairs, has repeatedly justified its long campaign for administrative autonomy in the leasehold by citing the terms of the convention.

This book is an attempt to fill the gap in the literature by providing a history of the Convention of Peking.

The basic source material is almost exclusively in the English language, consisting primarily of records of the British and Hong Kong governments. I do not pretend any knowledge of the equivalent Chinese documents and I do not attempt a 'Chinese version' of the events and issues which form the subject-matter of the work. No doubt Chinese records would throw additional light on the acquisition and occupation of the New Territories, and a complementary study by a sinologist would be of great interest and value. Not possessing the skills for such a task, I have relied on official correspondence between Hong Kong and Downing Street, between Peking and the Foreign Office, and between government offices in London. Despatches and telegrams from the secretary of state to the governor are not available in Hong Kong, apparently having been lost or destroyed during the Japanese occupation. When reference is made, therefore, to such correspondence I have assumed that the draft contained in the CO129 series is accurate. By colonial service regulations from about 1898 all official correspondence from the colonies was numbered sequentially every year except for that marked 'confidential' or 'secret'. I include these numbers unless they are, for some reason, missing. Where there are page numbers in a volume (which sometimes occurs in Colonial Office files of later years and often in the Foreign Office files) these are given. The CO129 series is bound in thick volumes with despatches and other correspondence in chronological order until 1927, when material is arranged according to subject-matter in files placed in boxes. The file number is given in brackets after the series and volume numbers. Inter-office correspondence is sometimes signed by and addressed to particular individuals; where it is not I have referred merely to the offices of origin and destination.

Hong Kong place-names have been rendered according to *A Gazetteer of Place Names in Hong Kong, Kowloon and the New Territories* (published by the Hong Kong government in 1960), and Chinese words have usually been transliterated in the manner adopted by the source-material. The spelling of 'Hong Kong', as two separate words, follows official practice laid down in 1926, and has been used even in quotations where the two words have been run together. I have discovered no reference, other than the *Gazetteer*, to the official naming of the 'New Territories': the name appears to have developed in popular usage from the original expression 'New Territory' and been gradually adopted by the Hong Kong government. It is used here as a singular. Although the expression 'extension', referring to the leasehold, begs the question of the status of the New Territories, I have employed it frequently.

This book is a revised version of a thesis presented to the University of Hong Kong in 1976. Its conception, gestation, and birth have occupied a good many years, and inevitably I have become indebted to many people whose encouragement and assistance it is a pleasure to acknowledge. The topic, or something similar, was first suggested by Professor Wang Gungwu, and my proposal to explore it at Hong Kong university was accepted and promoted by the supervisor of the thesis, Professor Dafydd Evans. Dr Alan Birch was of great assistance in many ways, and Dr James Hayes, one of the few these days to carry on the colonial tradition of combining government service with scholarship, contributed much to the book by his own writings, his infectious enthusiasm, and his willingness to answer enquiries. The community of scholars interested in Hong Kong's past is small but generous in its aid to the novice: my sincere thanks go to all its members who have offered advice. These include, in addition to those mentioned above, Dr Eugene Anderson, Mr Geoffrey Bonsall, the late Professor Maurice Freedman, Mr James Lethbridge, Mr Howard Nelson, Dr Margaret Ng, the Revd Carl Smith, and Professor Len Young. Responsibility for the final version is all mine, of course.

I must also thank the various librarians and keepers of records in England, Scotland, and Hong Kong, without whose guidance no scholarship of this nature would be possible. Permission for the reproduction of written material was kindly granted by Lord Salisbury, the Public Record Office in London, and the Merchant Company Education Board, Edinburgh. The illustrations were kindly provided by the Peninsula Group, the City Museum and Art Gallery, and the Government Information Services, Hong Kong. I gratefully acknowledge these sources. It is a pleasure to acknowledge, also, the fine typing of the final draft by Miss Barbara Chui and the labours of Mr H. K. Kwan of the Cartographic Unit, University of Hong Kong, in the preparation of the maps.

School of Law,   PETER WESLEY-SMITH
University of Hong Kong,
June 1979

CONTENTS

MAPS

PLATES

ABBREVIATIONS

Adm	Admiralty (papers)
AC	Appeal Cases
ALR	Australian Law Reports
All ER	All England Law Reports
Cab	Cabinet (papers)
CMC	Chinese Maritime Customs
CTA	Chinese Telegraph Administration
CO	Colonial Office (papers)
CP	Confidential Print Eastern No 66 (see bibliography)
DLR	Dominion Law Reports
Ex D	Exchequer Division
FO	Foreign Office (papers)
HKLJ	Hong Kong Law Journal
HKLR	Hong Kong Law Reports
HMG	Her/His Majesty's Government
IMC	(Chinese) Imperial Maritime Customs
KB	King's Bench
LHK	Laws of Hong Kong
LJ PC	Law Journal (Privy Council)
LR	Law Reports
PC	Privy Council
QB	Queen's Bench
tel.	telegram
WO	War Office (papers)

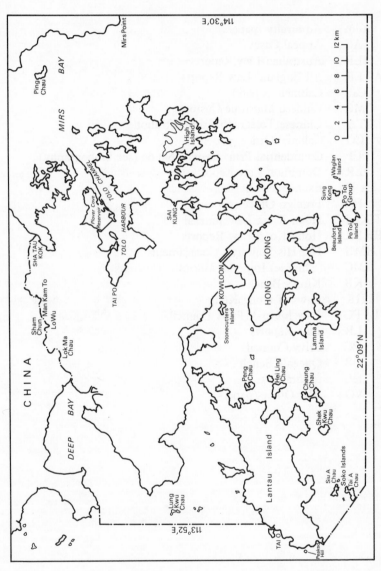

1. THE COLONY OF HONG KONG, SHOWING THE NEW TERRITORIES BOUNDARIES

PROLOGUE

ON 9 June 1898, the Convention Respecting an Extension of the Hong Kong Territory was signed in Peking.[1] Representing Her Britannic Majesty Queen Victoria was Sir Claude MacDonald, the British minister to Peking whose full title read 'Envoy Extraordinary and Minister Plenipotentiary to the Emperor of China and to the King of Corea'. On the Emperor of China's behalf the convention was signed by the famous diplomat Li Hung-chang and by His Excellency Hsu Ying-kuei, president of the board of civil office. The copies of the treaty to be signed had been made out by the British legation, Chinese officials having agreed that foreign paper was superior.[2]

Two days later, on 11 June 1898, the Kuang-hsu emperor issued an edict which began the abortive 'hundred days of reform'.

Ratifications of the convention were exchanged in London on 6 August 1898. The Chinese envoy in London, Sir Lo Feng-lu, took with him a Chinese version of the protocol of ratification. This aroused the suspicions of the Foreign Office officials who had gathered for the ceremony, but the Prime Minister, Lord Salisbury, wished to be civil and he agreed to take the document on trust. A clerk in the Foreign Office minuted: 'I had it verified afterwards by one of our qualified translators, on leave, who pronounced it to be what it purported to be, so *that* was all right.'[3]

Thus was ratified the Convention of Peking which leased to Great Britain, for ninety-nine years, part of San On county of Kwangtung. That area became known as the New Territories, and it was absorbed into the colony of Hong Kong by Her Majesty's order in council of 20 October 1898.[4] The lease agreement expires with the day of 30 June 1997.

The terms of the convention are set out below.[5] First, the preamble: 'Whereas it has for many years past been recognized that an extension of Hong Kong territory is necessary for the proper defence and protection of the Colony.' There follows the basic agreement as to the territory leased:

It has now been agreed between the Governments of Great Britain and China that the limits of British territory shall be enlarged under lease to the extent indicated generally on the annexed map. The exact boundaries shall be hereafter fixed when proper surveys have been made by officials appointed by the two Governments. The term of this lease shall be ninety-nine years.

The clause which aroused intense opposition amongst British merchants in Hong Kong and which has been the most problematic part of the convention is the Walled City clause:

It is at the same time agreed that within the city of Kowloon the Chinese officials now stationed there shall continue to exercise jurisdiction except so far as may be inconsistent with the military requirements for the defence of Hong Kong. Within the remainder of the newly-leased territory Great Britain shall have sole jurisdiction. Chinese officials and people shall be allowed as heretofore to use the road from Kowloon to Hsinan.

This is succeeded by two clauses referring to Chinese shipping and proposals for a railway:

It is further agreed that the existing landing-place near Kowloon city shall be reserved for the convenience of Chinese men-of-war, merchant and passenger vessels, which may come and go and lie there at their pleasure; and for the convenience of movement of the officials and people within the city.

When hereafter China constructs a railway to the boundary of the Kowloon territory under British control, arrangements shall be discussed.

Another provision which has been of considerable significance since 1898, especially in relation to the Hong Kong government's land policy in the New Territories, is the non-expropriation clause: 'It is further understood that there will be no expropriation or expulsion of the inhabitants of the district included within the extension, and that if land is required for public offices, fortifications, or the like official purposes, it shall be bought at a fair price.' The convention's substantive terms conclude with clauses dealing with extradition and Chinese war ships:

If cases of extradition of criminals occur, they shall be dealt with in accordance with the existing Treaties between Great Britain and China and the Hong Kong Regulations.

The area leased to Great Britain as shown on the annexed map, includes the waters of Mirs Bay and Deep Bay, but it is agreed that Chinese vessels of war, whether neutral or otherwise, shall retain the right to use those waters.

It is not at all clear what this convention means; indeed, one of the main purposes of this book is to clarify the meaning of the convention through a study of its negotiation and the subsequent practice of the parties. One thing seems obvious from the outset, however: the Convention of Peking 1898 is an unequal treaty. It is unequal in the sense that only one party appears to derive any benefit from it. There is no *quid pro quo* which China receives as compensation for her temporary loss of territory. In addition, as will be seen, the contracting parties were not in a position of equal bargaining power when the convention was drawn up.

The concept of the unequal treaty originated with western writers of international law treatises, but their modern successors no longer consider the concept worthy of detailed discussion. Chinese scholars and diplomats, however, seeking theoretical legitimacy for China's attempts early in this century to throw off the shackles of nineteenth-century European, American, and Japanese imperialism, have frequently resorted to it.[6] Treaties which are not concluded on the basis of mutual recognition of the equality and sovereignty of the contracting states, and which do not contain the crucial element of reciprocity where rights are conferred and obligations imposed, have frequently been condemned by both the Nationalist régime and the government of the People's Republic. Such treaties offend against notions of justice and of patriotism. Just as an agreement between individuals is not a true contract if made under duress or without consideration, so, it is said, states should not be bound by treaties founded on inequality.

China has long regarded the Convention of Peking 1898 as an unequal treaty. Claims for the return of all leased territories in China were made at the official level in 1919 and frequently thereafter.[7] In 1963 the *People's Daily* newspaper included the convention in a list of unequal treaties,[8] and this was confirmed by the Chinese delegation at the United Nations in 1972.[9]

But classification of a treaty as unequal does not necessarily mean it is invalid. As will be discussed towards the end of this work,[10] international law does not yet clearly recognize even that such a classification has any legal consequences at all. In assessing this question it is useful to consider the practice of the various Chinese governments which have 'administered' the New Territories convention; that is, we must examine the history of the lease agreement.

As we proceed to do so, several things should be borne in mind.

First, the negotiations for the Convention of Peking 1898 can only be understood in the context of colonial insecurity in Hong Kong and of growing imperialist rivalry in China. Secondly, China herself underwent dramatic changes almost immediately after the convention was signed; she soon began her long march to international equality, but it was a slow process interrupted by internal dissension, invasion, and civil war. Radical changes in the nature of government naturally affected Chinese attitudes towards the territory, both ceded and leased, at Hong Kong. Thirdly, international law is at best an unsatisfactory thing for those who wish to see the conduct of states determined by clear rules. The heady demands of politics are often more compelling on the international stage than the sober requirements of rules of law. Nevertheless, all states have a long-term interest in maintaining the international legal system, and it is unlikely that future Chinese practice in relation to the Convention of Peking 1898 will significantly change from now until 1997.

Finally, by way of prologue, it is instructive to take a brief look at some of the key personalities who play so prominent a part in the narrative. This is not to suggest that individuals are of special significance in the explanation of historical events, though it does deny that they are of no importance at all.

The evolution of British policy in regard to the acquisition of the New Territories involved three major parties: the Foreign Office, the Colonial Office, and the government and merchants of Hong Kong. At the head of the Foreign Office during 1898 and before was the Prime Minister, Lord Salisbury, a man of 'imperturbability and well-known capacity for inaction'[11] (or, as Sir Richard Burton is alleged to have said, 'he was, in reality, a very nice old lady'[12]). The best short portrait of the marquess is by Barbara Tuchman, who sees him as the ultimate patrician, an aristocrat passionate in his defence of aristocratic values. 'The pressures of democracy encircled, but had not yet closed in around, the figure whom Lord Curzon described as "that strange, powerful, inscrutable, brilliant, obstructive deadweight at the top".'[13] But by 1898 Salisbury was a man mature in years and in poor health; when he recuperated abroad his place at the Foreign Office was taken by his nephew, Arthur Balfour, who, like the colonial secretary, Joseph Chamberlain, advocated vigorous action.[14] The most recent full-length study of Balfour sees him as 'consistently practical and occasionally ruthless' when dealing with imperial problems, though he approved of territorial expansion only where clear and precise British interests were served.[15]

The Colonial Office was dominated by Chamberlain's forceful personality.[16] Appointed secretary of state for the colonies in June 1895, he was an ex-Radical businessman from Birmingham who saw imperial and colonial affairs in terms of business principles. 'I regard many of our colonies as being in the condition of undeveloped estates, and estates which never can be developed without imperial assistance.'[17] Known to the public as 'Pushful Joe' the 'Minister for Empire',[18] he became much more interested in Chinese affairs after the Russian occupation of Port Arthur,[19] and he was a convinced advocate of the acquisition of the New Territories. He eventually resigned in frustration when his more grandiose ambitions were thwarted. But he and Sir Henry Blake in Hong Kong presided over the first crucial years of the territory's development.

The permanent under-secretary in 1898 was Edward Wingfield, who played a much more active role than the parliamentary under-secretary, the Earl of Selborne. The most influential officers, however, were the assistant under-secretaries, Frederick Graham, Charles P. Lucas, and H. Bertram Cox (legal assistant under-secretary). Beneath them in the Eastern Department were the clerks under the control of the chief clerk, Sir W. A. Baillie Hamilton. These men, whose minutes on despatches often proposed policies eventually adopted, were G. W. Johnson, T. C. Macnaghten, and A. Fiddian. Among their successors, the most capable and those whose names most frequently appear in this study were R. E. Stubbs (later appointed governor of Hong Kong), A. E. Collins, A. H. Harding, G. V. Fiddes, J. R. W. Robinson, H. R. Cowell, and G. E. J. Gent.

The most important minutes in the first few years were often written by Lucas, an experienced administrator and distinguished scholar of whom Lord Elgin thought most highly among the assistant under-secretaries.[20] But he was considered diffident in his relations with others and was twice refused elevation to the post of permanent under-secretary.[21] As a friend and former teacher of Stewart Lockhart, the colonial secretary in Hong Kong, he was perhaps particularly interested in the New Territories.

The general policy of the Colonial Office, at least in respect of its attitude regarding retention of the New Territories, was remarkably little affected by changes of government in Whitehall. One reason is that the background and experience of Colonial Office personnel were very similar. The staff officers[22] in 1898 were mostly Oxford graduates who had taken classics;[23] three of them had been called to the bar, and only Graham had no reference to his school or university in the *Colonial Office List* (though he had in fact graduated from the University of Edinburgh). Among the clerks, two were first class scholars at Oxford, one was from Trinity College, Cambridge, and Hamilton had at least attended Harrow! In terms of class and education, therefore, there was considerable uniformity in the department, and this was inevitably reflected in the main lines of policy. There was only one startling exception: the secretary of state himself. 'Chamberlain's methods, derived from his Birmingham business and political background, were anathemas to men conditioned in a different school of life. The colonial secretary, in Hamilton's words, "was not born, bred or educated in the way which alone secures the necessary tact and behaviour of a real gentleman".'[24] But there is no evidence in the records relating to the New Territories that Chamberlain's lowly social status was of any significance in the orderly evolution of policy.

Apart from the men in the Colonial Office, the story of Great Britain's acquisition and occupation of the New Territories is woven around four personalities. Sir Claude MacDonald negotiated the lease for Britain; Sir Henry Blake was governor of Hong Kong when the territory was taken over; James H. Stewart Lockhart was the official most influential in determining policy and establishing the administrative system; and the viceroy of Canton, T'an Chung-lin, became the Chinese scapegoat following the disturbances of April 1899. Each of these men deserves more extensive discussion than will be possible in the narrative.

Chronologically, MacDonald's contribution was the first. He began his career as an army officer, serving mainly in Egypt. From 1887 he held various posts in Africa and was appointed consul in the Cameroons in 1891. Five years later he was sent to Peking as the British minister where he negotiated the crucial concessions of 1898. He was later transferred to Tokyo.

Han Su-yin refers to him as 'Gunboat' MacDonald: a diplomat who was more at home with militaristic methods and policies.[25] Indeed, he once suggested the hanging of an official, preferably a viceroy, as the only way to stop piracy on the West River.[26] Cyril Pearl's description of MacDonald in 1897 is based largely on the papers of *The Times* correspondent G. E. Morrison:

Sir Claude, an elongated man of forty-five, with a long nose, reproachful eyes, and long, lovingly waxed thin moustache, had fought in Egypt and the Sudan, been Consul-General at Zanzibar, Commissioner of the Oil Rivers Protectorate, and gunnery instructor at Hong Kong. It was a training which, though varied, was perhaps inadequate for one of the most important and difficult posts in the diplomatic service. 'Everyone denounced the appointment,' Morrison wrote. 'He was attacked as imperfectly educated ... weak, flippant and garrulous ... the type of military officer rolled out a mile at a time and then lopped off in six foot lengths.' Morrison himself would have endorsed this popular estimate, though he wrote, in a manuscript intended for publication: 'such were the criticisms levelled against a British officer of singular charm of manner who had not sought the post thrust on him by Lord Salisbury, and who quickly inspired to an unusual degree the confidence of his famous chief.' A note in Morrison's diary was less flattering: 'When Admiral Bruce asked Sir Thomas Sanderson ... the secret of MacDonald, "Don't you know?" said Sanderson, "I thought everyone knew that Salisbury believes MacDonald has in his possession evidence to prove that Lord Salisbury and Jack the Ripper are the same person." '[27]

Other comments by Morrison are equally unflattering: he had 'as little wisdom as judgment' and was 'garrulous, inaccurate, long-winded'; another British diplomat 'spoke "with much frankness" of Sir Claude MacDonald's "ignorance and incapacity" '.[28] And Balfour once noted: 'MacDonald is an official of many merits: but among them intelligent comprehension of the policy of his chiefs is not to be counted.'[29] In general, however, HMG probably concurred with Chirol's judgment of his work in the early part of 1898: MacDonald 'has had an up-hill battle to fight, and he has fought it admirably'.[30] He certainly achieved his immediate objectives, though a little more homework on the New Territories lease might have produced a document less open to misinterpretation and less pregnant with future difficulties.

Like MacDonald, Sir Henry Arthur Blake had had no experience of dealing with the Chinese when he first arrived in Hong Kong on 25 November 1898, and old China hands were quick to ridicule his mistakes. He had begun his career with the Royal Irish Constabulary and in 1882 was one of the five special resident magistrates selected to devise and carry out measures for the pacification of a large portion of Ireland. His first governorship was in the Bahamas in 1884, moving to Newfoundland three years later, Jamaica in 1888, and then Hong Kong. He was awarded what many considered the top post in the colonial civil service when he became governor of Ceylon in 1903.[31]

Very little has been written about Blake,[32] though his role in preventing the entry into Hong Kong of Chinese revolutionaries is well known.[33] The Colonial Office obviously held him in high regard, but mention was sometimes made of his financial incapacity.[34] Some sort of picture of him emerges from the account below of his role in New Territories affairs: he was clearly a competent governor and a humane man.

He was fed up with Hong Kong, it seems, in August 1901, when he asked Chamberlain for the governorship of Ceylon. The Hong Kong climate was too severe and the place too remote and small: he abhorred the 'deprivation of movement to which an active man has been all his life accustomed'[35] and was glad to leave in 1903. 'I have finished my experiment with John Chinaman.'[36] Many of the colonials in Hong Kong were glad to see him go, for his policy was too 'pro-Chinese' for them. The *China Mail* commented:

> His Excellency's intercourse with the Chinese has been more intimate than we are accustomed to see in a British colony. It is easy to see the pure motives that have prompted his policy and to give him all the credit that his sentiments inspire without approving of that policy; and when we say that a very large section of the European community has been alienated by His Excellency's policy we merely chronicle a well-known fact.[37]

James Haldane Stewart Lockhart, on the other hand, advocated firmness when dealing with the Chinese, though he was well-liked by the Chinese community. He was undoubtedly a capable administrator: the officer administering the government, Major-General Wilsone Black, recommended him for the post of resident in the New Territories (though prematurely, for it was never available), and sent along a petition to that effect from various inhabitants of San On.[38] Black wrote that 'he has an open mind, and is by no means wanting in decision of character', while the petition noted:

> Mr Lockhart has been for a long time in the Civil Service of Hong Kong, and has earned a great reputation for rectitude and ability. In addition, he has a thorough knowledge and acquaintance of the manners, customs, and feelings of the natives, and if he were appointed by the British Government to administer the newly acquired territory and to rule over us, we feel sure that we could derive thereby the greatest benefit and blessing.[39]

Stewart Lockhart's career has recently been summarized elsewhere,[40] and it is sufficient here to sketch only the outlines of his work in China. An ardent Scotsman and competent sinologist, he had been appointed to Hong Kong under Sir Hercules Robinson's cadet scheme in 1879.[41] By 1891 he was a member of both the Executive and Legislative Councils and from 1895 was both registrar-general and colonial secretary.[42] Although he was then second only to the governor in the civil service hierarchy in Hong Kong, a military man was appointed acting governor in 1896, much to Stewart Lockhart's disappointment.[43] Chamberlain was unable to hold out hope of promotion to another colony[44] and, despite the accolades he received for his work in establishing administrative control of the New Territories, it was not until 1901 that he was appointed civil commissioner of Weihaiwei.[45] He stayed there until 1921, his talents largely wasted in that semi-colonial backwater of northern China.

Lethbridge calls him 'a scholar-administrator in the Confucian sense', drawn towards traditional and conservative forces in Chinese society, and 'a colonial official from a particular stratum of British society, who believed in his mission to govern, but to govern well'.[46] Referred to by a French journalist as 'a charming, plump, and unctuous man',[47] he was one of the few officials to escape the censure of G. E. Morrison's pen (Morrison wrote to him: 'Without flattery I say it, that I think you are the ideal administrator').[48] Supported by Lucas in the Colonial Office,[49] he nevertheless failed to win the promotion to a governorship that he desired and probably deserved.

While the acquisition of the New Territories gave Stewart Lockhart the opportunity to enhance his reputation, it largely destroyed the career of T'an Chung-lin, viceroy of Kwangtung and Kwangsi. He had replaced Li Han-chang in Canton in April 1895, and was himself to be replaced five years later by Li's younger brother, Li Hung-chang. Soon after assuming office he was confronted with 'the Canton plot' and had been ordered to Peking to apprehend the chief instigators:[50] Great Britain's refusal to extradite Sun Yat-sen no doubt prompted bitter feelings by T'an towards the British. He was an old man,[51] infirm and nearly blind;[52] an imperial censor was reported to have stated in 1897 that he had lapsed into senility and was 'the easy prey of intriguing and corrupt persons'.[53] Two attempts to retire had been denied by Peking,[54] and it was said that he had been so averse to the lease of the New Territories that he wanted to resign rather than have any connexion with the transfer.[55] There is no doubt that he was a thorough-going conservative: he refused to carry out the new policies of the reform movement in 1898, and it may be that only the re-assertion of her authority by the empress dowager in September saved him from dismissal.[56] When he did eventually lose his job, his successor contended that he was the cause of all the trouble which had occurred in 1899.[57] This was an unfair accusation, but T'an Chung-lin proved as helpless in his attempts to control the British as his more famous colleagues had been during the opium-war.

1

THE PRESSURE FOR COLONIAL EXPANSION

The Campaign in Hong Kong

THE Convention of Peking 1898 represented the successful conclusion of a well-organized campaign by commercial interests in Hong Kong. It was Catchik Paul Chater, the prominent Armenian businessman who helped to found the Hong Kong Land Company and other successful business concerns, who fired the first salvo in 1894, though the proposal to acquire additional land near Hong Kong was officially raised many years earlier.

In 1863, only three years after the cession of British Kowloon and Stonecutters Island, a battery on the northern shore of Lei Yue Mun Pass (which guarded the eastern approach to the harbour) was suggested, and the Colonial Office was informed that the secretary of state for war considered it very desirable to secure a military reserve there. In 1884, Major-General Sargent urged upon the War Office the acquisition of all Kowloon peninsula, extending to the northern hills, and of several islands; but the governor, Sir George Bowen, opposed the scheme. Sargent's successor, General Cameron, put forward a similar view, only to see it rejected by the Committee of Imperial Defence in 1886. The various authorities in London appointed to consider colonial defences at this time thought Hong Kong the most liable to attack of all important British coaling stations, yet the fact that the north shore of the harbour was Chinese territory did not seem to them any reason for concern.[1]

But in March 1890 the governor, Sir William des Voeux, reported a rumour that the Chinese government proposed to fortify Tolo Harbour and build batteries overlooking the colony, and the colonial secretary, Lord Knutsford, suggested that HMG's minister at Peking be instructed to make enquiries and convey to the Tsungli Yamen (the Chinese office for foreign affairs) that the British government deprecated any action which would be regarded as unfriendly. Sir John Walsham telegraphed from Peking that China was not seriously entertaining the project; however, he noted that were a railway built between Kowloon and Canton it was not improbable that the Kowloon station would be fortified.[2] The Colonial Office and the War Office were alarmed at this prospect, especially as some Chinese entrepreneurs, probably from Hong Kong, carried out preliminary surveys for such a railway in 1890.[3] There is no evidence to suggest that the fear of Chinese intentions regarding territory contiguous to Hong Kong influenced opinion towards negotiating an extension of the colony's boundaries, but it must have been a factor in the minds of some.

The Sino-Japanese war, however, provided the initial impetus to Sir William Robinson's campaign for the acquisition of additional territory; the Chinese government and empire, said the governor, were 'rotten weeds upon which to rely' and would be a source of considerable danger to Hong Kong if they survived the war: 'I desire to point out most forcibly that an adjustment and an extension of the boundaries of this Colony is peremptorily necessary and that the position of Hong Kong, the "Gibraltar of the East" is by no means so secure as it is supposed to be.' Robinson's despatch of 9 November 1894, in which the matter of extension was firmly brought to the attention of the Colonial Office for the first time, deserves quoting at some length:

This may be a startling assertion but in support of it I would call Your Lordship's attention to the following facts: Gap Rock and Waglan Islands, on each of which is a most valuable lighthouse, belong to China. The approaches to Lei Yue Mun Pass and Green Island, the Eastern and Western entrances to the Harbour, belong to China. The fortifications at Lei Yue Mun are dominated by Chinese territory. The whole of the Northern side of Hong Kong Harbour, with the exception of 2 miles in the centre, belongs to China. Kowloon City is Chinese, and within the Lei Yue Mun Pass which is only a mile or so from Victoria are Chinese waters.

China itself or a Foreign Power at war with China or England could by disembarking troops at the north of the Canton River, or outside Lei Yue Mun Pass in Mirs Bay and descending upon the Peninsula of Kowloon, not only take our fortifications at a disadvantage but easily shell Victoria from Chinese territory as well as cut off the entire food supply of the Colony.

The boundaries of Hong Kong should in my opinion be extended to Mirs Bay and from thence to the Bay [Deep Bay] on the Canton River on the opposite side or at the very least should extend from the entrance to the Lei Yue Mun Pass on the North-East to the top of the hills behind Kowloon tending in a Westerly direction so as to include Kap Shui Mun Pass at the entrance to the Canton River so as to make the approaches to this valuable possession of Her Majesty absolutely safe. Further and in any case Gap Rock, Waglan Island, Lamma Island and all islands within three miles of Hong Kong should be ceded to Great Britain.

Without some such arrangement and re-adjustment of boundaries, the position of this Colony in the event of any war must I think be very insecure from a defensive point of view.

If therefore it is the intention of Her Majesty's Government to intervene at any time between China and Japan I venture to hope that these crude recommendations will be carefully considered. It may not be a magnanimous policy to suggest but they should be forcibly urged upon China before she has had time to recover from the defeat that has been inflicted upon her.[4]

Enclosed with the despatch was a memorandum requested by Robinson from G. Digby Barker, the officer commanding the troops; it emphasized the disadvantages resulting from Chinese military command of the harbour, and alluded to two other factors considered of great importance as affecting the health and welfare of both troops and Hong Kong residents. These were the necessity of obtaining more land for cemeteries, and the presence of Kowloon City.

Robinson's second despatch was forwarded a few days later, this time enclosing C. P. Chater's letter. Enlargement of the colony's boundaries, he said, should be sought 'not for the sake of territory, but wholly and simply for the sake of its more efficient administration and protection'. Chater wrote:

If the possession of portions of the opposite mainland and complete control of the water approaches of the Colony would be absolutely essential to the security of the Colony against any European foe, how much more necessary against China herself.

China is now at her lowest ebb, but 50 years hence, possibly 20 years hence, judging from the progress Japan has made, China will probably be a powerful nation fully armed and with the skill and knowledge that will enable her to make use of her vast natural strength. If then the boundaries of Hong Kong are no more extensive than they are now, where will we be with a Chinese fleet in Kowloon Bay, and the hills and the islands close around, in Chinese possession. At their mercy any moment. . . .

The same arguments that prevailed in 1860 must prevail now. We want now only what we wanted then: what is essential to the safety of the Colony. What was enough then, has become from the changes in weapons and the alterations in modes of warfare wholly insufficient now, and we must have more. . . .

There can be no better time than the present. And the time is now or never. However great the success of the Japanese today, however tremendous the disgrace and humiliation of China, that Empire is too intrinsically strong, too full of resources, too patient and persevering ever to remain for any length of time in her present condition. This Japanese war will be followed by a tremendous upheaval, and China twenty years hence, will be another China from today. If anything is to be done, it is to be done now.[5]

Chater also referred to purely civil advantages from such an extension of territory: the evils of Kowloon City would vanish, the Chinese customs (and 'its cruisers, revenue stations, revenue farmers, detectives and spies') would be done away with, the colony's population would have room to spread, industries would have space and water supplies, and Hong Kong might become independent of Canton as regards cattle, poultry, and vegetables.

Robinson had arranged considerable support for his views on the subject[6] but there was, originally, little response from the Colonial Office. Lucas commented that it would be an immoral proceeding and a fatal mistake for Great Britain to take some Chinese territory at that time, while Edward Wingfield wanted to remind the governor that his advice on military and foreign policy matters was outside the scope of his commission. The Foreign Office simply acknowledged Robinson's despatches 'in schedule'. He did not, however, lose enthusiasm for the project, and when he returned to England in March 1898 he consented to a Reuter interview in which he again urged the acquisition of territory.[7]

Major-General Digby Barker, as president of a joint naval and military committee, had in April 1894 considered the defence capabilities of Hong Kong; and the Colonial Defence Committee was made aware of the problems associated with the close proximity of Chinese territory. The acquisition of territory to remedy the defects of Hong Kong's defences was not, however, specifically mentioned,[8] but in May 1895 the joint committee issued a 'Report on the Boundaries of the Colony of Hong Kong' in which extension was recommended.[9] The report was immediately approved by the secretary of state for war and by the lords commissioners of the Admiralty, though the Colonial Office was still doubtful.[10] Pressure for the 'rectification' of boundaries was, however, increasing, for the armed services departments and Hong Kong residents were becoming alarmed at the developing competition in the East between Russia, Germany, France, and England, and the newly arrived and potentially hostile Japan. Chater wrote another letter to Robinson, this time on behalf of his fellow unofficial members of the Legislative Council, and reiterated his belief that extension was absolutely essential to the continued existence of the colony. Very favourable circumstances then existed, he claimed, for obtaining 'the trifling extension of territory so urgently needed': all the other powers were adjusting, favourably to themselves, their rights in China, and the recent 'Ku-t'ien massacre' provided an admirable excuse for Great Britain to do likewise. In this incident, one Englishman and a dozen English women and children were put to death by a Chinese mob; Chater's unsuccessful attempt to exploit it for territorial aggrandizement anticipated German and French demands following similar attacks on missionaries in 1897 and 1898.[11]

Sir William Robinson added a further and pressing reason a month later, namely a Chinese scheme for the construction of a new town only 400 yards north of the Kowloon boundary. It was rumoured that the town was to be built near Sham Shui Po, and the *China Mail* commented that this was

... the pestiferous haunt of the worst type of Kwangtung criminals, the refuge of thieves, robbers, and murderers fleeing from Hong Kong's minions of the law. We have no personal knowledge of Sodom and Gomorrah, but judging from what we learn of these places in scriptural narrative and what we know from actual experience of Kowloon City and Chinese Shamshuipo, we should say that if there were points in favour of either of the couples, Sodom and Gomorrah held the odds.[12]

This imaginative prose failed to move the officials at Downing Street, but when the War Office remarked soon afterwards that the time seemed opportune for colonial expansion at Hong Kong, as the Foreign Office was then allocating the Sino-Burmese border,[13] the Colonial Office was spurred into activity. Lord Salisbury, however, could not give immediate satisfaction. Francis Bertie, undersecretary at the Foreign Office, wrote that 'as soon as the questions relating to the Burmah Convention are settled, a communication will be addressed to the Chinese Government inquiring whether they will grant a perpetual lease to this country of the territory required on payment of its value'.[14]

Although the matter now lay in the Prime Minister's hands it was not allowed to be forgotten. Robinson even persuaded Sir Claude MacDonald to agree with a plan to extradite Sun Yat-sen from Hong Kong in return for a cession of territory behind Kowloon. Salisbury and Chamberlain vetoed the idea.[15] Moreover, other negotiations with China were still pending and Lucas minuted in August 1896: 'this is very unsatisfactory'.[16] Then the Colonial Defence Committee memorandum no. 85M appeared. The committee had previously noted the growth of Japanese naval and military power, the great increase of Russian naval power in the Far East, and the large garrison then being maintained by France in Indo-China, and had commented that the defence of Hong Kong required various measures on Chinese territory which might be taken as a *casus belli* by China.[17] In the new document the committee urged the government to proceed with negotiations for the extension, and pointed to the growth of Kowloon City as one of several elements which had materially changed during the previous ten years.[18] The Admiralty and the War Office concurred and the Colonial Office again tried to prompt Salisbury to action, but he was emphatic that other negotiations had to be completed first. Further, he was doubtful whether China would agree to anything beyond a non-alienation pact of territory in the neighbourhood of Hong Kong.[19]

Thus, during 1897, 'the Hong Kong question' was put aside, even the War Office temporarily losing interest. It was not to be revived until the arrival of an opportune time, when German, Russian, and French demands upon China forced Salisbury to reconsider the British position. Opinion in the colony, however, continued to favour immediate action,[20] and following a further despatch from the governor, Sir William Robinson, the British minister at Peking was requested to consider the possibility of approaching the Chinese government through the viceroy at Canton.[21] At last the Foreign Office was doing something about the yearned-for extension, and Chamberlain minuted: 'I am watching this matter'.[22]

Though the determination of Hong Kong residents to have the colony's boundaries extended is undoubted, the real motive remains unclear. The defence argument was sound, as events later showed, though the building of fortifications did not in fact follow subsequent granting of the lease and the security of the island was therefore only marginally improved. The Navy League's assertion that the islands south of Hong Kong were necessary because the south side of the island was unfortified was convincingly refuted by MacDonald: 'The same result would happen even if we possessed the said islands unless we fortified them, in which case we had better fortify the South side of the Island of Hong Kong.'[23] Those reasons so frequently articulated, such as the need for cemetery space, a rifle range and an exercise ground for troops, were so trivial that a more obscure motive may be sought. MacDonald indicated one when he pointed out that:

Many of the Colonists have been for years past buying up ground on the Kowloon promontory and adjacent islands as a speculation on the chance of our getting what we are now more or less on the point of getting; and a thundering good thing they will make out of it. Several of these land speculators are prominent members of the local Navy League.[24]

Nevertheless, there were genuine advantages of a more public nature to be achieved. Among these were British control of the Walled City of Kowloon, amelioration of the so-called 'customs blockade' in the waters surrounding the colony, and security for the lighthouse at Gap Rock. These matters loomed large in the negotiations for the lease of the New Territories, and their existence was particularly important in the build-up of pressure for colonial expansion.

The Walled City of Kowloon

No longer walled, and never in any normal sense a city, the Walled City was once a fort and administrative centre to the immediate north-west of a Chinese town called Kau Lung Gai (Kowloon City).[25] This town, which might be considered in some respects the suburbs of the Walled City, was frequently condemned during the 1890s as an obstacle to law and order in British Kowloon, and worthy Hong Kong citizens seeking 'rectification' of the colony's boundaries constantly referred to it as an evil that should be overcome. One of its main industries was gambling, and the tables were a favourite haunt of many prominent Hong Kong residents. Special steam-launches, operating well into the night, provided a free passenger service for gamblers from the colony, and complimentary coffee and cigars were handed out en route. Representations by Hong Kong authorities to the viceroy at Canton and to Peking eventually succeeded in having the houses closed down, but it is doubtful whether their doors remained closed for long.[26]

Thus Major-General Digby Barker in November 1894 noted the demoralizing influence of the gambling dens, and pointed out the potential danger to Hong Kong of the large junk traffic associated with the city and of the periodic visits by the Chinese fleet to its own waters in Kowloon Bay.[27] The Colonial Defence Committee reported in 1896 the necessity of maintaining a considerable military force on the mainland to protect the defence works and stores there from pilferage by Kowloon City residents.[28] No specific complaints were at this time made by Hong Kong against the fort, but the town was seen as a source of dangerous criminal activity.

To the imperial Chinese government the fort was an important centre of civil and military administration for that part of San On county: the deputy magistrate, with limited powers of arrest and detention, and certain army officers resided there.[29] Indeed the British in Hong Kong found the 'Kowloon mandarin'[30] a useful fellow, for he was in constant correspondence with the colonial police.[31] The military commander had a garrison of more than 500 men and was said, though probably erroneously, to exercise jurisdiction over the 200 civilians who lived within the walls.[32]

In 1898 the Walled City was about a quarter of a mile from the sea shore, though reclamation has now placed it much further inland. Its fortified stone wall, built from 1843 to 1847 with an average height of 13 feet and an average width at the top of 15 feet, was almost the shape of a parallelogram and enclosed an area of 6½ acres. Inside were several public buildings, a well-regarded school, two temples, and a number of quite substantial residences along the wide streets. By contrast the suburbs contained numerous factories, shops and gambling dens in its narrow, evil-smelling roadways. Whereas the Walled City, being an administrative town, eschewed commercial activities, the suburban area was used as a market centre by surrounding villages. Other landmarks were a defence wall rising to the top of the hill overlooking the city, an ambitious stone pier where the road from the city met the sea, and a rest-house for travellers.[33]

In 1841 at least one Chinese fort on Kowloon peninsula was destroyed by British forces,[34] and it is probable that construction of the Kowloon City wall was begun soon after as a specific response to the British presence in Hong Kong.[35] After the cession of Kowloon in 1860 the Walled City and its suburbs obviously grew in population and importance, attracting those elements which honest, God-fearing British traders found execrable. These two factors made Sino-British conflict almost inevitable: Hong Kong residents distrusted Chinese officials and objected strenuously to the very existence of the fort and the suburban area, whereas to the Chinese in Peking the Walled City was a government installation, a visible symbol of imperial control constructed for the very purpose of discouraging British interference in the region. China could not be expected to surrender it without fierce opposition.

The Hong Kong Blockade

If the Walled City of Kowloon represented irreconcilable differences between China and mercantile interests in Hong Kong, the vexed question of smuggling was an even more potent source of friction. China relied on the various taxes and duties levied on traded goods generally, but especially opium, for much of her imperial and local revenue, and she had a commensurate interest in the proper collection of such fees. But Hong Kong's openness as a free port contiguous to Kwangtung favoured the development of smuggling operations so large and well-organized that Chinese revenue inevitably suffered, and all schemes designed to protect that revenue inevitably endangered the freedom of Hong Kong trade.

The Chinese attempted to prevent the avoidance of duty on goods by establishing what apoplectic local traders termed 'the Hong Kong blockade'.[36] This originally consisted of two parts: in 1868 the Canton viceroy opened stations near Kowloon for the collection of *likin*, a form of inland trade tax, on Chinese-carried opium, and in 1871 the Hoppo (superintendent of customs at Canton) established depots where the treaty tariff duty on opium could be paid. These depots, at Kap Shui Mun, Cheung Chau, Fat Tau Chau (Junk Island), and just outside the Walled City of Kowloon, were all in the area later to become the New Territories.

The basic factual situation causing the conflict between Hong Kong and China was well stated by the governor, Sir Arthur Kennedy, in 1875:

> It is beyond doubt that a not inconsiderable number of Chinese junk owners are in the habit of consulting their individual interests by violating Chinese customs laws, and making this Colony the basis of smuggling operations, for which its geographical position affords every facility, and the profits, it is to be presumed, exceed the loss and risk, or the practice would not be continued....
> The Chinese Customs Officers and Revenue Collectors, with a knowledge of these facts, lose no opportunity of seizing and confiscating every Chinese junk for which they can find a pretext, and the characterless class of persons employed as subordinates in that service makes it too probable

that honest and innocent traders are often grievously harassed and plundered. I entertain no doubt that such is the case.[37]

But no entirely satisfactory solution was found. After an opium agreement in 1886 the Chinese Imperial Maritime Customs largely displaced the Canton authorities for the collection of *likin* and native customs duties from Chinese vessels trading with Hong Kong, and was permitted to open an unofficial office in Victoria staffed by a commissioner of British nationality. This arrangement went some way towards mollifying local criticism but, despite a new ordinance in 1887 designed to control the opium trade, the opium farmer's notorious illicit export of the drug into China was not prevented and the 'blockade' was vigorously maintained. The main problem was that the Hong Kong government relied heavily on the opium farming system as a source of revenue. Opium was too valuable a commodity and the colonial exchequer too impoverished to permit scrupulous regard by Hong Kong of international obligation. As Sir Henry Blake admitted at the close of the nineteenth century: 'The opium question presents very considerable difficulties as the loss to the Colony will be serious, and effective prevention may have the effect of transferring the opium trade from Hong Kong to Macao.'[38]

The Convention of Peking 1898 extended the northern boundary of the colony from just over two miles to sixty miles, thereby facilitating smuggling; enclosed within the enlarged boundaries were several Chinese customs stations. Yet China was as desperate as ever to protect her revenue, and Hong Kong was no less anxious to be rid of the panoply of customs depots, cruisers, and detectives. The differing interests of Chinese empire and British colony remained irreconcilable.

Gap Rock

The tiny island of Gap Rock was to become the subject of much discussion by the British at the time of the New Territories lease. It is situated about thirty miles south-south-west of Hong Kong, well-placed for a lighthouse station. The Admiralty having found it unsuitable for target practice, the chamber of commerce in Hong Kong proposed in 1886 that a lighthouse be constructed there. It had in fact been added to the lighting programme of the Chinese maritime customs nearly twenty years before, but it was given low priority as it would primarily have served the port which detracted most from the tonnage dues collected by the customs and available for coastal lights work. The governor, Sir William des Voeux, made it a pet scheme, and in January 1888 he suggested that a lighthouse be built on Gap Rock at the expense of the colony; he even inquired whether China would cede or lease the island to Great Britain. But later in the year he concluded an agreement with the Chinese customs whereby Gap Rock remained Chinese territory although a lighthouse was to be constructed and maintained there by the Hong Kong government. The foundation stone was laid on 1 September 1890 and the light began operating on 1 April 1892.[39]

The lighthouse was a great boon to Hong Kong shipping and was in use until dismantled in 1941.[40] It was feared, however, that its continued operation could not be guaranteed while it remained under Chinese control, and des Voeux's original idea was revived during the 1890s. The most important recommendation for the acquisition of Gap Rock came from the joint naval and military committee on defence, which suggested its inclusion within re-adjusted colonial boundaries in 1895. This was considered desirable 'from a naval and military point of view'.[41]

The defence argument, although in this particular case it was not to prevail, was crucial, and is one aspect of the larger question which had occupied the minds of colonial administrators since the early 1880s. A series of international incidents in the Far East pro-moted investment in Hong Kong's defences, with the construction of fortifications, the reservation of Stonecutters Island for military use, an increase in the size of the garrison, and a re-organization of the Volunteers. Concern was already being expressed about the designs of rival imperialist powers in China and the consequent vulnerability of Hong Kong.

Foreign Imperialism in China, 1894–1898

At the same time as residents of Hong Kong were urging the exten-sion of colonial boundaries, the traditional supremacy of Great Brit-ain in China was being threatened by Russia, Germany, France, and Japan.[42] Each power sought, by diplomatic means, to increase its influence with the decrepit Manchu leadership in China and to reserve for itself an increasing share in China's commerce. This was a development which could only be viewed with increasing alarm by Great Britain, and it demanded some subtle diplomatic ma-noeuvring in response. Imperialist rivalry intensified, allowing the powers to refine the cynical art of imperialist diplomacy: choose convenient friends, oppose convenient enemies; secure concessions by a false front of friendship with China, secure concessions by threat and *fait accompli*.

The historian seeking to describe the 'background' to the granting of the 1898 leaseholds need not go further back than the Sino-Japanese war of 1894–5. Japan's victory demonstrated, with profound results, the military weakness of China and confirmed the successful modernization of Japan, while setting in train events of crucial importance in the pattern of shifting alliances and intrigues. When the peace treaty was signed at Shimonoseki on 17 April 1895, China lost a portion of her territory for the first time since the cession of Kowloon,[43] and it was the Japanese claim to the Liaotung peninsula which brought Russia, Germany, and France to the supposed defence of China in the so-called 'triple intervention'. The indemnity loans gave imperialism another tactic as the major powers consolidated their Far Eastern policies: Russia coming down from the north and seeking control over Peking, France seeking her sphere of influence from the south by way of Indo-China, Germany determined to find a territorial foothold on the coast, Japan concerned about Korea and intent on extending her influence generally. To Great Britain it was primarily a matter of preserving her predominance in the Chinese market and framing a suitable policy to prevent, if possible, dismemberment of the Chinese empire.

Russia's principal objective was the control of an ice-free port as terminus for the trans-Siberian railway. She was therefore suspicious of Japanese intentions in Korea and had initiated the triple intervention in 1895. Russian ministers immediately realized the value of providing China with finance: the first indemnity loan, arranged by Russia with French assistance, indicated the beginning of Russian preponderance in China, for it suggested a Chinese political and financial dependence upon Russia secured in the loan agreement. The Russo-Chinese Bank was established in December 1895 and the Chinese Eastern Railway Company in 1896, and by the secret Li-Lobanov treaty of 1896 Russia was allowed the use of Chinese ports in the event of war and the right to construct the trans-Siberian across Manchuria. Although a Russo-Japanese condominium was established in Korea in 1896, Russia's attempt to gain greater control the next year with a view to securing a fair-weather port was rebuffed by an Anglo-Japanese show of strength.

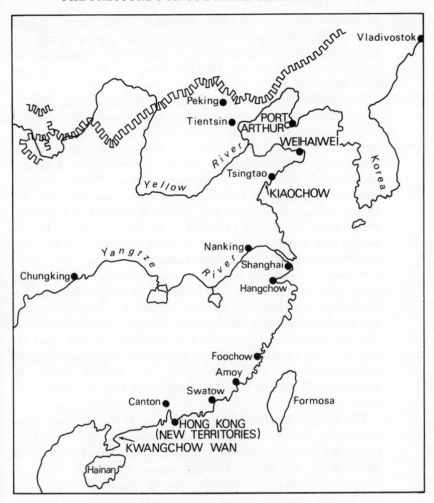

2. LEASED TERRITORIES IN CHINA, 1898

In apparent alliance with China, therefore, Russia looked forward to 'peaceful penetration' of the north with rights to a port and terminus. But when grand secretary Li Hung-chang refused further railway concessions in May 1897 the Russians were ready to take more direct action.

During this period Russia also had a firm alliance with France, and French interests were pursued just as vigorously. France sought, particularly, railway and mining privileges in the south. By agreement in June 1895 France won various concessions which consolidated and justified her position in South-East Asia and threatened more directly the interests of Great Britain. Further concessions in June 1897 included not only mining rights but the right to connect Indo-China and Yunnan by rail, while a Belgian-French syndicate secured a contract for the Peking-Hankow line. It seemed that Russian and French railways were about to tap Chinese resources from both north and south.

Meanwhile Germany was just as anxious to find a naval and commercial base in China. The achievement of this end required Russian support and thus German support for Russia, a policy also prompted by Germany's desire to divert Russian attention from Europe and to weaken the Franco-Russian alliance. And Japan, in actual occupation of Port Arthur and Weihaiwei until the indemnities were paid, maintained her general policy of increasing influence in China in competition with the continental powers.

Throughout the 1890s Great Britain was on the defensive. Misjudging the consequences of the triple intervention in 1895 and the advantages to be gained from joining, she was thenceforth isolated diplomatically and without a suitable answer to the dual alliance of France and Russia. As the predominant power in China she stood to lose most from the growing ambitions of the others. The issue facing Lord Salisbury and his ministers was 'to preserve in an age of competition what we had gained in an age of monopoly'.[44] Britain's interests were primarily commercial, and the defence of trade largely dictated British reactions to the policies of the other powers. For this reason Salisbury had no wish to discourage Russia's construction of the trans-Siberian, which would bring commercial advantages to all; for the same reason he opposed and sought to neutralize the French schemes. The plans of Germany and Japan were less likely to conflict with British interests. At the same time the Prime Minister bore in mind imperial considerations, and was content to see Russia engaged in the East to the detriment of her activities in India and Europe.

Salisbury's main objective was maintenance of China's territorial integrity. His government competed for the second and third indemnity loans and for mining and railway concessions in China, but attempted to discourage the alienation of territory. This policy was to become obsolete in 1898 when Great Britain was forced to join the scramble for territory after Germany's acquisition of Kiaochow.

Soon after Shimonoseki, Germany had approached the Manchu government for a suitable port as 'compensation' for her part in the triple intervention. Although the demand was rejected, German officials investigated various sites and favoured Kiaochow in Shantung. Russia, having wintered her fleet there, had a prior claim and China had considered fortifying it; its opening as a treaty port had been suggested to forestall any individual power taking control over it. But Germany was impatient: as early as 3 January 1897, Chamberlain wrote to Salisbury that the Germans 'appear to be really resolved to take some territory in sovereignty. We shall have no choice but to do the same'.[45] The murder on 1 November 1897 of two German missionaries in Shantung gave a pretext—the same pretext that had been futilely urged by Chater, after the Ku-t'ien massacre, for the extension of Hong Kong—for the German occupation of Kiaochow. Apparent blessing from the Tsar had been obtained and Salisbury, anxious to maintain Anglo-German friendship, indicated that Great Britain had no objection.

Russia originally protested and Sir Claude MacDonald resisted the more extreme of the German demands. But in return for German acceptance of her own plans in the Far East, Russia acquiesced, while Salisbury initially considered that if they stayed where they were they would act as an irritant to Russia but would not hurt Great Britain. And when Russian vessels entered Port Arthur, the German occupation of Kiaochow became less important. China was helpless; early in January 1898 she agreed to a ninety-nine year lease of Kiaochow, and the treaty was signed on 6 March.

Three points should be noted in connexion with this demand for territory. First, the extension of Hong Kong's boundaries had been suggested as a possible response. O'Conor, formerly in Peking, was opposed, on the grounds that extension could be achieved at any time and that it would not counter German and Russian action in the north. While Salisbury reiterated his preference for a Chinese promise of non-alienation, he generally agreed that advantage might be taken of the German action by insisting on such an extension of Hong Kong as was required for the safety of the colony.[46]

Secondly, a German crown council, in fear of military action by China, had noted that Chinese sovereign rights were to be protected wherever possible in Kiaochow and suggested, therefore, a lease rather than a cession.[47] This was the decisive precedent which set the pattern for the terms of subsequent territorial concessions on the China coast. Lastly, the German occupation of Kiaochow precipitated Russia's abandonment of her policy of peaceful penetration.

During the loan negotiations MacDonald suggested that Talienwan be given treaty port status. But China had no wish to annoy the Russians, whose intentions were revealed in February 1898 by an offer not to oppose a British loan to China in return for a lease of Port Arthur and Talienwan. Although this was rejected, the Bank of England provided the capital for a loan and Russia took over the Liaotung peninsula early in March.

On 23 November 1897 Count Muraviev, the Russian foreign minister, suggested occupation of Port Arthur and Talienwan; in mid-December Russian ships entered the port and refused to leave, while protests were made about British ships there. Salisbury complied with the Russian request for withdrawal. The demand for the lease was made on 3 March and China was again in no position to refuse, for none of the other powers would support her. The agreement was signed on 27 March, being a lease for twenty-five years. It is probable that the British insistence upon equal trading rights in any Chinese port under foreign control, and her initial doubts about the Russian initiative, combined with the German precedent to prevent actual annexation of Port Arthur.[48]

The eventual choice of a British counterpoise for Russian and German acquisitions in the north was Weihaiwei, which China had offered in February 1898 and which was still occupied by Japan. In pursuing his policy of discouraging the alienation of Chinese territory, Lord Salisbury considered that discussion of the lease to Great Britain of Weihaiwei was premature unless the action of other powers materially altered the position.[49] But the Russian request for Port Arthur and Talienwan did just that, and on 7 March a secret telegram instructed MacDonald to insist on a first refusal of Weihaiwei if the Russians were successful.[50] The British minister thought it futile to try to stop Russian pretensions to Manchuria and possibly Mongolia, and recommended that 'our line is to make best possible terms with Russia for not opposing lease of Port Arthur and Talienwan and in public utterance to diminish its importance'.[51] He noted that Germany intended to occupy Weihaiwei if Japan retired, and that any annexation by Britain would be followed by the French annexation of Hainan. Cabinet was initially prepared to accept his advice, raising no objection to the Russian action if Moscow did not protest against the construction by an Anglo-Chinese company of a commercial railway from Hankow to Peking; further, to avoid the cost of occupation, a non-alienation agreement regarding Weihaiwei was preferred to a lease.[52] But on 22 March MacDonald was told:

> Please inform Yamen that Her Majesty's Government concur with them in thinking that they ought not to lease Port Arthur to Russia. We see no objection to their leasing Talienwan as a commercial Harbour.
>
> If this course is pursued Her Majesty's Government would engage not to occupy Weihaiwei when Japanese leave it, but we must insist on pledge that it is not to be alienated or leased to any other European Power.[53]

The next day Balfour stressed that even though the Yamen refused to co-operate with Russian policy Great Britain should not be precluded from occupying Weihaiwei,[54] and on the 25th, following China's accession to Russian minister Giers' demands, he instructed MacDonald to obtain the first refusal of Weihaiwei after Japanese departure on terms similar to those granted for Port Arthur. The British fleet was then on its way from Hong Kong to the Gulf of Pechili. MacDonald, however, was unenthusiastic: he thought Weihaiwei too costly to occupy, a lease would incur Russian and German hostility and unite the two powers, and Chusan was equally an answer to the Russian presence on the Liaotung peninsula.[55] Balfour remained convinced that the taking of Weihaiwei was the only possible make-weight to that presence, and noted that Chusan should be kept in reserve in the event of undue concessions to France in the south.[56] Thus Weihaiwei was occupied by the British on 24 May and the convention was signed on 1 July.[57]

Weihaiwei was also acquired under the terms of a *lease*. Although the acquisition was specifically a counterpoise to German and Russian influence in the north, it represented the active abandonment of Salisbury's traditional policy regarding the alienation of Chinese territory and it must therefore have materially reconciled him to the acquisition of further territory near Hong Kong. China, on the other hand, was alarmed lest the lease of Weihaiwei be followed by further British demands for territory, though MacDonald was unable to offer the Tsungli Yamen any solace. He pointed out that 'they must distinctly understand that [their wishes] were in no way conditional to the lease', and he could give them no hope that territorial concessions given to other powers would not be followed by similar demands on the part of Great Britain.[58]

After Weihaiwei, foreign activity in China consisted primarily of 'concession hunting', taking the form of a scramble for rights to construct railways and operate mines. But France was determined to share in the general acquisition of *territory*, and in January 1898 had sent ships to Kwangchow Wan, only 210 miles south-west of Hong Kong. As a result of her continuing alliance with Russia, France had not opposed Russian demands on China and was rewarded by Russian support for her own demands presented on 7 March. These included an agreement for the non-alienation of Kwangtung and Kwangsi and a ninety-nine year lease of the bay at Kwangchow. Great Britain's response was, in part, to seek the lease of the New Territories.

2

NEGOTIATING THE TREATY

Preliminary Discussions

WELL-ORGANIZED opinion at Hong Kong provided the rationale, and imperialist rivalry in China provided the opportunity, for the longed-for extension of Hong Kong boundaries. This was to be achieved in mid-1898.

Even before 1897 was out an oblique approach had been suggested through the Chinese authorities at Canton for the lease of battery sites to secure the harbour.[1] When the Foreign Office asked MacDonald to comment on the viceroy's apparent willingness to entertain the proposal, he took it as

... indicating that the provincial authorities expect that the territorial acquisitions of other powers in China will be followed up by similar demands on our part, and that they hope by offering a small concession at once to prevent Great Britain from making larger demands of territory which they know that the Central Government would be unable to resist; and there would not, in my opinion, be any advantage in approaching the Chinese Government in the manner suggested. . . .[2]

MacDonald was busy at the time with negotiations for the third indemnity loan and had been instructed to wait until their conclusion before raising directly the question of an extension at Hong Kong.[3]

Unhappily for the colonial lobby these negotiations were rather protracted, for the Tsungli Yamen was faced with trying to reconcile both British and Russian eagerness to float the loan. The Yamen's attempts to find the money without bringing upon themselves a series of British and Russian demands for compensation delayed the negotiations and hence the occasion when MacDonald could press for territory behind Kowloon. Further, Cabinet was unwilling to make it a demand consequent upon China's acceptance of the Russian offer; instead it wanted the feared distortion of the balance of power to be corrected by freedom of inland navigation, the grant of territory required for the Burmese railway, and the occupation of Chusan.[4]

On 17 March 1898 MacDonald reported that France had demanded from the Tsungli Yamen an assurance, similar to that given to Great Britain over the Yangtze region, regarding the four southern provinces of Yunnan, Kweichow, Kwangtung, and Kwangsi. He suggested a protest to Paris, for if the French demand was conceded any plans for the future extension of Hong Kong would be frustrated.[5] The Cabinet's initial response was to raise no objection so long as Chinese engagements to France extended no further than the Yangtze Valley promises to the British and were made equally to Britain as far as Kweichow and Kwangtung were concerned; furthermore, Nanning should be opened as a treaty port, France should obtain no preferential rights in the southern provinces, and China should cede the Kowloon peninsula to Great Britain.[6] The view in Whitehall, therefore, was clearly that the extension of Hong Kong had to be achieved before concessions to the French made it impossible.

Lest the demand for it interfere with the granting of other claims, Balfour was prepared to accept a promise that the Kowloon peninsula should be ceded 'if at any time we require it', but on the same day it was reported that France had pressed for a cession of Kwangchow Wan.[7] 'You should warn Chinese Government', MacDonald was instructed by telegram, 'that it will expose them to similar demands by ourselves and other powers if it is conceded',[8] and he told the Chinese ministers that if a coaling station were given to France compensation would be required at Kowloon. The extension demand, he said, had been delayed in order to avoid exposing China to demands from other powers.[9] The British policy-makers decided that they were not in a good position to remonstrate in either Paris or Peking: pressure on their part would lead to suspicions that they meditated excessive demands. But they considered they had a fair claim to insist on whatever concessions were necessary for the safety of Hong Kong.[10] Then, on 23 March, the following significant instructions were cabled:

> Language implying that Kowloon would be regarded by us as an adequate *quid pro quo* for a French coaling station had better be avoided. It stands on a wholly different footing, and though we are not anxious for its immediate possession we could never allow it to be interfered with by other powers, and under certain circumstances might have to insist on immediate possession.[11]

Five days later MacDonald was told to demand assurances to Great Britain relating to Kwangtung, Yunnan, and Kweichow similar to those desired by France but with Kowloon being excluded from the agreement; if the French claimed a coaling station he was to demand the promise of Kowloon whenever Great Britain asked for it.[12] MacDonald was not anxious to hasten the dismemberment of China, and thought it in the British interest to ask for no more than was sufficient to strengthen the defences of Hong Kong, even if France obtained the lease of Kwangchow Wan.[13] The Foreign Office agreed but warned him not to let China know that if territory was conceded to France, England would make no further demands.[14]

Serious negotiations for the New Territories lease now began. Already, on 2 April, MacDonald had informed the Chinese ministers that Hong Kong was not satisfied with its present limits and wanted them extended. At the next meeting, according to the record book of interviews, he stated that he thought HMG would probably be content with that concession:

> As he had already mentioned more than once, this was a step which the Government of the Colony had long urged on his attentions as necessary for defensive purposes. He might mention that some time ago the Viceroy of Canton had expressed the opinion to Her Majesty's Consul that a small extension could be easily arranged.
> Li c.t. [grand secretary Li Hung-chang] thought so too, if the extension required was not of large extent.[15]

The Tsungli Yamen was willing, on submission to France, to lease the Kowloon promontory, but earnestly begged that parliament be informed that the concession was the result of previous negotiations between the viceroy and HM's consul at Canton, and not as a *quid pro quo* for the French lease.[16] Balfour's response was to promise no new territorial demands in return for several further concessions, including a non-alienation agreement as to Kwangtung and Yunnan and the immediate conclusion of negotiations for giving Great Britain all the land required for the military defence of Hong Kong. '[W]e want no more than is necessary from a military point of view but all this we must have whether it includes the town of Kowloon or not.'[17]

At a meeting on 16 April the ministers saw no objection to an extension of Hong Kong's boundaries but wanted to see a map showing what was required before deciding. MacDonald, however, sought to 'let the local people arrange the details as at [Kwang-chow Wan]'. Li rejected that and MacDonald hoped to get a map from Hong Kong soon.[18] On 25 April he reported to London that, on the previous day, he had strongly pressed five demands upon the Yamen, including an extension of Hong Kong to a line from Mirs Bay to Deep Bay. He personally considered that the amount of territory asked for was excessive, and noted that the great difficulty was Kowloon City.[19] He was poorly supplied with documents, being able to refer only to Robinson's 1894 correspondence with the Colonial Office and having only Major-General Digby Barker's 1894 chart of the territory.[20] The Colonial Defence Committee memorandum no. 139M had not yet been prepared, and the committee's recommendation in that document of a smaller leased or ceded area and a sphere of influence was not considered.[21] Balfour replied to MacDonald that 'the town [Kowloon City] is necessary to us however much we limit our demands, and we are advised that all the territory South of line from Deep Bay to Mirs Bay and including the waters of those two Bays and adjacent islands is desirable for purpose of military and naval defence'.[22] But the Chinese government strongly objected to such a large extension and would not consider a cession: only a lease could be hoped for.[23]

It was agreed at a meeting on 28 April that MacDonald should draw up a draft agreement. Li Hung-chang wanted all land required by HMG to be paid for (which MacDonald accepted on the spot), retention of the right to use the Kowloon City landing-place, Kowloon City to remain under Chinese control, and an understanding that the Hong Kong government vigorously police its newly acquired waters and take steps to prevent smuggling; MacDonald recommended that these requests be granted.[24] Balfour allowed him to accept 'a lease without fixed period terminable only by mutual agreement' and suggested the phrase which was eventually adopted covering Kowloon City. Two days later he authorized a ninety-nine year term. On 4 May MacDonald telegraphed the exact boundaries and, although notified immediately of entire approval of his arrangements, the Colonial Office and the Admiralty both urged alteration to include the whole waters of Deep Bay and Mirs Bay and to reduce the western extension.[25]

Further consideration of the boundaries, Kowloon City, and customs jurisdiction was to complicate matters enormously and require several more interviews. But at least the notion of a territorial concession at Hong Kong had been raised and accepted in principle by the Chinese government. Subsequent negotiations were concerned only with the details of the agreement. These were nevertheless crucial to the convention's impact and its consequences.

The Boundaries

Sir William Robinson, it will be recalled, advocated in 1894 a northern boundary extending from Mirs Bay to Deep Bay and including Kap Shui Mun Pass at the entrance to the Canton River, and the cession of Gap Rock and all islands within three miles of Hong Kong. Major-General Digby Barker provided a sketch-map of the area he considered necessary which, apart from its southern extension to embrace Gap Rock, is similar to maps presently in use. The report of the joint naval and military committee on defence in 1895 was more explicit, providing exact lines of latitude and longitude, though the proposed acquisition was surprisingly modest, omitting Lantau, Gap Rock, Deep Bay and Mirs Bay and extending no further to the north than the Kowloon hills. Nevertheless until 1898 this was the only definite scheme to which the British government could and did refer.

But when MacDonald was authorized to begin negotiations with the Yamen he seems not to have possessed a copy of the joint committee's report. On the basis, therefore, of the 1894 correspondence and the sketch-map he demonstrated to the Chinese ministers the strategical necessity of the line from Mirs Bay to Deep Bay and of the islands to the south and west, and it was only against great opposition from the Yamen that he succeeded in gaining their agreement to the lease of such a large area. He was not, of course, relying solely on colonial demands, and was instructed to acquire all land necessary for the defence of Hong Kong—yet this was to include the islands and the waters of the two bays.[26]

May of 1898 was a crucial month in the working out of the final territorial demand to be negotiated with China. The Colonial Defence Committee had originally merely endorsed the joint committee's proposal, but in April 1898, in response to a Foreign Office request, it reconsidered the extent of territory deemed necessary for defence purposes. Although it confirmed the 1895 limits, an extra zone was added to counteract the French acquisition of Kwangchow Wan: the committee adopted the controversial idea of a sphere of influence with the right of eventual occupation, and the boundaries it recommended were similar to those eventually chosen for the leased area itself. The absolute administration of the territory within this larger boundary was not considered essential for the protection of Hong Kong, and land commanding the channels giving access to Canton was excluded from the projected exercise of 'sovereign rights' lest it provide an excuse for retaliatory action by other powers with regard to treaty ports.[27] Thus it was now admitted that, in the light of French activities to the south of Hong Kong, the joint committee's scheme was too modest for the achievement of its purpose. On 5 May the Admiralty transmitted to the Colonial Office, Foreign Office, and War Office a letter from Admiral Sir Alexander Buller, former commander-in-chief on the China station, in which he recommended the acquisition of all islands in the vicinity of Hong Kong, Mirs Bay, and Deep Bay, and Kowloon peninsula within a boundary line drawn between the two bays. Lucas minuted that Mirs Bay was essential.[28] Six days later the Admiralty expressed concern that MacDonald had not included all of Mirs Bay, and hoped that his naming of 114° 26′E as the eastern boundary was a clerical error; 'such an arrangement would leave part of Mirs Bay under Chinese authority with very serious strategical disadvantages and ... it is extremely important to include the whole of Mirs Bay in the area proposed to be leased by Great Britain and the consequent extension of the eastern boundary to the meridian of 114° 30′E'.[29] The western boundary gave control over the Canton River, but neither the Admiralty nor the Colonial Office was prepared to alter it on that ground. Lucas raised the question of Deep Bay, affecting both northern and eastern boundaries, and suggested that it be put before the Foreign Office. Meanwhile Buller amplified his previous remarks about German interest in Mirs Bay.[30]

These representations were the result of MacDonald's initial negotiations, communicated by the Foreign Office to interested departments at the beginning of May. The secretary of state for the colonies, Joseph Chamberlain, had desired that there be no distinction between leased territory and sphere of influence, and all the territory which the Colonial Defence Committee had wanted as the latter was to be acquired under lease. But the northern and western parts of Mirs Bay and the northern part of Deep Bay were excluded, and this seemed to Lucas rather an important omission; approval had, however, already been telegraphed by the Foreign

Office. MacDonald confirmed that the eastern boundary was 114° 26'E. The other boundaries were 113° 47'E longitude on the west, 21° 48'N latitude on the south, and a line from Starling Inlet to Deep Bay at the point where they were nearest each other.[31] Yet Salisbury was still not satisfied; on the 20th he repeated that the waters of the two bays were necessary for strategical reasons, though the southern and western boundaries exceeded what was essential. They included, moreover, the western channel of Canton, which it was thought might give rise to questions with other powers. Those boundaries which would satisfy the Admiralty were:

... a line along the meridian of 114° 30'E from Mirs Point to the parallel of 22° 9'N, along that parallel to the Western end of Achau Island; thence to the Southern point of Lantau Island, and northward along the shore of that island to the meridian of 113° 52'E and up that meridian to the parallel of 22° 32'N.[32]

This was in conformity with the Colonial Defence Committee's recent proposals for the outer zone, though whether it was practicable for MacDonald to alter accordingly the verbal arrangement he had made with the Yamen was left to his judgment. When he next met the Chinese ministers he assured them that Mirs Bay would be free to Chinese men-of-war, and evaded a question about the three-mile limit of territorial waters by saying that this was not an issue with regard to Mirs Bay as there was no point in it three miles from the nearest land. The Yamen proved co-operative, though one doubts the quality of the advice they received: 'The new map was inspected with the help of the Yamen's geographical expert, who took a prominent but unintelligible part in the discussion. His incoherency was such that the Grand Secretary at last asked him whether he was speaking English or Chinese.'[33]

The court at Peking recognized the necessity for extension but contemplated, wrote MacDonald, 'only such a limited extension as would enable the British authorities to fortify both sides of Hong Kong Harbour and to defend the hills overlooking it'. They sought by various counter-proposals to evade leasing the whole area, but the Walled City clause weakened their resistance.[34] The convention stated that the exact boundaries were to be fixed after proper surveys by officials appointed by the two governments. Those sea boundaries drawn on the convention map were, on the west, 113° 52'E longitude; on the south, 22° 9'N latitude; and on the east, 114° 30'E longitude.

The Walled City of Kowloon

If it was important to the Chinese ministers to surrender as little territory as possible, it was absolutely vital to them that they retain control over the Walled City. They first objected to the inclusion of the city in the lease agreement on 24 April, declaring that they had no power to yield it.[35] MacDonald telegraphed that the necessity of withdrawing permanent officials was much resented, the Yamen assuring him that none of their recent leases had involved such an indignity. This was technically incorrect, for it was only in Weihaiwei that the seat of imperial government in the leasehold was permitted to remain,[36] yet MacDonald asked if the city at Kowloon could be left in the hands of Chinese officials until the experiment proved unworkable.[37] A minute by Lucas suggested offering either employment or compensation to the officials,[38] and Balfour asked MacDonald:

Is it a question of dignity or of money? Would a lease get over it? If money compensation is required we could offer reasonable terms, or some arrangements might be made leaving Chinese officials in the town undisturbed but subjecting them to paramount British authority and placing by their side nominal British subordinates who would do the work.[39]

Li Hung-chang himself proposed the appointment of Englishmen to help the Chinese authorities.[40] MacDonald replied to Balfour that it was almost entirely a matter of saving face, and that some such arrangement as was suggested might possibly be effected later.[41] The Foreign Office immediately telegraphed: 'Chinese Administration in leased territory to continue so far as it may not be inconsistent with the military requirements for the proper defence of Hong Kong',[42] and on the next day MacDonald reaffirmed the condition that Chinese officials be allowed to remain in Kowloon, and stated his belief that the Yamen would consent to British officials being appointed.[43] In a long despatch he summarized his negotiations on the question of jurisdiction:

The retention of Chinese jurisdiction within Kowloon city was the point on which the Yamen showed the greatest determination, and the concession made to them went far to reconcile them to the general demand. Apart from the fact that there were Japanese, German and Russian precedents for such an arrangement, the Ministers, of whom two of those chiefly concerned in the negotiations were Cantonese, showed considerable anxiety as to the effect on public opinion in the Canton Province of any sudden and conspicuous change in existing conditions. If the administration of law in Kowloon city were transferred to the Hong Kong Government, the latter would, of course, be obliged to inforce a number of rules to which the population are at present not liable, and I think it probable that the Yamen was right in anticipating that this would lead to trouble.

It is not to be supposed that the city of Kowloon will long remain outside British jurisdiction with the surrounding district subject to it, but I think that no harm can result from allowing it to do so for a few years longer, and that little inconvenience will be caused by it, especially as the authority of the Chinese officials will be exercised subject to the stipulation that it does not interfere with military requirements. I should recommend that every effort be made by the Hong Kong authorities to work smoothly with these officials—at all events at first—and to induce them to cordially co-operate in all matters where their assistance is needed. I do not, as I have already said, expect the Chinese jurisdiction in the city to be of long continuance, but I should be sorry, for the sake of general British interests in China, if, after the Chinese have met our wishes in so friendly a spirit, we were at once to set to work to obtain a further concession.[44]

But discussions on the proposed placing of the boundaries continued, and on 4 June Lucas minuted his dissatisfaction with the Walled City clause. MacDonald had earlier pointed out the understanding regarding the prevention of smuggling,[45] and the Colonial Office seized on this as a possible *quid pro quo* in further attempts to modify Chinese jurisdiction in the city. Salisbury was asked to instruct MacDonald that a new formula was desirable: 'Chinese jurisdiction shall continue concurrently in Kowloon City so far as is not inconsistent with military requirements and with European law and custom.' The Yamen might be assured that there was no intention to interfere with the position and emoluments of Chinese officials; all that was wanted was the assimilation of Chinese to British procedure in order to prevent the possibility of friction and scandal.[46] In any case, the Colonial Office doubted whether the Chinese *imperium in imperio* would last very long. Salisbury declined, however, to inform MacDonald for fear of greatly delaying conclusion of the agreement,[47] and the Colonial Office reluctantly decided that the thing was settled: a way out would be found somehow, 'notwithstanding the (no doubt perfectly justifiable) vaticinations of Mr Lockhart'.[48] Whatever these were, the report which Stewart Lockhart wrote on the new territory later in the year was optimistic: the garrison could not be allowed to remain, and the consequent departure of the dependent civil population from the Walled City would leave no one over whom a Chinese official could exercise jurisdiction.[49] In any event, MacDonald opined, if the Hong Kong authorities could not get the Walled City mandarins under their thumb they must be a 'thundering poor lot'.[50]

The Chinese Imperial Maritime Customs

The Tsungli Yamen was able to insist upon inclusion of the Walled City clause but, although the ministers were determined that the blockade should not be affected by the lease, there is no mention in the convention of customs arrangements. MacDonald had entered into a merely informal understanding with the Yamen that the leased territory would be properly policed and measures taken for the prevention of smuggling.

Previous to the inclusion of Mirs Bay in the lease I was authorised by the Colonial Office, through your Lordship, to promise an energetic enforcement of existing arrangements, and with that inclusion the necessity for the assistance of the Colonial authorities becomes much greater. Protection of the revenue of China is not primarily the duty of the Colonial Government, but that duty is morally imposed on them by the circumstances under which they obtain an increase of territory, for our demand was based on, and justified solely by the necessity of providing for the better protection of Hong Kong.

I do not mean to suggest that the Hong Kong Government would be slow to do whatever can be rightly expected from them, but I think that by pledging themselves before the extension of territory is actually assured they may find it more easy to reconcile the local public to measures otherwise perhaps distasteful.[51]

A few days later the ministers were promised that the Hong Kong government would take all possible precautions to prevent the leased territory from being used to facilitate smuggling into China or in any other way that was detrimental to Chinese interests.[52]

Reliance on a British promise to take action against smuggling, and the failure to include in the convention any agreement as to the future of customs houses in the New Territories, was a foolish mistake by the Chinese negotiators. They had not suspected that the dues-collecting stations would be removed,[53] and they accepted assurances that everything would be done to protect the interests of Chinese revenue. But in Hong Kong there was no reticence to state opinions as to the best methods of implementing the British pledge, and all such opinions disregarded the moral duty imposed on the Hong Kong government.[54] Even Stewart Lockhart, who recognized the duty, suggested that fulfilment of it be used as a *quid pro quo* for a further concession.[55]

Gap Rock

The final issue requiring settlement was the fate of Gap Rock. Opinion in Hong Kong favoured its cession to Great Britain, the joint naval and military committee recommended possession in 1895, and the Colonial Defence Committee, the War Office and the Admiralty supported the joint committee.[56] However, there is no mention of Gap Rock in MacDonald's despatch summarizing his negotiations with the Yamen, and it did not appear in the chart upon which he relied. A possible reason is given in a handwritten, undated note opposite the Cabinet copy of the Colonial Defence Committee memorandum no. 139M:

> Gap Rock was not included in the British sphere under the convention of 1898, Sir C MacDonald's instructions (telegraphic) not including it. The Hydrographer informed me on 18/10/99 that his recollection was that at the time of the negotiations by telegraph the Naval Lords did not ask for Gap Rock (i) because it is practically British already and (ii) because they did not wish to appear to be threatening the approaches to a treaty port.[57]

Nevertheless, during 1898 and 1899 proposals for its acquisition were frequently made.[58]

The Final Draft

On 19 May 1898 a draft agreement was made out and on 9 June the final treaty was signed. At first reports the inhabitants of Hong Kong were jubilant,[59] though somewhat dismayed at the reservation of Chinese jurisdiction in Kowloon Walled City and the pledge regarding customs. Nevertheless, the extension was seen as 'another wedge of civilisation driven into Kwangtung'.[60]

MacDonald, in his despatch summarizing negotiations with the Chinese,[61] noted that he had no great difficulty in inducing the Yamen to accept the extension in principle. But the Yamen contemplated a very limited grant of territory and hoped that British demands would go no further. When those demands did go further, to involve over 350 square miles of territory, the ministers tried to put Weihaiwei into the balance and suggested various other counter-proposals, and it was only through British compromise on other matters that they eventually agreed to lease the whole area. The major compromise was over the Walled City and the reservation of its pier. MacDonald conceded these with reluctance, but he had to do so if the main demand was to be achieved without friction and resort to threats. Other concessions were the railway clause and the right of Chinese vessels of war to use the waters of Mirs Bay and Deep Bay. The promise to take steps against smuggling was unpopular but essential for the speedy conclusion of the negotiations. Finally, the ministers successfully resisted Mac-Donald's demand for an absolute cession by arguing that other nations with Chinese leaseholds would follow suit, at probable inconvenience to Great Britain. The Chinese managed, therefore, to salvage something from the negotiations, though in practice the British 'concessions' have meant very little.

A curious omission from the agreement was any mention of rent. Despite Balfour's instructions that rent was 'to be fixed hereafter'[62] and the Foreign Office statement in late 1895 that China would be approached for the necessary territory 'on payment of its value',[63] the issue was apparently raised only once, by the Chinese delimitation commissioner:

> Mr Wong Tsun Shin: What rent will be paid for the lease of the new territory?
> Mr Stewart Lockhart: I do not know. That is a question which cannot be settled by me. Is any rent paid for [Kiaochow] by the German Government or for Port Arthur by the Russian Government? I think China may rest satisfied that Great Britain, animated by feelings of friendship, will deal as fairly with China in this matter as any other Power.[64]

In fact, no rent was paid by France, Germany, or Russia for their respective leaseholds. MacDonald commented: 'doubtless they [the Yamen] are afraid of being denounced for selling their country'.[65]

Another curious feature of the convention negotiations, in view of the Foreign Office recognition of the necessity of extension more than two years previously, is that the British minister should not have been in possession of all relevant documents. The joint committee's report of 1895, proposing limits which were exactly specified and including Gap Rock, was not sent to him; from the colonial point of view this was probably fortunate, as its suggested boundaries were somewhat smaller than those eventually obtained. Even when MacDonald first asked the Yamen to consider an extension at Hong Kong he had no idea how much territory was required, and had to apply to the governor for some guidance. The 1894 material did not arrive until 13 April, well after initial discussions had taken place. It might have been expected that the Foreign Office would have given explicit instructions as to the boundaries from the outset, and MacDonald's task was not made easier by telegraphic changes of mind. One might also have expected prior preparation of a model leasehold treaty or, at least, submission of the draft convention to the law officers, but Major MacDonald, a soldier with no legal training, was required to draw up the thing himself. In consequence it is a vague and imprecise document allowing no easy interpretation. It may be that, just as MacDonald had reported the German lease of Kiaochow to be in reality a disguised cession,[66] he understood the New Territories to be a permanent addition to the empire, and that therefore the terms of the transfer were not very important. Events were later to prove, however, that the terms were not as unimportant as had been assumed.

In his representations to the Chinese, MacDonald justified his demand solely by 'the necessity of providing for the better protection of Hong Kong'; other reasons for extension which had been put forward by Hong Kong residents, such as the importance of acquiring cemetery accommodation, exercise grounds for troops, industrial land and so on, were ignored, for the Yamen would have countered with offers of all the territory required for the purposes named. Colonial defence had all along been the major stimulus of agitation for extension, and in the end it was the only important factor.

But defence against whom? It was neither solely nor mainly defence against France, as is often suggested as the major stimulus behind the convention, or against any other specific power. Those advocating territorial expansion held a long view, based on recognition of Hong Kong's value to British interests generally and of rapidly-developing imperialist rivalry in China; they did not ignore the possibility of defence being necessary even against China herself, and hesitated to point the finger at any particular country. They did not know who was most likely to threaten Hong Kong's security in the future, nor did they care very much; all they saw was a vital trading-post at the mercy of any hostile force in control of the Lei Yue Mun Pass and the Kowloon hills. This was the argument which eventually prevailed, a carefully prepared argument accepted by the Cabinet when conditions allowed.

MacDonald, in his official despatch, reported that he had told the Yamen: 'we should, long before this, have invited China to make over to us what was necessary for the Colony's safety had we not been afraid of setting an example to other Powers. The time was now opportune for China to make the concession to us without any risk of counter-claims'.[67] This, of course, was hardly accurate: the reason previously advanced for the delay in applying for the extension was the existence of other negotiations, and the first half of 1898 was hardly a period when China could consider herself free from any risk of counter-claims. But it did seem the right moment for Great Britain to discard her traditional policy, and she lost little time in following other nations' demands for railway and mining concessions. In this context the acquisition of the New Territories seemed only reasonable and just.

More important to British thinking was the changing balance of power, represented by Germany and Russia in the north and France to the south of Hong Kong. The Far Eastern situation during 1898 was in a state of flux; international relations touching the Chinese empire were fluid, and the uncertainty made more urgent the protection of Britain's major vested interest. As Lord Salisbury said in parliament:

... though I cannot say that any immediate danger is apprehended—indeed, I do not see from what quarter it can come—yet it is in conformity with the ordinary rules of military prudence that all strategical conditions should be so devised that if an accident we cannot foresee takes place we should not be exposed to any danger or disadvantage ... (cheers).[68]

Even so, it was ten months before occupation of the leased territory was undertaken.

Statements in the House cannot be considered always reliable or honest, and both the Intelligence Division and the Admiralty had reported, in response to Foreign Office enquiries, that Kwangchow Wan could adversely affect British naval power centred in Hong Kong.[69] Yet the particular significance of French diplomacy to the Kowloon extension was not the acquisition of a coaling station but the demand for a non-alienation assurance in relation to Kwangtung. This would have precluded a long-standing and strategically necessary scheme for defensive improvements to Hong Kong, and colonial expansion had either to be insisted upon when the French claims were first known or else abandoned; thus the appearance of the extension being granted as a *quid pro quo* for Kwangchow Wan was illusory. 'Rectification' of Hong Kong's boundaries was not a make-weight to counter the French as was Weihaiwei in regard to the Russians; Chusan was being kept in reserve for that. Changing power relations meant that lease or cession of the territory behind Kowloon could be delayed no longer. The final decision was not prompted by seeing Frenchmen at Kwangchow Wan, Germans at Kiaochow, or Russians on the Liaotung peninsula; rather, these concessions gave the Foreign Office the opportunity to remove a persistent colonial complaint.

Thus the convention was sought only when distortion of the Far Eastern balance of power made it necessary and, further, made it possible. Given the history of pressure by Sir William Robinson, the War Office, and the others, emphasis should be given to the arrival of a time suitable for the pressing of demands upon a demoralized and feeble Ch'ing government rather than to the immediate defensive needs created by rival territorial gains in China. The Foreign Office had recognized the value of an extension of Hong Kong's boundaries in 1895; it was faced with a united front of War Office, Admiralty, and Colonial Office and, no doubt, would have gladly submitted had it thought general interests could be preserved. This could be achieved in 1898.

But the Foreign Office was necessarily mindful of considerations other than colonial security: the type and extent of demands which could reasonably be made upon China, the opportune time for making them, and the effect they would have on the Far Eastern policies of imperialist competitors. As the chief clerk of the Colonial Office complained privately: 'We *cannot* get them [the Foreign Office] to look at the matter from our ie the Colonial point of view, and all they care about is their general programme of Chinese policy, regarding Hong Kong and the new territory as mere items in the programme, and of no special importance.'[70] Salisbury's policy was, until 1898, firmly opposed to dismemberment of the Middle Kingdom, and he feared initiating a scramble for concessions such as developed after the German occupation of Kiaochow. So he did nothing, except reiterate that the time was not ripe, until the occasion presented itself when the action urged for so long by the colonialists could be undertaken with clear conscience by the imperialists. His prevarication was not the result of neglect but of overriding policy, of his desire to preserve the integrity of the Chinese empire and to protect British investment in free trade.

Yet it is significant that the serious negotiations began when Lord Salisbury was away. The crucial telegrams to Peking were signed by Balfour, and it may be that, had Salisbury still been in effective command of the Foreign Office, the extension lobby would have been frustrated once again.[71]

In the process of negotiation, general imperial interests had to take precedence over the narrower interests of colonialism. Thus the crucial concessions of the customs pledge and the retention of Chinese jurisdiction in the Walled City of Kowloon. Only a lease could be obtained: as Bertie claimed, HMG had 'deliberately adopted the leasehold course so as to follow the example of Germany and Russia, and to avoid accusations of going one better and beginning the break up of China'.[72] Gap Rock was omitted from the demand partly because, it seems, Great Britain feared the response of her rivals. The importance of colonial defence could not be the sole consideration in the minds of Her Majesty's negotiators.

The Chinese ministers had one overriding objective: to limit the British claim to the barest minimum. Their greatest success was retention of Chinese jurisdiction in the Walled City of Kowloon. The more obvious political factors seem insufficient to explain the peculiar tenacity with which the Kowloon mandarin's interests were defended, and it may be that a 'cultural' analysis is required. It can therefore be suggested that the tenets of Chinese culture which loss of an administrative centre offended were too fundamental to be breached without the use of force. Immanuel Hsu refers to *t'i-chih*, the Chinese equivalent of England's unwritten constitution, as 'the sum total of all tangible and intangible traditions, beliefs, codes, statutes, governmental systems, and religious observances';[73] included in it are filial piety (the emperor's obligation to preserve the institutions established by his forefathers) and imperial familial law. Ancestral admonitions, edicts, decrees and practices were presented to the emperor as sacred and inviolable, his function being to preserve the dynasty for his ancestors. The Yamen probably recognized the futility of asking the emperor to approve a treaty which involved loss of a governmental installation established by one of his predecessors.[74]

3

OCCUPATION OF THE NEW TERRITORIES

Hoisting the Flag

THE day chosen for the formal taking of possession of the New Territories was 17 April 1899. Although it seems to have been a coincidence, this was the fourth anniversary of the signing of the Shimonoseki treaty which had ended the Sino-Japanese war and encouraged the agitation for extension of Hong Kong's boundaries. A public holiday had been declared in the colony, and the good citizens of Hong Kong looked forward to what one newspaper called 'a pleasant little outing and an opportunity for indulging in an outburst of patriotic fervour'.[1] But the population of the new British possession was less enthusiastic about the proceedings than was hoped for in the city of Victoria. The flag had to be hoisted a day earlier than planned.

His Excellency Sir Henry Blake remained behind his desk in Hong Kong, but the ceremony on the newly-named Flagstaff Hill in Tai Po was as impressive as urgent improvisation could allow. Stewart Lockhart had taken along his full official uniform and a silk flag; the officer commanding the troops and his naval equivalent, Commodore Powell, were present with four hundred men from the Hong Kong Regiment and two fully-dressed ships; and the artillery provided a stirring salute with the navy's guns. The troops, forming three sides of a square, presented and shouldered arms; the union jack fluttered proudly above as the colonial secretary read the convention and the order in council; and from 2.50 p.m. on Sunday, 16 April 1899, the inhabitants of the New Territories became subject to British jurisdiction. They indicated disrespect a short time later, however, by renewal of the hostilities which had disrupted the great event. The soldiers of their new colonial masters had no difficulty in dispersing them.[2]

On 17 April, Lady Blake did the honours outside the customs

station at Kowloon City. The gentlemen present raised their hats, the military presented arms, printed copies of an address were distributed, and the wife of the governor handed out silver coins to local children. Other such ceremonies were enacted at various places in the New Territories.

The Long Delay

The convention had been in force since 1 July 1898, but formal possession had been delayed for a variety of reasons. One difficulty was that the Hong Kong government knew surprisingly little about the area it had officially coveted for nearly four years. Until some survey of the population's size, composition and needs had been completed, and details of policy worked out between the Colonial Office and the local authorities, the assumption of administrative control would have been futile. Great importance, therefore, was attached to the sending out of a fact-finding mission whose report could be used as a basis for policy-making. The man chosen for the job was the colonial secretary and registrar-general, James H. Stewart Lockhart.

Although the special commission was obviously desirable if British administration in the New Territories was to begin efficiently there were some voices raised in protest. Fears were expressed that the consequent delay would stimulate other powers to thwart the extension by making fresh demands on China,[3] and the selection of Stewart Lockhart was not universally applauded.[4] Nor were the commissioner and his team everywhere welcomed by the inhabitants. The San On magistrate, though apparently ordered by Peking to let Stewart Lockhart copy his land register, evaded all requests for it and eventually refused point blank. 'Mr Lockhart', said a local scribe, 'then personally called on this contumaceous official and after administering to him a severe rating finally procured the books wanted, which he retained possession of for three days, copying out necessary details.'[5] Opposition took place at the village of Kam Tin, stronghold of the powerful Tang lineage: one thousand villagers appeared before the commission and shouted abuse. 'Nothing is said here of the rotten eggs that emphasised these cries....'[6] It was only by bringing up seventy-five men from HMS *Plover* with two maxim guns that Stewart Lockhart was able to induce the villagers to open the Kat Hing Wai gates. A French journalist gleefully wrote:

The villagers obeyed—and that is how relations were established between the English Government and its new subjects. The old ladies of foggy Albion's Tract Societies will have much difficulty in understanding the state of mind of these despicable wretches who ought to be so grateful to philanthropic England for having sent during the last half century so many merchants to enrich themselves at the expense of so many Chinese and so many missionaries to sell bibles of all shapes.[7]

Stewart Lockhart, however, was unamused by the villagers' insult to his authority: he reported the matter to the viceroy (who was to deal with it 'in a proper manner') and a deputation was obliged to express regrets in Hong Kong. Further, HM's representatives in Peking demanded that the district magistrate be removed, the offenders punished, and the official at Kowloon ordered to apologize.[8]

Such obstruction did not markedly impede the progress of the commission, and the report was submitted on 8 October. Stewart Lockhart had carried out his instructions admirably, and the document is an immensely valuable survey of the physical and human aspects of the New Territories, its administration by the Chinese and its proposed administration by the British, and of other matters needing consideration by Her Majesty's Government. Some of its recommendations are discussed elsewhere in this work, and it is only necessary to note here that possession of it provided the British authorities with the information they needed for intelligent shaping of policy.

More than three months were required for this project, a plausible reason for delaying occupation of the newly-acquired territory; it would also have been unwise to take it over during the acting governorship of Major-General Wilsone Black or before Sir Henry Blake had had time to settle in as the new governor. But there was a further reason why the British authorities prevaricated before taking the decision to occupy the territory, and it pertained to a matter of imperial rather than colonial policy. On 23 April 1898, Black telegraphed that there were six United States ships of war in Hong Kong, part of Admiral Dewey's squadron then prosecuting the Philippines war against the Spanish.[9] The ships were required, by the rules of neutrality, to leave Hong Kong and coal in no other British port within the succeeding three months.[10] Dewey proceeded to Mirs Bay, thereby infringing China's neutrality—but no one seemed very concerned about that. The problem was that if the waters of Mirs Bay became British under the convention the Hong

Kong authorities would be obliged to request the US fleet to sail elsewhere and thus deprive them of a base relatively close to the war.

MacDonald first pointed out the difficulty on 26 May, submitting that if the convention came into force on 1 July Dewey's ships would have to leave immediately.[11] Salisbury minuted that an excuse might be found for postponing the date of the lease. Thus both MacDonald and the Prime Minister seemed to think that the date of the *lease* was crucial to the question of neutrality. No discussion of this interesting theoretical issue was discovered in the records, but the Foreign Office evidently changed its mind, for it subsequently considered the date of *taking possession* to be the time from which the neutrality rules should run. Texts on the law of war do not mention this problem; the latter view taken by the British authorities, however, accords with common sense, for HMG was in no position to enforce the territory's neutrality until in actual possession.

The policy adopted, therefore, was that the occupation of the New Territories should be postponed in the hope that the American-Spanish war would come to an end. MacDonald was informed that formal possession would not be taken on 1 July as 'preliminary arrangements' would take some time. The telegram ended with the secret question, 'Have Americans ceased altogether to make use of Mirs Bay as a Naval base?'[12] He passed the question on to the acting governor, Wilsone Black, who wrote to the Colonial Office that he would inform MacDonald as soon as he learned that supplies had arrived at Manila direct from America, as after that date he supposed that Mirs Bay would not be needed. Chamberlain thereupon left the date of occupation to be decided by Salisbury.[13]

By December it was thought by the Foreign Office that the territory could be ceremonially taken over early in February 1899, but three important questions were still outstanding. The first of these concerned the collection of Chinese customs duties and the prevention of smuggling.

Before the actual signing of the convention the Tsungli Yamen had addressed a note to MacDonald setting out matters in which co-operation was required: certain procedures were to be followed with respect to opium, customs collectorates were not to be moved (though alternatives were mentioned), and Great Britain was to defray the cost of building more branch stations.[14] The proposals had been submitted by Sir Robert Hart, the inspector general of customs, who later drew up a more complete list in the forlorn belief that Her Majesty's Government 'desire to give China liberal and sustained support in the protection of her revenue. . . .'

Hart's scheme was as follows. The right of the Imperial Maritime Customs (IMC) to maintain its office in Hong Kong should be formally admitted and the Kowloon commissioner of customs recognized as a Chinese official. Sub-stations at Cheung Chau, Kap Shui Mun, Lai Chi Kok, and Fat Tau Chau should be retained and others instituted inside the territory if needed; the office in Hong Kong should have the right to collect duty and *likin* on any opium and duties on general cargo shipped to or from China on any native vessel. The right to build special jetties for the examination of cargo and the right of customs cruisers and launches to continue their operations in the leased waters should be granted. Opium was to be handled only under permit from Hong Kong; the opium farm was to be maintained and its activities open to inspection by the Chinese customs, and the whole opium system was to be strengthened. Arms or contraband goods should not be shipped to a Chinese port without the authority of China, and Hong Kong was to pass the legislation necessary for proper and zealous compliance with all these provisions.[15]

Alas, not a single British individual or association whose voice was raised in the corridors of power advocated acceptance of the Hart plan. The acting governor, Wilsone Black, considered nearly all of Hart's suggestions quite objectionable, for to submit to them would mean handing over the free port of Hong Kong to the domination of the IMC. Sir Henry Blake advocated the collection of duties by Hong Kong on China's behalf, which would, of course, mean the ending of the 'blockade' and the total removal of the IMC from Hong Kong. The China Association wanted to make such an offer conditional upon a further rectification of the northern boundary. Even the *Daily Press*, which saw no objection to the foreign branch of the customs watching over a discreditable smuggling trade, baulked at the idea of retaining the iniquitous opium farm.[16]

The Colonial Office, following the Hong Kong lead, took exception to Hart's proposals and rejected the alternative suggestion of H. M. Hillier, the Kowloon commissioner of customs, that cargo be examined and duties paid to the IMC station at Kowloon City. Despite certain reservations, the Colonial Office favoured the idea that the colonial authorities should collect duty on opium and pass it over to China. On 30 November Lucas wrote to the Foreign Office: 'In return it should be stipulated that not only must there be no Chinese customs houses or offices within the Colony or the leased territory, but that they should be removed from the immediate vicinity of the Colony, in order to prevent a repetition of the difficulties and annoyances which have been so constant in past years.'[17] A further concession, the inclusion of Sham Chun in the lease, might be invited from China on account of Hong Kong's generous offer. Salisbury concurred; MacDonald was instructed to arrange matters with China accordingly, and Blake to prepare the details of the scheme as one of his earliest duties and to submit proposals to Chamberlain soon after.

Not only, however, was the Tsungli Yamen quite unwilling to grant any further concession: it refused to countenance the removal of the customs stations. On 9 March 1899, the ministers claimed that such an event was contrary to the original agreement and would open the door to smuggling; the Colonial Office, on the other hand, considered that the maintenance of Chinese customs houses and cruisers inside territory under British administration could only result in constant friction between the two governments and consequent loss of revenue.[18] Meanwhile, the governor, Sir Henry Blake, had informed Hillier that the stations must be withdrawn by 1 April, 'or China will be responsible',[19] but postponed action for two weeks pending instructions, following a request from China. The Yamen had argued that opium revenue was only 30 per cent of total customs revenue and that smuggling losses would therefore be great without the existing collectorates, and MacDonald was sympathetic to the complaint; he suggested the devising of a compromise. But Chamberlain was not interested: he merely repeated that smuggling was chiefly concerned with opium and suggested that Blake go ahead with the take-over. The British chargé d'affaires in Peking, H. Bax-Ironside, was told on 5 April to inform China 'that Her Majesty's Government regret they cannot agree that, either in the Colony or the new extension, any form of Chinese customs jurisdiction should be permitted to continue.'[20]

This decision, which Hart declared had done immense harm,[21] was never altered, though the island stations (but not Kowloon City) were allowed to continue operations until the next October while new stations were being built. Blake had raised objections, but Chamberlain considered it of greater importance that the negotiations for the formal occupation of the New Territories should not be further interrupted.[22]

The second outstanding question which needed to be resolved before taking possession of the leased territory related to Chinese jurisdiction in the Walled City of Kowloon, for the signing of the lease did not mean the end of British agitation for correction of the anomalous retention of foreign jurisdiction. The Hong Kong press refused to believe first reports, and the intrepid triumvirate of treaty port pressure groups, the Chamber of Commerce, the China Association, and the Navy League, collapsed into paroxysms of rage. In the words of the acting governor, the views of 'some of the Societies who interest themselves in public affairs and freely give advice thereon'[23] carried considerable weight with the British government at this time,[24] and the jurisdiction exercised by China in Kowloon City was to be restricted as much as possible. Stewart Lockhart was instructed to give special attention to the matter, and he stated in his report that the Walled City, not the suburbs, was obviously what was referred to in the convention.[25] His interpretation was simple: the Kowloon City clause was virtually a dead letter, for Chinese writ ran no further than the walls of the fort and did not extend to military affairs. Salisbury accepted this view and called upon China to withdraw the garrison.[26] The Tsungli Yamen did not, surprisingly, object.

The third matter to be disposed of before occupation was the delimitation and demarcation of the northern land boundary. During the last half of 1898 several interested parties made proposals for increasing the territory leased, either as modifications of the convention or as further territory to be included on delimitation. Some such proposals came too late in the day to be considered, but more credence was given to a report by Ormsby, director of public works in Hong Kong, who contended that boundaries between countries should be either a large river or the ridges of hills separating valleys. He suggested leasing the whole of San On district, as its boundary followed the ridges of a chain of mountains; alternatively, a line along the top of a chain of hills just south of Nam Tau should be chosen. Failing either proposal, inclusion of the Sham Chun valley was recommended, necessitating the selection of meridian 113° 50′E as the western boundary.[27] An extract from the report was forwarded to the Foreign Office and a map supplied to Stewart Lockhart.

The special commissioner borrowed Ormsby's arguments when

he set forth his objections to the northern boundary as laid down in the convention. The Sham Chun valley would be bisected, thus dividing villages closely linked by family ties and common interests. The influential head council of the local government was in Sham Chun and should be incorporated into the leased territory; a river boundary would create endless disputes as to water rights on each side; smuggling was facilitated by the convention line; and Sham Chun would be a source of friction between the governments of Hong Kong and China in much the same manner as Kowloon City had been. Further, to have undisputed rights over the waters of Deep Bay and Mirs Bay required control of the surrounding land. Stewart Lockhart recommended that all San On be leased, or, alternatively, the northern boundary should pass to the Chinese side of Sham Chun and of land north and east of Mirs Bay and west of Deep Bay.[28]

In the Colonial Office Hamilton thought that settlement of the customs question satisfactorily to China might provide a *quid pro quo* in the form of a further rectification of the boundary; it would be worthwhile trying for at least the inclusion of Sham Chun. Lucas' minute suggested leaving the 'natural boundary' argument alone and proposed asking for Sham Chun or, if refused, that the Hong Kong government take charge of the customs house there.[29] The Colonial Office letter with which Stewart Lockhart's report was forwarded to the Foreign Office remarked:

It is obvious that constant difficulties, as regards both smuggling and general details of administration, are likely to arise if this town [Sham Chun], which appears to be the administrative centre of the district, is left just outside the boundary, and its inclusion in the leased area, while not likely to be regarded as of any great importance by the Chinese Government, would be of considerable importance to the Government of Hong Kong. Mr Chamberlain would, therefore, recommend that these considerations should be pointed out to the Chinese Government, and that they should be pressed to allow, at any rate, the inclusion in the leased territory of the town of Sham Chun.[30]

Salisbury considered that Stewart Lockhart's more ambitious proposals differed too widely from the convention boundary to be put forward in Peking but, with the subsequent support of the Colonial Defence Committee, he agreed on the reasonableness of asking for Sham Chun. MacDonald was instructed accordingly.[31] The proposal to include Sham Chun, therefore, had wide support in the British government, though it was not to be successful.

Delimitation of the northern boundary was entrusted by HMG to the Hong Kong authorities acting in concert with MacDonald, and the indispensable Mr Stewart Lockhart was appointed as commissioner for the task. Viceroy T'an nominated Wang Tsun-shan (Wong Tsun-shin), his foreign secretary, as the Chinese delimitation commissioner. Wang and Stewart Lockhart held meetings on 11 and 14 March during which the main process of delimitation was completed.

Much of the first interview was concerned with irrelevant matters such as the collection of *likin*, supression of piracy, customs, and rent. Wang first suggested following the line drawn on the convention map and determining the position of divided villages by counting the number of houses on each side of the boundary and labelling them Chinese or British according to the higher number. This unworkable scheme was replaced by the search for a natural boundary, the best one, in Stewart Lockhart's opinion, running along the base of the hills beyond Sham Chun to the mountain Ng Tung Shan and to the north of Sha Tau Kok. Chinese agreement on this would be gratefully acknowledged by British assistance in the matters of opium—a system allowing easy and effective collection of duty by China—and the smuggling of arms. Wang was personally disposed to accept Stewart Lockhart's boundary but could not act without authority, and he went off to Canton to discuss the proposal with the viceroy.

Authority was not forthcoming, however, and Stewart Lockhart therefore decided to submit a more southern boundary. He had previously argued that the Sham Chun River, being tidal, should be regarded as part of the waters of Deep Bay, and on the 14th he insisted that its northern bank would be the boundary. Wang agreed, and further discussion was to be reserved for the authorities at Peking. Blake wanted the river boundary formally agreed to as a provisional measure to enable him to take over the territory, and the following memorandum was signed:

It is agreed that for the present the river past Sham Chun to Sha Tau Kok shall be the boundary to its source north west of Sha Tau Kok and thence to Mirs Bay immediately to the west of Sha Tau Kok, the north bank of the river referred to being the boundary. The question of including Sham Chun and Sha Tau Kok to remain open for further reference to [Peking].[32]

Blake sent the appropriate map to MacDonald, and Bax-Ironside told the Tsungli Yamen that an opium ordinance would be passed in Hong Kong at once and the Chinese customs given time to leave British territory if the ministers agreed to lease Sham Chun and district. But they firmly declined to accept such an arrangement. Sham Chun was therefore to remain Chinese, and although it was later occupied by Hong Kong forces its ultimate rendition took place before the year was out. There was some consolation to Britain, however, in securing complete control of the Sham Chun River, for its inclusion within British territory had not been indicated on the convention map.

Stewart Lockhart left Hong Kong on 16 March to begin demarcation and it was completed on the 18th. Next day he and Wang signed a lengthy memorandum in which the northern boundary was described in some detail. No mention was made of Chinese rights to the Sham Chun waters. This boundary was defined briefly in a notification, checked and altered by Stewart Lockhart, which was issued by the San On magistrate.[33] Initially only an occasional peg was driven into the ground to signify the boundary's changes of direction, though Wang had stated that properly inscribed stones should be erected along the line; Stewart Lockhart had suggested the possibility of a palisade such as existed at the northern limits of British Kowloon.[34] In fact the Public Works Department marked out the northern boundary in 1905 with stones inscribed 'Anglo-Chinese Boundary, 1898'. Chinese officials were not present.[35]

As soon as the demarcation was complete, Chinese jurisdiction in Kowloon City had been restricted to the fort, and the IMC given its marching orders from the territory, only a few formalities were necessary before hoisting the flag. But two issues of policy arose in 1898 which are important in that they illustrate British and Chinese attitudes to the meaning of the convention. They were firmly settled before the occupation.

The first of these was raised by Major-General Black's recommendations for the future administration of the New Territories. He suggested a system of government not dissimilar to government by the 'father and mother official' of the Ch'ing dynasty, a system which, for the first few years at least, might well have been considered particularly appropriate for a predominantly peasant society with its own traditions of local government. But Hamilton quickly ruled out Black's scheme: the word 'Resident', the title Black had suggested for the man who was to head the administrative system, was normally applicable only to areas outside British territory, and 'this new territory should be regarded from the first as essentially part of the Colony of Hong Kong'.[36]

The second issue concerned the viceroy of Canton's list of 'regulations' which were to be accepted before he would co-operate with regard to boundary delimitation. Most of them dealt with matters contained in the convention, and specific rules for demarcation, jurisdiction in the Walled City, and the retention of Chinese customs stations were laid down. These could not have been altogether unexpected, but the tenth regulation contained a startling innovation: 'Land owned by Chinese subjects within the new settlement must pay the land tax to the Chinese Authorities.' Further, if the land tax was to be levied by Great Britain, then a rent was to be calculated by China, and the English inscription on boundary stones was to read 'Boundary of the Settlement', not 'Boundary of the Colony'.[37] These provisions were a flat contradiction of Hamilton's desire to treat the New Territories as an integral part of the colony, and could never be allowed. In September 1898 the Tsungli Yamen addressed MacDonald on the subject and saw no objection to the viceroy's proposals, but the reply was curt: 'It is ... out of the question that the Governor-General of Canton should be permitted to draw up Regulations for the loan of his district. His action is quite uncalled for, and his Regulations are unworthy of consideration.'[38] MacDonald referred to the viceroy's 'gratuitous interference'[39] and Lucas suggested that the Chinese government be warned against putting forward 'unfounded pretensions'.[40] Salisbury noted that the regulations appeared to be an attempt to treat the leased territory as if it were a settlement at a treaty port,[41] and they were, of course, rejected.

Final Preparations

A useful legal formality before the commencement of British administration was the issue of an order in council providing for the exercise of jurisdiction in the leased territory. Chamberlain thought it desirable to deal with the leasehold as British territory rather than foreign territory over which Her Majesty had acquired jurisdiction; the draft order in council was therefore based on the 1861 order incorporating the ceded tip of Kowloon peninsula rather than on the provisions of the Foreign Jurisdiction Act, for during the period of the lease the new territory was to be emphatically regarded as part of Her Majesty's dominions. It was accordingly declared to be 'part and parcel of Her Majesty's Colony of Hong Kong in like manner and for all intents and purposes as if [it] had originally formed part of the said Colony'. Salisbury concurred in Chamberlain's interpretation of the convention, and the law officers approved the draft order as 'sufficient and proper for the purpose proposed'.[42]

The Prime Minister had, however, objected to the first draft because it had omitted all reference to the convention's Kowloon City clause and of any definition of the new boundaries. Chamberlain demurred, replying that the retention of Chinese jurisdiction should not be emphasized, but Salisbury considered that to ignore it would not be a proper performance of Great Britain's treaty obligations.[43] He also objected to a rather underhand attempt by the Colonial Office to imply ultimate sovereignty over the Walled City to Britain:

> As regards the further suggestion, that it might be sufficient to pass a Colonial Ordinance maintaining Chinese Courts for the trial of Chinese subjects according to the law of China, but on the understanding that no torture should be inflicted, and that sentences of imprisonment should be carried out in the Colonial prisons, Lord Salisbury considers that it would be much better not to assume any responsibility with regard to Chinese judicial methods in Kowloon City.[44]

MacDonald was reminded to ensure that a suitable proclamation be issued by the viceroy for posting in the New Territories, and Stewart Lockhart prepared a similar proclamation on behalf of Her Majesty's Government. Its original English version declared:

> Whereas the Queen of Great Britain has leased from the Emperor of China the territory immediately adjacent to British Kowloon, and whereas all affairs within that territory will be administered and all revenues collected by British officials ... this proclamation is issued to notify you inhabitants accordingly. At the same time you should clearly understand that the long inherited manners and customs of the people will not be interfered with, that vested interests in land will be duly respected, and that all real grievances and just complaints will be carefully and thoroughly investigated. All law-abiding persons will be allowed to pursue in peace and without disturbance their usual vocations. Any disorderly conduct or disregard of the law will involve immediate punishment. You inhabitants are therefore urged to assist in maintaining good order and bringing bad characters to justice, whereby the welfare of the people may be secured and good government promoted.[45]

By December 1898 it was thought by the Foreign Office that the territory could be ceremonially taken over early in February 1899.

The Colonial Office, however, doubted whether policy matters could be settled in the time allowed, and Blake was instructed to keep in touch with MacDonald and postpone the occupation for a few weeks if necessary.[46] The governor, immediately upon being informed of the possible delay, expressed concern that land speculators would increase the price of land necessary for public purposes still further.[47] Eventually, 17 April was set down as the day for occupation and the formal commencement of British administration. A month before that date Blake reported conflicting accounts of the feeling of the people, but he thought that 'in the main it is friendly'. He was wrong about that, but his next sentence was more prescient: 'The inhabitants on the Deep Bay side do not bear a very good reputation, and it will be necessary to have a fair show of force when hoisting the flag.'[48]

The only other matter needing attention concerned preparations for rejoicings and adequate tiffins on the great day when the British Raj would formally extend over yet another small portion of the globe. These were, however, frustrated by the restlessness of the natives.

The Resistance Movement

The instances of hostility met by the special commissioner and his party in October 1898 were not entirely spontaneous and unorganized. On the day Stewart Lockhart submitted his report it was noted in the press that preparations for resistance had been common talk amongst the local Chinese for weeks past, and the Chinese authorities were accused of 'proceeding with their old, time-honoured tactics' and 'secretly inciting the natives to resist the foreigner'.[49]

Following a rumour concerning dispossession of land a subscription was begun among the extension's population, and over $100,000 had been raised. All the 'rowdy characters' in the district had been encouraged to join the disturbances planned on the taking over of the territory. The San On magistrate applied to Canton for troops to suppress an anticipated rebellion, which was chiefly directed against the British assumption of authority; rumour had it that the movement's recruits were originally paid two dollars and that a considerable number of people willing to bear arms had been enrolled.

The allegations made by the *Weekly Press* were investigated by the Hong Kong government, and the evidence which has survived, though scanty, sometimes contradictory, and largely based on the uncorroborated testimony of individuals, supports the claim that preparations were being made as early as October 1898 to resist the British. According to one report, by prominent Hong Kong citizen (later Sir Robert) Ho Tung:

> It is a fact that the [Kam Tin] village had expressed its intention of subscribing money for the use of resisting England's jurisdiction over the land. Some time ago the gentry of the said village had once summoned the gentry of the neighbour villages to a meeting, and said that if the various villages would mutually agree to assist in opposing England and subscribe more or less, the [Kam Tin] village was willing to exert itself to pay the rest of the expenses. Now it is heard the matter was dropped. In the end no subscription was made.[50]

Another report, however, confirmed that Kam Tin was ready to offer opposition to the British should their ownership of land be disturbed, and a large fund was in hand. The captain superintendent of police, F. H. May, ascribed an informant's denial that a subscription was being raised to fear of the consequences. It was generally agreed that Sham Chun was in a very disturbed state: many people from the district had sought refuge in Hong Kong during October and three hundred Chinese soldiers were ordered there on the 20th.[51]

The situation was confused by two facts: land jobbery (to be discussed in chapter 4) and traditional arrangements in San On for self-defence. Many walled villages had acquired an armoury of weapons for inter-clan warfare and defence against bandits, and the existence and improvement of armaments, during a time of political instability and confusion arising from the transfer of territory to Great Britain, did not necessarily indicate militant opposition to the new rulers. One of the two Chinese legislative councillors, the Hon. Mr Wei Yuk, thought that the efforts of one village to raise funds for protection against a triad uprising may have been misinterpreted as a plot to oppose the British occupation. F. H. May, however, would not wholly accept this explanation, and insisted that Kam Tin, at least, had made plans for active resistance. Flags for the collection of money had been flown at various places but Ho Tung claimed that the motive was criminal rather than political.

The truth of allegations that resistance was being planned seemed to be confirmed when Hong Kong officials moved into the leased area to begin preparations for the formal taking of possession. On 24 March 1899, Captain May selected a site for a matshed at Tai Po Hui, to be used as police headquarters; but local villages forced the contractor to desist for fear of upsetting the *fung shui*, or geomantic propitiousness, of the area. May, at first declining, eventually ordered the matshed's frame taken down and removed to a new site pronounced satisfactory by elders from the nearest village. On 1 April the workmen were again threatened by local people, and Blake was given a copy of a placard posted nearby which declared hatred for the English barbarians and determination to resist them, and offered 'proficiency rewards' for patriots who drilled with firearms every day. Blake at once decided to pay the viceroy a visit in an attempt to secure Chinese protection for the work-parties and punishment for the rebels, and he proceeded to Canton early next morning, having determined to hoist the flag as soon as possible: 'further delay would involve danger'.[52]

Blake was ceremonially greeted by viceroy T'an Chung-lin at 11.00 a.m. in a crowded audience hall apparently open to all comers. He first asked that the writer of the inflammatory placard be punished, but no such assurance was forthcoming. The more important item on the agenda, however, was to ensure that agitators were not permitted to operate in the territory while it remained under Chinese jurisdiction. But viceroy T'an wanted to talk about the customs houses, and said: 'this country is only leased: it is China, and there is nothing about Customs in the Convention'. Blake demurred, of course, and went on to more specific matters: the posters were to be removed and ample protection provided for the matshed parties and road surveyors. The viceroy eventually agreed, before proceeding to the temple to continue his prayers for rain, to send out some men and to instruct the magistrate at San On. He issued a proclamation warning the inhabitants against disorder or opposition and dispatched soldiers to prevent disturbances and to arrest the author of the placard.[53] The governor, Sir Henry Blake, returned to Hong Kong well satisfied with the result of his visit but to the ridicule of British residents, who believed he was 'possibly attracted by the glamour of an official reception by an Oriental satrap'.[54]

April was an eventful month, however, and the Hong Kong authorities had no time to rue their reputation with the public. Blake had given the viceroy until the following Wednesday, the 5th, to carry out his promises and to avoid a full-scale British occupation on the next day; Bax-Ironside in Peking, deputizing for MacDonald, was ordered to make immediate representations to the Yamen and to urge that the viceroy be instructed to prevent any hostile action by the local Chinese. But on the 3rd, Captain May and his party were attacked by a mob at Tai Po Hui. He had gone there with several Sikh policemen, a few Chinese soldiers from Kowloon City, and an interpreter to inspect the matshed under construction, to withdraw the two Indian constables on guard (Blake not wanting to place British police in an equivocal position in the event of conflict before the 17th) and replace them with the Chinese soldiers, and to discuss the site of the matshed with village elders. At the Tai Po temple the elders again declared that the matshed interfered with the *fung shui* of the neighbourhood and should be removed. When May refused, the crowd became angry, tried to seize the Chinese interpreter and threw bricks at the retiring party. May ordered a bayonet charge, enabling the Chinese soldiers, who had become separated from the others, to rejoin them and apply their rifle muzzles against their compatriots. The Hong Kong Chinese with the party were sent back by junk to Victoria while the others remained to protect the matshed. That night, however, a large number of locals gathered to attack the hill, whereupon May withdrew and watched the firing of the bamboo shed before marching back to Hong Kong through Sha Tin.[55]

At midnight on 3 April, Blake asked Major-General W. J. Gascoigne, the general officer commanding in China and Hong Kong, to send 200 men to Tai Po Hui and Stewart Lockhart to accompany them and request an additional 200 men from the commandant at the Walled City: the Chinese troops were to have the responsibility of protecting the matshed. The commandant, aroused from his slumbers at 3.30 a.m., agreed to telegraph to the viceroy and to despatch messengers to the San On magistrate and to Major Fong, who was in command of the three hundred troops to be sent to various points in the extension. The British troops marched to Tai Po Hui, where Gascoigne addressed the elders and promised that after 17 April any disturbance would be promptly quelled. He believed that the swift despatch of the armed forces had impressed the inhabitants and that no further trouble would arise in Tai Po Hui.

Blake considered hoisting the flag at once, but the Executive Council agreed that it was better to wait until the appointed day. The viceroy had been asked to send troops to preserve order and to instruct the magistrate to arrest the guilty parties. With the news that 600 men had been posted to the leased territory there seemed no reason for panic, as the occurrence was in Blake's opinion nothing more than a sudden affray: so he thought, at least, in late April when reporting the events of the month to the secretary of state.[56] But in his despatch of the 7th, he wrote:

Mr Stewart Lockhart, whose knowledge of the people is great, and who has means of obtaining special information, is of opinion that this attack is part of a general movement against our occupation on the part of the *literati* who have hitherto lived by irregular squeezes from the people and of the gamblers and bad characters banished from Hong Kong, and I am disposed to agree with him. But the heaviest punishment that we could inflict, even if we could define the offence of which the people have been guilty, remembering that we have so far no legal standing, would not equal the expense and discomfort of having to support the Chinese soldiers sent into the territory today by the Viceroy, in fulfilment of his undertaking. The probable result will be to welcome our appearance on the 17th instant with the disappearance of the Chinese troops.[57]

The governor soon became confident that this firing of the matshed on 3 and 4 April was an isolated instance of hostility which was unlikely to be repeated: 'Such a sudden access of militant irritability is not uncommon in Ireland, and subsides as rapidly as it arises.'[58] On the 12th, nine elders from Tai Po Hui district performed the *kow tow*, pleaded for clemency, and presented a petition blaming false rumours of a Sanitary Board and other undesirable innovations for their part in the disorder. Blake wrote to the Colonial Office that everything was quiet and the people civil. He enclosed a translation of the viceroy's notification to the leased territory's inhabitants, in which the people were exhorted to abide by the law, and his own proclamation of the 7th, expressing the wish of Her Majesty the Queen 'that all her subjects in every part of the world shall be prosperous and happy ... All must render implicit obedience'.[59]

No further incidents were reported for a few days, and negotiations continued with the Chinese government over the future of customs administration. HMG's decision to expel IMC officials and to insist upon revenue collection being carried out beyond the land and sea boundaries of the leased territory provided the occasion for apparent obstruction by the viceroy. He wrote to R. W. Mansfield, British consul at Canton, on 10 April, that Blake had personally agreed to the non-removal of customs stations, and as this understanding was now violated it would be needless for the occupation to go ahead as planned. Yet despite the viceroy's note, and the despatch of 600 Chinese troops to Kowloon City on 14 April, Blake was determined not to alter his arrangements, and Stewart Lockhart asked Mansfield to request the presence of an officer of suitable rank at the ceremonial transfer of jurisdiction and to intimate the necessity of withdrawing all Chinese troops on that day. As a concession it was decided in London to allow temporary retention, pending other arrangements, of some of the customs houses, and Chamberlain hoped that the Yamen would prevent further difficulties impeding a peaceful and orderly occupation. But the Chinese ministers would give no definite promise of co-operation.[60]

Blake's optimism was shattered by a police party's discovery that the matsheds at Tai Po Hui, supposedly being protected by the viceroy's troops, had been reduced to smouldering ruins. On the northern hills was a menacing force of about 150 Chinese, and Captain May returned with his small party of seventeen men to Hong Kong. They were sent back the next day, the 15th, with a company of the Hong Kong Regiment under Captain Berger. The governor did not expect this force to be attacked, but at Tai Po Hui they were met by a large number, estimated by Berger to be about 1,200, of 'apparently Chinese troops in regular uniform' in position on the hills and manning an entrenched battery of artillery. The Chinese opened fire until routed by the regiment with reinforcements from HMS *Fame*.[61] Major-General Gascoigne proceeded on the 16th with a much larger force to the scene of battle, accompanied by Stewart Lockhart, and the hoisting of the flag took place soon after arrival.

The Battle of Tai Po

The sight of the union jack at Tai Po and the presence of a few British troops were no deterrent to the rebels, and it required more emphatic measures to dissuade them from further resistance. A party of 'sportsmen' from Hong Kong had been fired on at Deep Bay, and on the evening of 16 April the Volunteers were called out to protect Yau Ma Tei and Kowloon against an expected attack from Castle Peak.[62] The next day several thousand Chinese armed with heavy weapons bombarded the camp at Tai Po, and only a direct assault repelled them. They took up strong positions on hills overlooking the Lam Tsuen valley but were again repulsed, this time retreating to and regrouping at Sheung Tsuen. Their next attack, at a point two miles from Kam Tin, was their last: a resounding British victory convinced the villagers and agitators who had advocated rebellion that further fighting was useless.[63] The British forces were too powerful, too well-organized and too determined, while the rebels had suffered heavy casualties.

Stewart Lockhart now proceeded to impose strict control preliminary to the rapid organization of an administrative system for the territory. From a base camp at Ping Shan he travelled to the surrounding villages, dispelling the rumours which had contributed to the decision to resist, endeavouring to discover and arrest the ringleaders, and impressing upon the inhabitants the new government's determination to govern them fairly but firmly. At each village the temples and halls were searched and the elders lectured; informers were questioned and evidence collected; arms were demanded and, if produced, confiscated, while villagers were exhorted to return to their normal occupations. Gates in walled villages were demolished[64] and numerous ricks of grass were burned. The rebellious inhabitants were forced to acknowledge defeat, accompanied in some instances by sullenness and in others by abject appeals for leniency.

During the April disturbances, the Hong Kong authorities had to make all the important decisions: although Blake was in constant telegraphic touch with London there was little control that the secretary of state could effectively exercise. The role of the Colonial Office in the affair was to make representations to the Foreign Office for transmission to Bax-Ironside at Peking, though the governor was instructed to keep him directly informed. He impressed upon the Chinese ministers the necessity of precautions being taken to prevent trouble arising, but Peking was also too far removed from Hong Kong to inhibit very much the policy of the local authority: a promise to arrange the withdrawal of Chinese troops from the Walled City was extracted on 20 April but soldiers were still there when the place was occupied on 16 May.[65]

It was this matter of Chinese troops within the leased territory which seemed to Britain clear evidence of the viceroy's duplicity. Blake had, of course, requested their presence for the protection of the matsheds and various work parties, and viceroy T'an had complied, sending 300 men to be posted to several parts of the region by Stewart Lockhart. After the initial assault on May's party a 'considerable force' was asked for, and 600 troops proceeded into the leased area to preserve order. But on 25 April it was discovered that a further 300, under deputy Wang, had been despatched by the viceroy to Kowloon City and 300 to Sham Chun; Blake protested, and insisted that they be withdrawn. Wang thought that, knowing the viceroy's feelings, there was little chance of obtaining the authority to move, while the governor was convinced that protection of the customs had been the viceroy's motive. The Yamen insisted that T'an had merely complied with Blake's request for men to keep order.[66] Eventually, as will shortly be described, colonial troops expelled their Chinese counterparts.

A second cause for representations to the Yamen was the acquisition, through an informer, of a portion of a telegram purportedly sent by the viceroy to the commandant of coast forts: 'Should more than three British men-of-war enter harbour unauthorised, then, no matter whether they break into interior, open fire on them resolutely.' The Yamen naturally questioned the telegram's authenticity.[67]

Bax-Ironside's services were called upon, finally, with regard to compensation for the disturbances, and the consequent negotiations are discussed below. It is sufficient to note here that HMG was on the one hand outraged, and on the other delighted, at being provided with an excuse for the pressing of further concessions; the Chinese government was indignant but impotent.

From the Chinese point of view the resistance movement was futile: many rebels were killed, while the gravest injury to the British forces was caused by an enraged and patriotic buffalo; normal occupations were interrupted; much damage was done to property; some of the territory's leading inhabitants fled, two others were hanged. Yet the rebels had fought bravely, with a high degree of organization. The military orthodoxy of their gun emplacements and intrenchments at Tai Po Hui and their uniforms suggested official support and control, and the question of their status naturally arose.

In Kwangtung during the last decades of the Ch'ing dynasty, and even earlier, there were three varieties of soldiers: regular troops, *yung* (braves) and *t'uan-lien* (militia). The second class were the 'bare sticks', irregular mercenaries officially organized; the *t'uan-lien* were gentry-trained, and consisted mainly of ordinary peasants assembled occasionally for a particular purpose and then disbanded.[68] Blake referred to the five Chinese soldiers from the Walled City who had accompanied May's party to the matsheds on 3

April as 'braves', and possibly they were *yung* recruited to supplement the army at this time and place of disorder. The viceroy had sent ordinary soldiers from Canton. But it was the 'local corps' who were engaged in the fighting against British soldiers, 'village train-bands' wearing uniforms and carrying flags in similar fashion to government troops yet free from government control.[69]

The first indication in 1899 of preparations for resistance appearing in the admittedly unsatisfactory British records was a gathering of Tang elders in the Ha Tsuen ancestral temple on 28 March. Further discussions were held next day at Yuen Long, attended by representatives from Pat Heung, Shap Pat Heung, Ping Shan, Ha Tsuen, and Castle Peak, and again on 31 March, when people from Sheung Shui, Fanling, Tai Po Tau, Ping Kong, and San Tin appeared to join the proposed resistance movement. On 10 April, a 'Great-Peace-Public-Council Hall', the Tai Ping Kung Kuk, was established. Prior to formation of the *kuk* the matshed at Tai Po Hui had been burned and an armed body of men from Ha Tsuen proceeded to Tai Po. Tang Tsing-sz, one of the principal organizers, travelled to various villages inciting them to resist the British; another Tang went to Canton with a petition for the viceroy. On 12 April, Major Fong arrived at Castle Peak in a gun-boat and, although he apparently had no orders to interfere with the villagers' plans, was forcefully resisted by Castle Peak residents. The Tang villages of Kam Tin, Ha Tsuen, and Ping Shan coerced smaller villages in the Shap Pat Heung district into sending men.[70]

During the actual hostilities against the British troops, men from Lam Tsuen, Pat Heung, Kam Tin, Shap Pat Heung, Ping Shan, Ha Tsuen, Castle Peak, and Yuen Long, and from various places across the border, were involved. A table drawn up by Stewart Lockhart, containing the names of ring-leaders mentioned in captured documents and in statements by informers, mentions forty-two persons, twenty-nine with the family name of Tang; no other clan was represented by more than two names, though each of the 'five great clans' of the New Territories (Tang, Hau, Pang, Liu, and Man) was included.[71] All were Punti, that is, they were members of what was originally the dominant land-based Chinese ethnic group in the area.

The tactics of the ring-leaders were the spreading of false rumours and the use of coercion. Those who argued against resistance were accused of accepting bribes from a land company which had allegedly been operating in the area or of receiving a licence

from the British government; those who co-operated with the barbarians were condemned as traitors and rewards were promised for
their arrest, and several were brutally murdered. Preparations were
thorough, and included the raising of money by subscription,
arrangements for medical treatment of the wounded, prohibition of
the export of grain, recruitment of men from over the border, and
the stock-piling of arms and ammunition. Perhaps the most important centre of organization was the Yuen Long market, which was
used as a base by villages in the marketing area. The Tai Ping
Kung Kuk, headquarters for the resistance movement, was established at Yuen Long. A temple at Shek Wu Hui, shared by seven
lineages, become the centre of operations in that region, and in the
Tai Po area the Man Mo Miu temple was headquarters for the
military activities of the *ts'at yeuk*, which was a union of over
seventy villages based in Tai Po.[72]

All this suggests a degree of organization and determination to
resist the foreigner of which the British authorities were aware only
after the event. Resistance to the British occupation was not suspected, and not taken into account, when the extension of territory
was demanded in Peking. If problems were to arise on the assumption of authority they could be dealt with by the men on the spot,
men who, despite Stewart Lockhart's reputation and the careful
report he had prepared in 1898, were insufficiently informed of the
true situation. The details of the rebellion imply prior *t'uan-lien*
activity in this part of San On and the existence of enduring sets of
relationships (kinship ties, identification with marketing com-
munities, and gentry leadership) which reflected the cohesive social
structure of rural Kwangtung.[73] Colonial expansion at the expense
of a tottering Chinese empire was beset with initial difficulties quite
unimagined at the time of the convention.

From the British point of view, resistance to the occupation
necessitated a great deal of extra and costly work and a considerable
loss of prestige. The governor was sorely disappointed and scath-
ingly criticized. A *Daily Press* article summed up the general
response of the local British community: France at Kwangchow
Wan and Russia at Liaotung had both resorted to force resulting in
the deaths of many Chinese[74]—but the British 'were going to show
the world how such things should be done'.

Those who have been through the country before the transfer will bear
in their minds a picture of a fairly happy and contented population, well
fed, well clothed, and well housed, living in a law-abiding sort of way—

barring an occasional clan fight or armed robbery—and who had few taxes and few policemen to trouble them, and desired only to be left alone.... Now the consequences are before the world in their full unpleasantness and our French and Russian friends may jeer at the superior person— JOHN BULL to wit—who has not brought things off quite so well as he intended—no better, in fact, than they themselves.[75]

4

THE AFTERMATH OF CHINESE RESISTANCE

The Policy of the Hong Kong Government

DURING the last week of April 1899 Stewart Lockhart toured the New Territories collecting evidence, receiving petitions from contrite and fearful villagers, and making preliminary plans for administration. Thereafter he remained for the first part of May at Tai Po. The policy he wished to pursue against the graduates and local notables responsible for the disturbances was one of uncompromising retribution. 'It will, I fear, tend to shake the belief of the people in British justice if the rascals who have created all the trouble are allowed to escape unpunished.'[1] But Sir Henry Blake, anxious to receive the goodwill of the Chinese community and somewhat patronizing in his attitude towards the resisters, disagreed. He did not think it just or expedient to follow a vindictive policy, and did not intend to exact any punishment; he advised the colonial secretary to ignore what had passed. Stewart Lockhart, however, persisted in his rather different approach, advocating that those responsible for the resistance movement be banished and their property confiscated: 'These men did not wish to enjoy the benefits of British rule, so it will be no great hardship to them to transfer their energies to a soil more congenial to them.'[2]

This was a significant conflict of opinion between an old China hand and a new governor, between the official responsible in practice for the early administration of the New Territories and his superior officer, formally responsible to Downing Street. Blake's policy was the more humane, in that he considered the events of April from the point of view of the unfortunate inhabitants who took exception to being handed over to the jurisdiction of a foreign government; and ultimately his policy was probably more sound from an administrative point of view. 'It is to my mind not improbable,' he wrote to Chamberlain, 'that in the future the leaders in the movement may be our most useful assistants in carrying out the local arrangements in the new territory.'[3] Stewart Lockhart's proposals, on the other hand, seemed to contemplate a violation of the non-expulsion provision of the convention. Chamberlain concurred that ring-leaders should not be punished, for at the time of their offence they were outside British territory and to adopt severe measures against persons who could only be treated as prisoners of war would be most impolitic.[4]

Fung shui provides a neat example of the ruthlessness of Stewart Lockhart's approach. The colonial government has always been sensitive to the 'superstitious' ideas of its Chinese subjects, and geomantic objections to constructions plans have generally been listened to with patience, if not sympathy. But Stewart Lockhart decided to ignore them even where they were not voiced by formerly rebellious elders, and insisted on placing police stations on whatever sites were considered most suitable. Petitioners from Cheung Sha Wan were informed that Britain would not tolerate the obstruction of necessary public works by agitators making improper use of the superstitions of the people.[5] In this instance Blake agreed, but with respect to petitioners from Sha Tau Kok division he could not accept his colonial secretary's proposals.

A committee of the Tung Wo Kuk had, on 12 April, presented a case to the San On magistrate for the prevention of the British occupation. Excessive taxation and oppressive government were feared, and the Sanitary Board in Hong Kong was accused of poisoning suspected plague patients with arsenic: 'Chinese and British rule in their good and evil effects are as far removed from each other as heaven is from earth.' The San On magistrate's reply reminded the petitioners that the lease had been sanctioned by the emperor and that the foreign officials would treat the people exceptionally well. His promise to investigate the truth of the statements in the petition was taken by Stewart Lockhart as being acquiescence in the 'atrocious libels' contained in the document, for which the magistrate should be punished. As for the *literati* who presented the petition, they could be banished and their property taken with a clear conscience since they did not desire to be governed by the British. This was an extraordinary reaction to an inaccurate but fairly reasonable petition by Chinese subjects to a Chinese official, and Blake would have none of it. He could not see any grounds for taking action against the petitioners, especially as some of them might usefully be appointed to the district council.[6]

Two incidents revealed in practical form the opposing attitudes of governor and colonial secretary. The first was the detention, on 24 April, of the messenger sent to post a notice issued by viceroy T'an and governor Luk of Kwangtung, a notice which, strictly speaking, should not have been issued and for which Stewart Lockhart recommended calling the viceroy and the San On magistrate to account. Blake ordered the messenger's release, for he had committed no offence.[7] Hong Kong was indignant that official Chinese notices should be published in the territory after it became British, although Blake's own proclamation was distributed before that date.

Ng Lo-sam, an alleged agent of 'land jobbers' and confidant of Stewart Lockhart, had engaged three persons for the latter task: one was threatened at Castle Peak and robbed, another was seized and released at Ha Tsuen by villagers who promised to kill him later, and the third, Tang Cheung-hing, was arrested at Kap Shui Mun on 16 April by Ha Tsuen men and taken to Yuen Long. He was locked in a room at the Tai Ping Kung Kuk, and four days later his body was recovered from a creek. This appalling murder had taken place at Ha Tsuen on the night of the 17th, ordered by Tang Tsing-sz and others and carried out by a sometime gambler and thief, Tang Nin. Three other men were murdered at about the same time, though the fact was not discovered for two months.[8]

Stewart Lockhart, who was at Ping Shan when first informed of the outrage, immediately set off for Ha Tsuen with a party of the Hong Kong Regiment. Elders of the district confirmed that three men named by the dead man's widow had taken part, and on his own authority Stewart Lockhart had some houses belonging to these men burnt down. The villagers were informed that Tang Cheung-hing's widow would have to be supported by them. 'If no legal power at present exists for dealing with property in this matter,' wrote Stewart Lockhart to Blake, 'I am of opinion that it should be obtained at once...'[9] The troops then proceeded to Yuen Long and destroyed the meeting house in which the murder was arranged. Back at Ping Shan, Stewart Lockhart ordered Ha Tsuen, Kam Tin, Pat Heung, Shap Pat Heung, and Ping Shan to contribute a total of $1,200 towards the support of the widow.

Blake thought the means adopted as retaliation for the murder were unfortunate, because without legal sanction. 'I have no doubt that the burning of the houses was effective, but we have come to introduce British jurisprudence, not to adopt Chinese.'[10] Stewart

Lockhart was not impressed: the crime was political, having been committed by men who had played a primary role in the resistance movement; the deceased and the murderers all belonged to the same lineage, the heads of which had frequently co-operated with the British in their investigations. This was considered important to people living under a system where the basic unit was the clan rather than the individual, and the villagers heartily approved the punitive measures taken. Prompt retaliation had considerably encouraged the return to order of the Yuen Long area. Blake, however, preferred to offer a large reward for evidence leading to conviction of any of the murderers, for such a course of action contrasted a system of law with the previous system of benevolent despotism.[11] In addition, it was ultimately to prove successful.

Stewart Lockhart admitted to his diary his personal feelings on the matter. He described Blake's minute as a polite form of censure and observed that it was:

... disappointing to say the least of it, not to receive the support which one has a right to expect from one's Chief, especially when there can be no doubt that the prompt action taken has had the effect of satisfying the people and making them believe in the justice of our rule. British jurisprudence is excellent in theory, but in practice was quite inapplicable to the state of affairs we found in existence when we took over the territory. I have not the least hesitation in saying that had we acted otherwise than we did and sat still doing nothing until we had tried to obtain strictly legal proof, which may never have been forthcoming, a most unfavourable impression of British justice would have been created among the people.[12]

Stewart Lockhart was being thoroughly Chinese in his approach to this matter, for what he recommended was very similar to the *pao chia* notion of group responsibility. But the governor's view prevailed, of course, and the establishment of the administrative system in the New Territories was not to be hampered by seeking vengeance against the leaders of the resistance movement.[13]

Occupation of Sham Chun and the Walled City

The Colonial Office lost no time in seeking imperial advantage from the essentially provincial rebellion. On 17 April Salisbury was asked to inform Bax-Ironside that Sham Chun would have to be included within the new boundary and customs stations immediately withdrawn; Lucas referred to the 'clear proof' of Chinese bad faith. Next day demands for the removal of Chinese officials and troops from the Walled City and the abolition of all Chinese jurisdiction there were added. The director of military intelligence further suggested that the southern and western boundaries be extended to include Gap Rock and the islands dominating the approach to Canton. Blake reiterated that Chinese jurisdiction would have to go, and Chamberlain endorsed this view in correspondence with the Foreign Office. The Navy League joined the chorus, demanding in addition the extension of the northern boundary to the East River and conversion of the lease into perpetual cession.[14]

Public and Colonial Office opinion coincided, but Salisbury had larger issues of imperial policy in mind; he was not initially willing to insist explicitly upon the withdrawal of Chinese jurisdiction, and noted that the Tsungli Yamen had promised to evacuate its troops from the territory. By the 26th, however, Bax-Ironside was instructed to intimate to the Chinese ministers that HMG reserved its demands for satisfaction following the disturbances, pending further consideration of the form they should take. The ministers received this message with excited and angry indignation, but Salisbury had no sympathy: failure to consider properly his chargé's representations would force Britain to conclude that the Yamen could not control the viceroy at Canton and to deal locally with the matter without reference to Peking.[15]

On 26 April Blake telegraphed that the disturbances were at an end, though 300 native soldiers remained in the Walled City despite the request by the consul at Canton that the viceroy remove all troops, arms, and ammunition by the 24th. Chamberlain's plan to blockade the city and starve out the garrison was put aside by Salisbury, but on 7 May Blake informed Peking of plans by Chinese north of the boundary to invade the leased territory. On 9 May the Foreign Office suggested that Hong Kong be instructed to occupy the Walled City. Blake was encouraged by a plea from the commander at the Walled City that he ask the viceroy to remove him, as he and his soldiers had not been paid for over a month. Despite the Yamen's instructions to the viceroy that he arrange all matters with Hong Kong in a friendly spirit, Chamberlain, by telegram on 14 May, ordered the occupation of both the Walled City and Sham Chun.[16] This was done two days later.

Despite the secrecy with which preparations were made, a large crowd of spectators was gathered on the beach by the time the troops given the Walled City detail had disembarked at the Kow-loon City pier. Royal Welsh fusiliers and 100 Hong Kong Volun-teers assembled in front of the old customs house building, which had been converted into a police station, before marching into the dark, evil-smelling streets which led to the fort. The city was found to be almost deserted, the main gate open, and uniformed Chinese soldiers nowhere to be seen; the mandarin remonstrated wildly but he made no attempt to resist. The union jack was hoisted, troops presented arms, and the Volunteers provided a twenty-one-gun salute from their seven-pounders. A search for arms and ammuni-tion revealed a collection of fighting irons, bows and arrows, gingals (long, telescope-like guns), flintlocks, repeating rifles, boxes of ammunition, and uniforms, and these were all later sent to Canton, while about 150 inhabitants were rounded up. A small force remained in occupation when the main body of troops withdrew; commented a local newspaper: 'The trip was immensely enjoyed by all who took part in it.'[17] The residents of the Walled City departed by junk next day. The commanders of the garrison, however, refused to leave, and the viceroy was informed that unless he re-called the officers by 20 May they would be forcibly removed. His answer ignored the stipulation and protested against the occupa-tion.[18]

The failure of Chinese troops to withdraw was arguably a viola-tion of the condition regarding Hong Kong defences in the Kow-loon City clause of the convention, even as China understood it. This ground for occupation of the Walled City does not, however, seem to have been stated explicitly in British communications to the Chinese government, and the unilateral act of occupation was made to appear more as a punishment for the viceroy's alleged con-nivance in the disturbances.

Sham Chun, just over the boundary beyond the river which bears its name, was both a standard marketing town and the inter-mediate market for other standard markets in the area. Stewart Lockhart had advocated its inclusion within the New Territories for two main reasons: to allow surrounding villages to continue using it as a market without interruption, and because it housed the primary local government authority. It had a population in 1898 of 2,000 Punti.[19] 'The country round Sham Chun', wrote Major-General W. J. Gascoigne, 'is fertile and prosperous, and the town itself compares favourably with many, certainly with Kowloon city.'[20] After 1899, however, it replaced the latter as the mecca of

Hong Kong gamblers and high-spirited philanderers. 'No scenic beauties has Sham Chun. As a health resort, it would never be in the running. What, then, is its attraction? Just this. It is the latest gambling hell in South China, replete with facilities for roulette, *fan tan* and other games of chance; in short, a veritable Monte Carlo of the East.'[21] Yet today it is well known as the border town where passengers from Hong Kong to China change trains.

The proposal to occupy Sham Chun was apparently made on the initiative of the Colonial Office, for Salisbury did not suggest it; the stimulus was a report that a large force of 'rowdies' was preparing to invade the new territory from the north. Failing intervention by the viceroy, Blake promised to 'take such measures of self-defence as may lead to complications'.[22] He noted that over 140 fighting men from Tung Kun had gathered to join Sham Chun residents in the proposed attack, and suggested sending 2,000 men. The manoeuvre was easily effected without opposition and it was said that the troops were cordially received by the Chinese.[23]

Three large columns of men converged on Sham Chun and, by 5.45 p.m. on 16 May, the town was under British military occupation. Gascoigne issued a proclamation in Chinese, informing the locals that Sham Chun was now British territory to be governed by British laws: the viceroy of Canton was declared to have no further jurisdiction in the district.

The whole operation had been completed most satisfactorily, yet the haste with which it had been conceived and executed left the Hong Kong authorities in something of a quandary concerning subsequent procedure. The major problems facing HMG were the exact limits of this new extension, the duration of the occupation, and the form of administration.

Blake had written on 28 April:

The district north from [Sham Chun] River to the East River includes the most turbulent portion of all China. It contains the headquarters of the Triad Society, and the districts are composed of practically robber clans. Such a district as even [Sham Chun] to the summit of the hills would entail an additional regiment and so large an increase of the police force as to create a serious addition to the expenses of the Colony. In my opinion, the river boundary as already settled is the best for the Colony, and so far as Colonial necessities are concerned I do not consider further extension desirable.[24]

While not wishing to retract this view, the governor also considered that to hold Sham Chun effectively the whole valley to the northern hills should be retained, and that a withdrawal from Sham Chun would be misunderstood. On 26 May he contemplated taking Nam Tau, the seat of the San On magistrate, but the garrison was not thought sufficient if complications arose to threaten Hong Kong. Eventually the positions established by 17 May remained, without extension, until evacuation: Lord Salisbury pointed out that any further occupation might give the impression that Britain was involved in dismembering China, an impression which the Russian minister at Peking would use to create distrust of Her Majesty's Government in the minds of the Tsungli Yamen. Chamberlain agreed that the line delimited in March should remain the boundary of the New Territories.[25]

If British troops were to be stationed across the river in temporary occupation only, however, the opportune time for their withdrawal had to be determined. This depended on the progress of the indemnity negotiations, but there was considerable delay and the British authorities on the spot became more and more concerned about the effects of rendition. Blake was informed on 13 June of the decision regarding eventual restoration of Sham Chun to China,[26] and he soon began a campaign to have that decision either changed or effected at an early date.

He first noted such serious unrest at Canton as to endanger withdrawal; then he informed the Colonial Office of much dissatisfaction being expressed in Hong Kong at possible retrocession. There was also dissatisfaction in the Sham Chun valley; villagers who had been friendly to the troops feared repercussions if the territory became Chinese again. Open war between Russia and Japan, which appeared not unlikely, would necessitate the return of troops to Hong Kong, and the Sham Chun community was becoming demoralized under the lengthy military occupation. New sites for the three remaining customs stations, which were to be removed by the end of October, could not be chosen, to the inconvenience of the IMC and the considerable encouragement of smugglers.[27] And use of the valley north of Sham Chun as a recreation ground for troops was recommended, for the men were prey to 'licentious habits' resulting in a serious weakening of the garrison by venereal disease.[28] Such matters did not significantly affect the negotiations going on in Peking, and it was not until 22 November, nearly six months after the initial occupation, that Blake was ordered to evacuate the troops. He made a final and rather ludicrous attempt to hold on to Sham Chun:

...is it necessary to withdraw at this moment when British population of the Colony is very despondent over reverses in Africa and the German community as I am informed are drinking success to Boers in their Club. It will be less hurtful to our prestige if I may suspend action until African reinforcements have arrived and tide has turned?[29]

This was, understandably, not thought deserving of serious consideration.

The third problem facing the British authorities in May 1899 concerned the style and details of administration: should the Sham Chun district be governed from Hong Kong or left under the control of the military? The latter course was selected, but Blake was most dissatisfied and promoted the appointment of a political officer to take charge. This idea was rejected and the Colonial Office and Hong Kong therefore had little to do with Sham Chun, responsibility devolving upon the army and, ultimately, the War Office.[30]

The Sham Chun valley was notoriously lawless, and Blake's major cause for concern was that restlessness there would spread to the leased territory proper and, if the area was ever to be formally annexed, the task of civil administrators would be exceedingly difficult. At the end of May the Revd Martin Schaub, of the Basel mission at Li Long (about nine miles north of Sham Chun), wrote to Blake that elements of the Tang clan at Pan Tin were engaging men and assembling weapons in readiness for an attack on the occupying forces. Blake at first considered the report exaggerated, or that the Tangs were organizing to prevent the capture of Tang Cheung-hing's murderers, the viceroy having issued orders for their arrest, while the later consensus maintained that the Chinese wanted only to resist an expected British invasion of Tung Kun district. But the governor had determined to protect the mission station if necessary, for it appeared to him undesirable that the German government should be presented with an opportunity to intervene. The Foreign Office approved and, although Hamilton thought this showed Salisbury's inconsistency, it was in line with standard British policy in China of maintaining the balance of powers and avoiding occasions when other European nations could become further involved. HMG could not afford a recurrence of the situation leading to German occupation of Kiaochow.[31]

The viceroy was informed of the putative resistance movement and he reacted vigorously to prevent the feared attack: there could be no complaint, this time, of non-co-operation by the provincial authorities. The missionaries were told that, if seriously threatened, they could apply for and receive protection from the troops at Sham Chun, and Lieutenant-Colonel N. V. O' Gorman of the Hong Kong Regiment was instructed to go to their aid if satisfied there was actual and immediate danger of attack. But no incident occurred: the British troops did not venture beyond Sham Chun, the wealthy Chinese wanted the 'rowdies' dispersed, and the summer rains began. By 5 June the danger had abated.[32]

Though conditions in the surrounding area continued to be relatively lawless, Sham Chun itself remained peaceful under military rule. But when news leaked out that Sham Chun was to be restored to China minor disturbances broke out and brought into prominence the central problem of the occupation: the legal régime which was to apply. Chinese jurisdiction had been ousted by conquest confirmed by the major-general's proclamation, and despite appeals to the Chinese authorities to deal with their own people by their own law, the maintenance of order and the settlement of disputes were solely within the army's domain. Blake, unable to appoint his own officer to administer the territory, suggested the resumption of local government by village elders and gentry under army supervision, but Schaub's opinion that the people of Sham Chun were incapable of governing themselves was accepted by Gascoigne. The governor's primary concerns were that matters affecting the New Territories, such as gatherings of 'rowdies' preparatory to crossing the border, should be properly dealt with under martial law and that information and assistance be given to the Hong Kong authorities. Gascoigne, however, was not anxious to interfere where troops or their safety were not concerned, and with the support of the acting attorney-general he refused to assist Hong Kong police seeking to subpoena a Sham Chun man to give evidence in Victoria.[33]

It was clearly an unsatisfactory situation, though when Salisbury at last suggested retrocession the Colonial Office delayed ordering the withdrawal of troops for a further month while attempting to gain more concessions. On 2 November, however, the immediate evacuation of troops from Chinese territory was ordered, the viceroy being informed that failure to provide protection for friendly villagers and the maintenance of law and order might lead to a second occupation. Major T. J. W. Prendergast, who had been given control of the Sheung Po camp near Sham Chun, assembled the last of his men on 13 November and marched them to the New

Territories, amid 'expressions of goodwill, and regret at their departure'.[34] A force of the Regiment was stationed in British territory near the border to deter any exhibitions of Chinese grief uninhibited enough to constitute disorders and uprisings.[35]

Indemnity Negotiations

The most popular item in any list of reparations for the resistance movement—expulsion of Chinese officialdom from the Walled City of Kowloon—was achieved by *fait accompli*. But the opportunity for further concessions was too good to miss; for nearly six months indemnity negotiations continued, with the presence of British troops in Sham Chun being used by Salisbury as a bargaining ploy. One scholar has referred to this as 'one of the most involved and bizarre episodes of British diplomacy in China . . .'.[36]

No further territorial demands were to be made on China, as such were expected to lead to similar claims by other powers.[37] It seemed for a moment, however, that the cession of Gap Rock would be an exception. In June 1899 the Colonial Defence Committee had noted a memorandum by the harbour master at Hong Kong drawing attention to the disadvantage arising from Chinese control of Gap Rock, and had again urged the cession of the island. The possibility of exchanging Sham Chun for Gap Rock was canvassed by the War Office and the Colonial Office, but the Colonial Defence Committee abandoned its previous advocacy of the island in favour of the retention of Sham Chun. Chamberlain, however, agreed with the War Office and urged upon Salisbury that the view of HMG's military advisers be accepted. The Prime Minister concurred, replying that he was prepared to instruct the chargé at Peking to inform the Chinese government that Gap Rock would be retained when Great Britain withdrew from Sham Chun. But he added that proviso fatal to so much British initiative in China: 'It is however very doubtful whether the present is a favourable opportunity for pressing of a formal cession.' Then the Colonial Office seemed to lose interest; unless, wrote Bertram Cox, legal assistant under-secretary, a complete cession was asked for, which Chamberlain did not wish to press, there was little use in disturbing the arrangements then existing. Salisbury agreed to leave Gap Rock in China's hands,[38] and the matter was not to be raised again until 1912.[39]

The Colonial Office suggested $100,000 as compensation for the

April disturbances, which included $7,000 profit, but Salisbury decided on $150,000, though he was prepared to forgo payment provided satisfaction was given in other matters. The money was unimportant if more pressing affairs could be arranged. These were of no interest to the Colonial Office, which thereupon suggested, in the event of restoration of Sham Chun, that West River trade be fully opened to foreign commerce.[40]

The Yamen refused to pay any compensation, and in September Chamberlain, concerned about the long military occupation of Sham Chun, considered that it would soon be necessary to proceed on the assumption that the district was permanently annexed to the leased territory. Salisbury wanted further delay, however, until on 4 October he informed the Colonial Office that other matters had been satisfactorily dealt with by the Chinese and that therefore Sham Chun could be returned to Chinese jurisdiction. The $150,000 compensation was neither paid nor insisted upon. Chamberlain was quite dissatisfied and asked that China be pressed for a moderate indemnity covering the costs of the Sham Chun occupation; Salisbury was only prepared to seek a pledge that order be maintained and collaborators protected after the British withdrawal.[41] The Colonial Office noted that the continuance of the occupation was 'beyond question in the main dictated by considerations of Imperial interest...'.[42]

Comparatively minor gains, therefore, were achieved lest a new chain of demands by other powers be initiated; China was protected from more extensive reparations by Britain's traditional policy of safeguarding the Middle Kingdom's territorial integrity, and colonial interests were once again subordinated to the realities of imperial affairs. The acquisition of the New Territories was secured in order to satisfy the defensive requirements of an existing colony; as with Gap Rock, the further acquisition of Sham Chun was suggested for the same reason. The necessity of including Gap Rock and Sham Chun within the new boundaries, however, was not so compelling, and HMG used the occupation of the latter for other purposes. Once these had been achieved the town was restored to China. The Walled City, on the other hand, could not be returned to Chinese jurisdiction if the purpose of the leasehold was not to be frustrated.

The decision to evacuate Sham Chun, when first known by local inhabitants at the end of June, was commented upon by some of them in these terms: 'Now we see that [foreign devils] are after all like we Chinese, they are only looking for money. By giving up Sham Chun for $93,000 they make a very good business.'[43] When Sham Chun was eventually given up without any money consideration at all the profit was to the business interests of the British empire, not the colony. But Hong Kong won some compensation in another area. Property of the Chinese government within the leased territory, consisting of several customs stations, the lighthouse at Waglan, and civil and military premises at the Walled City, were taken over by Great Britain without monetary recompense of any sort, despite MacDonald's assurance to the Yamen that all property required would be paid for. A rough estimate set the value of the buildings evacuated by the Chinese Imperial Maritime Customs at almost $22,000, a small sum which would nevertheless have been an unwelcome expenditure in the colony's budget.[44]

The matter was first raised by Blake in mid-June. Some of the structures had been taken over as police stations, others were not required by the government. Hillier, the departing commissioner of customs at Kowloon, demanded payment for the property, but Blake refused, only giving him a receipt for each building. Chamberlain thought payment should be made, though he wanted the value of New Territories public buildings set off against the eventual compensation claim on account of 'the connivance of the authorities at the disturbances . . .'.[45] But there had been no payment for Chinese public property at Weihaiwei, and at the end of October HMG saw no reason for departing from that precedent. Although Blake was asked for an estimate of the buildings' value, in case the Foreign Office objected to non-payment, Chamberlain proposed that there be no refund to China, and Salisbury agreed to defer the question until the Chinese government put forward a claim.[46]

In March 1900, however, Li Hung-chang, then viceroy of Canton, submitted that the value of the premises used by the military before the take-over should be estimated and the money paid over; alternatively, the Chinese should be allowed to demolish the buildings, including customs stations, and take away the materials. Britain was not to be bothered by such claims:

... in view of the fact that Her Majesty's Government were put to expense greatly in excess of the value of the buildings in question, owing to the resistance offered to the occupation of the leased territory, they propose to regard the value of these buildings as a set-off against the above-mentioned expenditure, and are not prepared to pay any compensation, nor to allow the Chinese Government to pull them down and remove the materials.[47]

The rendition of Sham Chun had been delayed while concessions, on account of the trouble and expense suffered by Hong Kong during the take-over of the leased territory, were demanded and received. It is therefore unexpected to read Bertie's letter to the Colonial Office on 17 October 1899, in which he said:

> It is true that the conduct of the Viceroy of Canton was unsatisfactory in that no efficient measures were taken by him previous to the occupation of the leased territory for the preservation of order, but the evidence since received tends to show that neither he, nor any other of the high provincial officials, instigated the disturbances in any way, or was indeed privy to them.[48]

Perhaps the Chinese were consoled by the fact that, for this reason, the indemnity for the Sham Chun occupation sponsored by Chamberlain was not demanded.

The Chinese Response

The response of the Chinese authorities to the occupation of Sham Chun and the Walled City was, of course, vigorous protest. The Tsungli Yamen complained on 21 May:

> In connection with this affair China has shown the most accommodating spirit, and the conduct of England in sending soldiers to Kowloon City and expelling the Chinese officials and troops, and in forcing the withdrawal of officers and soldiers from [Sham Chun] and hoisting the British flag is indeed an unexpected return.[49]

The viceroy wrote twice to Hong Kong without receiving any reply, and then sent deputy Wang to interview Blake and discover 'how international business is to be conducted hereafter'. Sir Henry no doubt took great delight, considering the criticisms made of his Canton trip, in declining to receive the envoy: 'If the Viceroy wants to see me, he should come himself, just as I went to see him.'[50] Sir Lo Feng-lu, the Chinese minister in London, was given a lengthy review of the April disturbances and the May retaliation, and was informed that Sham Chun was to remain provisionally in British occupation for the protection of the New Territories.[51] The provisos concerned Salisbury's general policy in China, and the occupation of Sham Chun, initially for the sake of the colony and con-

tinued in order to further imperial interests, came to an end only
when those interests were satisfied.

In October the Yamen, having met British reparation demands,
asked for the restoration of jurisdiction in Kowloon. Chamberlain
expressed the hope that 'this matter may be taken as finally settled
and that under no circumstances or conditions whatever will Chinese authority in any form be revived in Kowloon City'.[52] The Foreign Office affirmed its decision, but China continued to protest and
hoped that the removal of viceroy T'an and his replacement by Li
Hung-chang would lead to faithful observance of the convention.[53]
Sir Claude MacDonald advised Li to discuss the matter with the
governor of Hong Kong, which he did in July 1900, but to no
avail; indeed, his reference to the Walled City was characterized by
one British official present at the interview as 'more or less perfunc-
tory and showing little insistence on the subject'.[54] By order in
council of 27 December 1899, 'the exercise of jurisdiction by the
Chinese officials in the City of Kowloon having been found to be
inconsistent with the military requirements for the defence of Hong
Kong', the Walled City was declared to be 'part and parcel of Her
Majesty's Colony of Hong Kong ... as if it had originally formed
part of the said Colony'.[55] As far as Britain was concerned the issue
was settled, and when the New Territories Land Court was established in 1900 its first office was the school building inside the Walled City.[56]

Reasons for the Resistance

Having investigated the resistance movement and its immediate
consequences, we can now look back and attempt to explain why it
occurred. Many theories were put forward at the time, though none
was completely substantiated. In particular, the British had a vested interest in claiming that the April disturbances were tacitly
supported, if not partly organized, by the viceroy of Canton in a
last-ditch attempt to save the customs stations. Chamberlain was
very anxious to prove complicity to assist him in seeking the
immediate evacuation of customs houses and the Walled City, and
Blake attempted to provide the evidence. Apart from such matters
as the arrival of 300 troops on 15 April and the military knowledge
and tactics of the rebels, he relied on the letter from Major Fong
promising to 'allow all the villages to carry out their own settled
plans'.[57] Stewart Lockhart discovered that 1,350 men from Chinese

territory had joined the battle against British troops yet Major Fong, stationed at Sham Chun, took no steps to preserve order; as an informant put it, Fong 'pretended to be deaf and blind!'[58] The viceroy, said Blake, had shown an utter disregard of his responsibility.[59]

Doubtless the viceroy was lax in his duty to protect British work parties before 17 April; doubtless he was not too dismayed by the first reports of resistance. Whether he can be accused of actual knowledge and connivance is quite debatable: the British case merely assumed that Chinese officials *must* have known and *must* have been deliberately neglectful of their responsibilities, without producing real evidence. Fong's letter is obscure in its meaning, and is anyway contradicted by another letter found at Yuen Long which implied a warning to the villagers; Fong was forcibly resisted at Castle Peak.[60] Two proclamations issued by the Chinese authorities were uncompromising in their command for the inhabitants 'to strive to be good and loyal subjects' who can 'all live together in peace without suspicion'.[61] The *t'uan-lien* were not totally ignorant of military strategy, and despite 'sanction' by the authorities could nevertheless act quite independently, without official control or knowledge; the brief analysis of their organization presented above indicates that they did so. Neither regular Chinese troops nor *yung* were involved in the fighting. It seems a quite sufficient explanation that the viceroy and his underlings were unable to prevent the disturbances; a genuine form of local government by strong lineages was powerful enough to ignore the provincial representatives of a weak and declining central authority. Viceroy T'an is more likely to have been incapable of controlling than secretly conniving in the resistance movement. This conclusion is in line with the Foreign Office view, quoted above, that T'an had neither instigated the disturbances nor been privy to them.

An alternative suggestion, that the viceroy was merely the agent of a throne become ultra-conservative after the collapse of reformism in September 1898,[62] has no support from the records. The various allegations by China-coast newspapers of official complicity,[63] founded, one suspects, on regular expectations of oriental cunning in such events, were also uncorroborated.

No one doubted that, whether the viceroy was involved or not, the inhabitants' fear that government by the British would mean interference with their established rights and customs was a primary reason for the resistance. Rumours were disseminated of evils 'so great that one could not bear to think of them',[64] such as the imposition of taxes, the prohibition of fishing and wood-cutting, the defilement of women, the registration of births and deaths, and the destruction of good *fung shui*. One theory blamed 'land jobbers' as the source of such rumours.

The *China Mail* noted in August 1899 that rank land jobbery was alleged to be widespread in the New Territories:

> Without doubt a good deal of land was sold under threats that if not handed over peaceably the British Government would take it forcibly without compensation. The name of one minor Government servant, which must be known to the Government, *i.e.*, to Mr J. H. Stewart Lockhart, the Administrator of the New Territory, is being mentioned freely enough in Hong Kong and in the Hinterland in conjunction with that of a Chinese gentleman, whose land speculations in the New Territory have evidently been carried on with a view to future purchases by the Government for sites of public buildings.[65]

Such allegations were being made and investigated as early as October 1898. It was said that the leaders of a syndicate formed to buy potentially valuable properties at low prices were the two Chinese legislative councillors, the Hon. Dr Ho Kai and the Hon. Wei Yuk.[66] Ho Kai has been described as a very far-sighted land developer, as was Wei Yuk, who was involved in plans to construct a railway from Kowloon to Peking through Canton.[67] The land company's agents, Ng Lo-sam (Ng Sui-shang) and Tang Yung-shen (Tang Ying-shang), had since before the Lockhart commission endeavoured to buy up title deeds at selected places. An informant stated that these men told landowners they would be dispossessed when the British took over the territory, tactics which resulted in the acquisition of land and houses at very cheap rates. The agents were said to be hated throughout the district, and Ho Tung claimed that coercive measures had also been used to induce owners to sell.[68]

Ng Lo-sam, a native of Tung Kun across the boundary, had been branded on his face and banished from China after committing a crime, and a proclamation issued by the San On district magistrate declared that Ng and others had bought land fraudulently and were to be arrested. Ng was alleged to be a 'hanger-on' of Wei Yuk. Tang Yung-shen was an ex-convict still wanted in Nam Tau; he was from Ping Shan, a Tang lineage village, and was accused by the Tangs at Kam Tin of improperly selling lineage property at Cheung Sha Wan. Both Ng and Tang seem to have unofficially accompanied Stewart Lockhart on his tour of the leased territory in 1898 and had provided much of the information upon which his report was based. Perhaps for that reason, they and the syndicate were staunchly defended by Stewart Lockhart, while Blake expressed fears that the colonial secretary may have been misled.[69]

But Stewart Lockhart himself had no such doubts; the land company was blamed, he said, by parties seeking an excuse to justify their resistance to British authority and to conceal the true reason.[70] He reported that Mr Li Shing[71] was the chairman of the company and the largest shareholder and that, as far as he could ascertain, no purchases of land had been made by the company since the signing of the convention. It was formed when there was talk of building a railway between Kowloon and Canton and its purchases of land had been at prices well in advance of the market rate. One seller of land to the company was discovered who said that the price was a fair one, that he sold the land willingly, and that he did not want to buy it back.[72] Nevertheless, although no details are available, the company was apparently investigated by the government. Stewart Lockhart suggested that this be done by the land officer at Tai Po rather than by a committee in Hong Kong, for the summoning of witnesses to Victoria would become known, and 'it is not unlikely that they would be got at'.[73] This may have been an admission that the syndicate had in fact indulged in jobbery in the territory.

Blake issued a proclamation on 12 July 1899, inviting any person who had been coerced or fraudulently persuaded to sell land at a low price to present a petition to the government for investigation. Six months later Stewart Lockhart wrote:

It will thus be seen that the Government has spared neither pains nor time in trying to discover whether land has been obtained by false misrepresentations. Up to the present time 25,540 claims to land have been registered and not a single complaint has, as yet, been received of any person having bought or sold land as has been rumoured.[74]

There is no more evidence on the company's dealings or of any action against it. Endacott writes that Blake wished to restore property bought cheaply as a result of false rumours, 'but the land problem proved too baffling for him to carry out his threat'.[75] The allegations of land jobbery are plausible, and could no doubt be imaginatively developed by any conspiracy theorist, but even if substantiated they would not entirely account for the hostility of San On peasants to British government. Further reasons for the resistance movement must be sought.

One provocative theory put forward by the viceroy was that confederates of Chung Shui-yung were involved. In October 1898 the British received intelligence that this gentleman, supposedly a follower of Sun Yat-sen, planned to attack Hong Kong from San On with triad (secret society) support. His slogan was said to have been: 'Since Our Emperor has leased to the British our territory, it is the duty of our brethren to hold the land ourselves, collect troops, gather taxes, and govern it ourselves. Those who can must be masters of the country.' Apart from a report by Ho Tung, however, which accused Chung Shui-yung of being a common criminal, there is no further mention of him in the records, and it is unlikely that the patriotic motives revealed in the slogan had much to do with the disturbances.[76] Similarly, there is no reason to suspect significant triad participation, though Blake had originally done so and the Tsungli Yamen sought to lay blame at the triad door.[77]

Stewart Lockhart, after intensive investigation, was quite clear as to the fundamental reason for the disturbances: the gentry, hoping to enrich themselves by posing as patriotic defenders of the homeland, were responsible.[78] One informer stated that the gentry intended to extort money from rich inhabitants, even that they wished it to be arranged that the jurisdiction of Chinese officials would remain so that the gentry could continue squeezing the people. Other statements refer to the initiation of discussions by elders of various lineages: though not necessarily gentry in the narrow sense of possessing an imperial degree, they were men of influence and some wealth. But it is difficult to see the object of resistance unless eventual victory could be expected, and even then the elders could not hope for more than maintenance of the status quo. While, undoubtedly, lineage members enriched themselves by their power over corporate property, the main concern of the elders is more likely to have been retention of the wealth and influence of the lineage as a whole. It has been shown that the Tangs played a leading part in the initial organization of the resistance movement and coerced smaller villages into compliance with their plans; the Tangs also had most to lose by the British take-over, for they possessed 'taxlord' rights which could not be recognized under any efficient administration.[79]

Blake had been dissatisfied with Stewart Lockhart's evidence: Chan Kwan-nam, whose statement Stewart Lockhart relied on as proof of his theory that the gentry were the guilty parties, gave no particulars as to the means by which the gentry were to benefit, and the colonial secretary was unable to elaborate. Not the gentry as individuals, though they would lose some prestige and influence, but the gentry as leaders of lineages would suffer most under the British. As subscriptions for resistance were commonly paid from corporate accounts into a special fund it is inconceivable that the organizers hoped to divert the money for their private use. The degree-holding gentry implicated in the documents numbered ten, five of them with the surname Tang from the Yuen Long market- ing area.[80] The higher-order lineage to which they belonged stood in greater jeopardy than any other social group in the New Ter- ritories. The more convincing reason for the elders' alarm was sug- gested by Ho Tung in October 1898:

... the villagers were very much displeased [by the lease of the territory], especially those of [Kam Tin] village, owing to the fact that, though the owners of the property in the neighbourhood of [Kam Tin] village hold deeds, they have to pay tax to the said village. If England got the place, it is feared that the benefit will be deprived of.[81]

Various statements collected by Stewart Lockhart indicated that, once the peasants were alarmed by the impending take-over, they passed beyond the control of their elders. 'But the people having been worked up to revolt, it was impossible to restrain them, so that the sorry spectacle was seen of the tail wagging the dog, instead of the dog the tail.'[82] Although this assertion cannot be corroborated by other evidence, it is likely that, had the elders reconsidered the wisdom of their plans, enthusiasm for the resist- ance movement removed any doubts or will to change course. Peasant fears of more taxes and fines, of interference with tradi- tional ways of livelihood and with *fung shui*, and, most of all, of the dreadful activities of the Sanitary Board overwhelmed the populace, contributing to inter-lineage co-operation and the rela- tively efficient and rapid organization of the *t'uan-lien*. As Wake- man points out, while the *t'uan-lien* 'may have attracted and abetted rebellious and heterodox forces of disorder, the basic values they invoked were conservative, familistic, and orthodox'.[83]

5

BRITISH ADMINISTRATION OF THE NEW TERRITORIES

Law and the Administrative System

As soon as relative peace prevailed in the New Territories, the most urgent task facing the Hong Kong government was the devising and establishment of a suitable administrative apparatus. Given the lack of sophistication of most of the villagers, the inaccessibility of many areas where Chinese peasantry had settled, the utterly different style of government to which they were accustomed, the confusion over land ownership and tenancy, and the resentment and fears of the inhabitants concerning the take-over, the extension of British control over the territory was a difficult operation.

Probably the most important issues of policy related to finance, the administration of justice, settlement of the land problem, and the style of government. The last two are relevant to the theme of this study in that they both raised questions regarding the obligations created by, and the interpretation of, the 1898 Convention of Peking.

The decision upon which everything else revolved was whether to separate the New Territories from Hong Kong and Kowloon and govern it as a virtually independent region. The acting governor, Black, had previously advocated such independence and the local Chinese had petitioned for the appointment as 'resident' of Mr Stewart Lockhart.[1] The Colonial Office had not been impressed then, nor was it impressed when Stewart Lockhart himself voted in favour. The colonial secretary suggested that general administration be the responsibility of a commissioner subordinate only to the governor, assisted by a treasurer, the head of the police, and an advisory council composed of the commissioner and native representatives, one from each of the administrative divisions, known as *tung*, which had existed under the San On apparatus of local government. Village tribunals should remain but under the strict supervision of a travelling magistrate, with appeals to the council of a *tung* and, as last resort, the commissioner.[2]

A lengthy minute by Lucas reveals two main reasons for administrative separation: localization of the seat of government, and avoidance of the bureaucratic red tape appropriate to the older parts of the colony but only likely to confuse unsophisticated villagers familiar with 'primitive' law and custom. Victoria, however, was considered as central to the whole territory as Tai Po Hui (where the headquarters of the New Territories administration was established), and the appointment of suitable men and the establishment of proper communications would answer the second point.[3] Chamberlain's instructions to Blake stated:

I should wish you to understand that in my opinion the new territory should from the outset be regarded as an integral part of the Colony of Hong Kong, and, as such, should be brought under the general administration of the Colony at as early a date as possible. It appears to me that future difficulties will be obviated by taking this course, and that it will be found to be at once more effective and more economical than treating the leased district as separate from the old Colony.[4]

The reference to 'future difficulties' provides a clue to Colonial Office thinking on the subject, confirmed by the conclusions of an informal conference attended by Wingfield, Hamilton and Lucas, Blake, Cecil Smith and Stewart Lockhart. The majority agreed with Lucas that to treat the leased area as an integral part of the colony was more politic: 'more politic because it confirms at once the view that the leased area is for all intents and purposes British territory, colony not protectorate...'.[5]

To understand the significance of this decision it is necessary to refer briefly to the position in imperial constitutional law. When a territory is conquered by British forces, or ceded to the British crown by virtue of an international treaty, it becomes part of Her Majesty's dominions, and Her Majesty has full prerogative powers in relation to it. The courts recognize the authority of Her Majesty's Government to establish an administrative system for the newly acquired territory; the crown's discretion in this matter is initially limited only by whatever provisions might be made by the British parliament. In the absence of imperial legislation, the crown may establish any kind of constitution and governmental system as is thought appropriate. Until the new apparatus is created by prerogative legislation, however, the pre-existing laws and legal system remain intact. Where the crown seeks to govern a territory which is not considered part of Her Majesty's dominions, further powers are needed, and these have been granted by parliament in the Foreign Jurisdiction Acts.

Thus Hong Kong island and Kowloon, being clearly ceded to the British crown, came under the general prerogative authority of Her Majesty's Government. But international leaseholds of the type imposed on China by the foreign powers in 1898 were inventions, mutant creatures adapted to the environment created by imperialist rivalry in the Far East. Their status and effect in international law had not been carefully worked out, and it was vital to colonial interests in Hong Kong that subsequent practice should affirm that the leased territory behind Kowloon had been transferred to Great Britain in the same manner as Kowloon itself and Hong Kong island. The New Territories was not to be just another part of China administered by a western power, but an 'extension' of Hong Kong; the convention was to be seen as a treaty for the 'extension' of established colonial boundaries, not just for the lease of territory. The fundamental decision regarding the style of administration in the New Territories was therefore a political decision prompted by the nature of the territory's acquisition. Colonial opinion and, to a large extent, subsequent practice sought to administer the leased territory as a separate area; but the view that it must be seen to be part of the colony of Hong Kong was the view which prevailed. Had there been no doubt of the leasehold's status the policy recommended by Stewart Lockhart, the man most knowledgeable about and most concerned with New Territories administration, might well have been adopted.

The corollary of the decision to integrate government of the New Territories with government of the existing colony was the necessity of applying to the leasehold the same legal régime as already applied to Hong Kong and Kowloon. There were no established constitutional principles in relation to a leased territory, but it was convenient, and politic, to assume that for this purpose a lease led to the same result as a cession. The crown would therefore possess plenary powers over the leasehold and could alter the previously existing legal system in any way it pleased. In the case of the New Territories, the régime of Chinese law and custom was to be almost totally replaced by the laws and legal system of Hong Kong.

This was done in three steps. First, the order in council of 20 October 1898[6] decreed that, from a date to be fixed by proclamation, all colonial laws then in force were to take effect in the New Territories. Secondly, the proclamation fixing the due date was issued on 8 April 1899.[7] Thirdly, particular laws considered inappropriate during at least the initial stages of British administration in the leasehold were exempted from operation there by an ordinary ordinance of the Hong Kong legislature.[8] No powers under Act of Parliament were resorted to: the crown was assumed to have ample authority for the governance of this new portion of empire. Just as importantly, it was politically desirable to *assert* such authority.

If the crown had not wished to claim sovereign rights over the New Territories, reliance would have been placed on the Foreign Jurisdiction Act 1890 as the source of governmental powers. This was in fact done in relation to the leased territory at Weihaiwei. The lease convention[9] is basically similar to the New Territories treaty, and refers to the exercise by Great Britain of 'sole jurisdiction' (except in Weihaiwei's walled city); the only fundamental difference between the two leaseholds was the contiguity of the 'Kowloon extension' to an established British colony. The Colonial Office originally intended to assume and maintain full sovereign rights over Weihaiwei,[10] and the law officers agreed that the territory was part of Her Majesty's dominions by virtue of cession from China.[11] But Lord Salisbury was concerned not to create a precedent that might be followed by Germany, Russia and France *vis-à-vis* their own leased territories in China,[12] and for this purely political reason the Weihaiwei order in council claimed British authority under the Foreign Jurisdiction Act. Thus Weihaiwei was treated as foreign soil and was not officially recognized as part of Her Majesty's dominions.[13]

Long-term practical convenience, however, required that the New Territories be incorporated into the ceded colony. Whether this was justified in law is a question which will be discussed later.[14] The important point to note here is that the vagueness of the convention as to the extent of the rights acquired from China, combined with the purpose of the lease from Hong Kong's point of view, made it imperative for HMG to integrate the governmental and legal system of the New Territories with that of the colony of Hong Kong.

Another decision of great practical importance was to retain an element of Chinese customary law in the New Territories. In Hong Kong generally (and thus in the New Territories when the Hong

Kong legal régime was applied to it) there were areas of law where pre-cessional legal rules remained in force.[15] The only specific legislative reference, however, to the maintenance of Chinese 'usages and good customs' in the New Territories is now contained in section 13 of the New Territories Ordinance:[16] 'In any proceedings in the Supreme Court or the District Court in relation to land in the New Territories, the court shall have power to recognise and enforce any Chinese custom or customary right affecting such land.' A government committee appointed to consider Chinese law and custom in Hong Kong thought that all questions affecting New Territories land should prima facie be governed by Chinese custom,[17] and in the Supreme Court of Hong Kong it has been held that section 13 is mandatory in effect.[18] Thus Chinese customary law controls land matters in the New Territories.

In summary, it was essentially with respect to *land* that customary law was retained, though there are exceptions contained in the ordinance. And it was customary law, not the imperial 'statutory' law of the Ch'ing dynasty, which was preserved—but early in this century some land questions were settled on the basis of imperial law, and many customary rights must have derived originally from, or more likely were confirmed by, dynastic legislation.[19]

Why was this policy adopted? No doubt it was thought that ease of administration required the maintenance of a land system familiar to the local inhabitants; perhaps, also, Chinese customary land law was preserved in execution of the promise made by Sir Henry Blake to the New Territories Chinese that their 'usages and good customs will not in any way be interfered with'.[20] But it may also be true that a land system quite different from that which had long existed in the ceded portions of the colony was thought required by the non-expropriation clause of the convention. Given that (as will shortly be explained) the original settlement of title to land by the New Territories Land Court was to be governed by Chinese law, it is likely that the choice of policy for subsequent land administration was at least influenced by what was conceived of as a treaty obligation.

Settlement of the Land Question

Although care was taken to imply British acquisition of full sovereign rights over the New Territories, there were promises made in the convention which it was not convenient to ignore and which affected the manner in which administrative control was assumed. This, and the kinds of difficulties created by the convention, can be illustrated by the steps taken to solve the problem of title to New Territories land. The matter was both urgent and complex, and the secretary of state wanted title to land settled as early as possible even if it proved very expensive. Anxiety on the part of the local Chinese prompted the Hong Kong government to invest large sums of money in a complicated survey, in the registration of claims to land, and in setting up a land court to deal with cases of disputed title.

The early realization that utter confusion in respect of land had prevailed in the New Territories under Chinese rule,[21] and that many inhabitants hoped to obtain titles by fraudulent means under British rule, required the establishment of a special court to hear and determine all disputed claims to land. The original bill was substantially amended and was not enacted in its final form until nine months after its first appearance in November 1899. Yet speed in this matter was of vital importance to the full extension of British administration to the leased territory. 'I hope,' wrote Stewart Lockhart to Fiddian in the Colonial Office, 'you will do your best to have this matter put through as soon as possible; there will be no real progress in the new territory until the land question has been settled.'[22]

The chief aim of the bill, in the acting attorney-general's words, was 'to provide owners and occupiers of land in the New Territories with a tribunal to which they can appeal, without incurring the expense of resorting to the Supreme Court, and to arrange amicably questions of disputed title and land and rent disputes generally'.[23] The achievement of this aim was, however, a complicated matter of policy and precise legal language, and various objections were raised. One of these was that, during the amending stage, the section on 'occupiers and trespassers' had undergone a subtle change. The original bill declared that occupation by any person without licence, etc., of land 'a certificate of title for which has been disallowed by the Court or for which no claim has been made under this Ordinance shall be deemed a trespass' (clause 12): the effect was to provide for verification and authentication of existing titles. But section 15 of the amended ordinance began: 'All land in the New Territories is hereby declared to be the property of the Crown' during the term of the lease, and occupation was trespass unless authorized by the government or unless a claim had been presented to the court. In the opinion of the Hon. T. H. Whitehead, the non-expropriation clause of the convention was thereby contravened.[24] Attorney-general Goodman's memorandum is worth quoting on this point:

> Now although the Land Court will not expropriate or dispossess persons having, at the time the New Territories were ceded [*sic*], *bona fide titles*, yet they must have these titles verified, and, *during the 99 years*, all persons must be made to understand they hold from the Queen and not from the Chinese Government. It is to the Queen, rent must be paid, not to the Emperor of China.... In theory, when the 99 years have expired and the land reverts to China (if it ever does) the descendants of the 'so called' perpetual Lessees can fall back on the title they possessed prior to the Convention.
>
> What Mr Whitehead apparently would like would be a Certificate that the claimant has 'a title from the Chinese Government'. If not, I do not understand his meaning.[25]

Fiddian minuted that as the ordinance did not provide for 'expropriation' or 'expulsion of the inhabitants' of the leased territory, and did not provide for the confiscation without compensation of land required for public purposes, it could not be considered a violation of the convention. Yet in strict legal terms every owner and occupier in the New Territories was, by section 15, duly expropriated of his land; from the coming into operation of the ordinance (28 March 1900, in the first instance) until the setting up of the Land Court and the lodging of claims, all land was the property of the crown. It is inadequate to talk of the government's intention or the practical results of the policy: in *legal* fact only the crown, not the inhabitants, had rights to land from 28 March to 1 June 1900 (when the Land Court was constituted). But the Colonial Office saw no reason to accept Whitehead's view on this matter.

With reference to Goodman's remarks it is worth noting the implication that there was a political motive: the desire to impress upon the inhabitants the supreme authority of the British monarch during the period of the lease.

The New Territories Land Court Ordinance received the governor's assent on 23 July 1900, though the court had earlier been constituted under the original ordinance of 28 March. It did not begin its judicial work until over seven months later, partly because what were termed 'ministerial duties' (mainly concerning demarcation) were extensive and complicated, and partly because its mem-

bers devoted much of their time to a study of the relevant law. That
law was Chinese law relating to land:

... the principles by which the validity of a claim was to be tested could be
none other than those of the law of China and it was necessary for the
Court to make itself familiar with the general provisions of that Law no
less than with the local customs modifying its operation within the area to
be dealt with under the Ordinance.[26]

The problems this created were immense, and they vastly
increased the time and cost of the settlement of land disputes. The
court did not finish its work until early 1905, and various expe-
dients were adopted in efforts to complete the process as soon as
possible. In the meantime, valuable crown rent was lost, government personnel were not available for other tasks, and general
development was hindered. No doubt any really satisfactory solution of the land problem would have taken a long time; but the
decision to follow assiduously an alien and imperfectly-understood
land-law system could only further delay successful settlement.
And the reason why strict Chinese law was adopted as the prevailing law was, almost certainly, the non-expropriation clause of the
convention.

An example of the Land Court's practice of hearing cases 'under
the strict letter of the Chinese law'[27] was in its treatment of 'taxlords'. A taxlord, or perpetual lessor, had been defined as: 'A person who pays, or purports to pay tax for land in which some other
person has an interest greater than a lease for years or a customary
mortgage.'[28] The necessity of formulating a coherent policy to be
followed consistently was shown by the united stand of cultivators
against lineage tax-collectors, whose position, wrote H. H. J. Gompertz, was 'not very secure before the convention, they have lost
ground steadily ever since and any attempt to re-instate them
would be bitterly resented and would, I think, be found to fail'.
The practical aspects of this form of tax collection, such as the size
of the grain measure, the quality of the grain, and the discount to
be taken off the nominal amount, had always caused strife. 'With
the signing of the Convention the tenants seem to have made up
their mind to shake off the tax lord, a half formed resolve which
had been gathering definiteness for a considerable time.' In Lantau,
the Li family's rent-collector was arrested by tenants and taken
before the Tung Chung police; judgments against perpetual lessees
had been impossible to enforce. To turn out the old lessees in Lan-

tau would have meant the expulsion of 2,000 people and the depopulation of all villages in the Tung Chung valley. Initial hopes that taxlords would compound with their tenants for a lump sum and thus drop out by natural process were not realized. They were a class 'absolutely out of touch with things': 'We cannot expropriate them and it remains to select the speediest and most painless method of extinction.'[29]

Another member of the Land Court was of opinion that the perpetual leasehold system originated in a fraud on the Chinese government. Since the titles of both lessor and lessee were unsound, the Land Court should disallow any claim of either party and the matter should be dealt with executively.[30] There was much discussion of the proper way of settling this issue until the acting governor, May, laid down the policy which was to be adopted: taxlord claims were to be evaluated according to official Chinese law at the date of the convention (though in appropriate cases the Land Court could make recommendations for compensation).[31]

The effect of this decision was to eliminate the taxlords as a class and thus upset the whole balance of local influence, wealth, and power in the region. Only the large and long-established lineages could claim taxlord rights, and without them their position *vis-à-vis* their less affluent neighbours was weakened. The Tangs of Kam Tin, for example, asserted 'ownership' of the whole of Tsing Yi island, but after the Land Court's judgment their rights were much reduced and, indeed, liable to complete extinction.[32] In the 1960s the Tangs of Ping Shan pointed out to one observer large sections of the Yuen Long valley which, they considered, belonged to Ping Shan but which were lost as a result of Land Court decisions.[33] Other powerful lineages were also deprived of what had been an enduring income, for the land claimed by taxlords affected a large proportion of the mainland.[34] This is arguably a significant factor in the relative decline of lineage groups in the modern New Territories.

In two important cases the judicial work of the Land Court was criticized and the decisions overturned on appeal to the Supreme Court. A certain Mr Ho Lap-pun claimed a large area of foreshore and seabed in Kowloon Bay, and the Land Court originally supported him. But it was subsequently decided that his title deed did not confer any rights at all over the seabed or reclaimed land, and on appeal by the attorney-general the Supreme Court considered that Ho's rights were extremely limited.[35] In another case, where the Land Court had allowed a claim to most of the sea frontage of Kowloon City, the Supreme Court declared a vital deed to be a forgery.[36] A third series of disputes arose over title to foreshore in Cheung Sha Wan. Eight lawyers were employed on the case, which was extensively argued before the Land Court, and the crown solicitor represented the government. Eventually the crown won judgment, the affair involving a prolonged study of the intricate Chinese law relating to reclamation.[37]

In respect of all these claims the determination of the Hong Kong government to abide by Chinese law properly construed is shown by the extensive investigations carried out by executive officers. Cecil Clementi, then assistant registrar-general, was deputed to make a special study of the title deeds and claimants' bona fides; he was assisted by James Scott, consul-general at Canton, and a Chinese expert made available by the San On magistrate. He travelled on several occasions to Canton and Nam Tau, and provided reports and affidavits which enabled the government case to be placed on an unassailable basis. The government was anxious, of course, to win these cases because of the importance and value of the land involved, yet it did not consider changing the basis of its policy. It is probable that that policy was determined by the wording of the convention.

In 1899 leases of portions of the seabed surrounding Ping Chau, from which coral and shells had long been dredged for their lime content, were granted for a term of five years 'until the investigations into this peculiar business are completed'.[38] Lantau marine lot no. 2, whose lessees paid 300 dollars as crown rent, was invaded by local fishermen who took coral without paying royalties; the lessees sued one of them in the Police Court for larceny. But the magistrate held that, being attached to the seabed, coral was not a subject of larceny; thereupon an action for trespass and conversion was brought in the Supreme Court. One judge supported the plaintiffs; the chief justice, however, who possessed the casting vote, held in favour of the defendant's alleged customary right 'by immemorial usage', the crown lease notwithstanding. This controversial decision was given on 29 June 1900, in what became known as 'the shell case', and it raised the whole issue of the meaning of the convention.

The basis of the chief justice's argument was that the non-expropriation clause of the convention limited the prerogative of the crown to grant leases in conflict with established rights to land;

and the validity of any so-called custom was to be determined by the rules of Chinese law. Although no evidence as to that law was presented, the judgment implied that in this case the custom claimed by the defence established a legal right which could not be taken away by mere executive action. The attorney-general, Goodman, strongly disagreed on two main points. As the onus was on the defendant, his failure to prove his position in Chinese law should have been fatal to the defence. The British crown did not have 'only a limited or qualified Sovereignty in the leased District', as the chief justice had held, but 'sole jurisdiction' for ninety-nine years; while a cession should not, under international law, affect private property, the Supreme Court had no authority to enforce that principle by declaring the marine lease *ultra vires*. Goodman feared that the judgment might tempt the Chinese or their astute legal advisers to make numerous ingenious claims to all kinds of alleged rights under Chinese law, and that the decision would be given in evidence on the question of the existence of the supposed custom in subsequent suits.[39]

The attorney-general therefore recommended that the government give financial aid to the unsuccessful plaintiffs to encourage their appeal to the Privy Council, but no appeal eventuated. The Colonial Office instructed Blake to take the issue to the highest authority if a similar case arose again,[40] but the governor preferred to solve the problem by another means.[41] The shell case prompted the highest judicial authority in the colony to hold that British sovereignty over the New Territories was limited and subject to restrictions. A right established in Chinese law prevailed over the grant of a crown lease.

The Land Court did not complete the crown rent rolls until 1905, though some rent had been paid since 1900. But in 1905 various inhabitants of the leased territory protested against increases in crown rent. Their main complaints were that new crown rent rates as proclaimed in June were excessive and that 'a Building tax in the said locality is new, such tax never before having been imposed'.[42] Although the governor, Sir Matthew Nathan, stated, quite correctly by British concepts of administration, that the novelty of a tax does not affect the validity of its imposition,[43] the implication of the petition was that in re-classifying land for the purposes of taxation the Hong Kong government was contradicting its policy of approaching the land question according to Chinese law.

This objection was circumvented, and the complainants

1. Official Ceremony in the New Territories (alleged to be the flag-raising ceremony at Tai Po on 16 April 1899, but the presence of the Chinese makes this unlikely. Perhaps the governor addressing elders after the take-over, possibly from Tai Po matshed) (*Government Information Services, 585/35*)

2. Governor Blake and Viceroy Li Hung-chang at Government House, Hong Kong, 1900 (*City Museum and Art Gallery, P70.1*)

3. The Kowloon City Pier, *c*. 1900 (*City Museum and Art Gallery, P64.158*)

4. The Walled City, with Fields in the Foreground, *c*. 1906 (*City Museum and Art Gallery, P64.161*)

5. The Walled City, with Kowloon Bay in the Background, *c.*1910 (*City Museum and Art Gallery, P69.31*)

6. The Walled City: The Top of the Wall, *c.*1930 (*City Museum and Art Gallery, P64.159*)

7. The Walled City: South Gate, 1935 (*City Museum and Art Gallery, P66.10*)

8. A Pavilion Inside the Walled City (Date Unknown) (*City Museum and Art Gallery, P66.20*)

9. Cannon Inside the Walled City (Date Unknown) (*Peninsula Group*)

10. The Walled City: Aerial View, 1973 (*Government Information Services, 8866/15*)

11. Customs Guard-Post (probably on the Kowloon boundary before 1898) (*City Museum and Art Gallery, P64.73*)

12. Customs Staff Near the New Territories, c. 1900 (*City Museum and Art Gallery, P71.3*)

mollified, by a proclamation issued on 11 July 1906, promising not to raise rents during the term of the lease.[44] But such a generous promise not only deprived the government of large sums in revenue; it was also contrary to specific instructions given by Chamberlain in 1899. The secretary of state had stated that land tax must be subject to revision at intervals of years: 'This is very necessary. The land will become more and more valuable, in human probability, and there should be no doubt as to the system on which tax will be levied and collected.'[45] But Blake's successor, and Chamberlain's, had probably forgotten this policy. Even when crown leases were renewed in 1973 the crown rent remained unaltered in respect of most lots in the New Territories,[46] despite enormous increases in the value of the land. In this matter the concern of the Hong Kong government to appear to be acting in accordance with rights guaranteed by the convention had important consequences.

The same is true when the administration of New Territories land is considered. The New Territories Titles Ordinance 1902, which provided for a modified Torrens system of registration of title, was repealed within a year. Registration of title was replaced by registration of deeds, as was the practice in the San On registry. Provision was also made 'for the registration of a manager where property is vested in a clan or family—a common custom in China—and to make such manager liable in respect of the land as if he were the owner, in the way that this is done under Chinese Law'.[47]

When the New Territories Land Court Ordinance 1900 was finally passed it did not settle the important question of the appropriate form of title: by section 17 titles were to be 'in such form or forms as may, from time to time, be directed by the Governor'. The acting attorney-general, Pollock, moving the second reading of the original bill, said that it was proposed to substitute a crown lease by a certificate of title, because the ordinary holding of land in the New Territories was a tenancy in perpetuity and 'this Government could not, under the terms of the Convention with China, grant a lease for more than 99 years from the date of the Convention'.[48] The title eventually granted was a lease from the crown for seventy-five years from 1 July 1898, subject to renewal for a further twenty-four years minus three days.

An attempt by the governor, Clementi, in the 1920s to substitute a longer period of crown lease was unsuccessful. At a Foreign

Office conference in November 1928 he urged that the northern side of the harbour would only develop rapidly if security of tenure was assured for a longer period than recognized by the convention; he should therefore be able to grant leases which would expire well after 1997. This proposal required very cautious treatment. Many objections were raised against it: the erroneous impression given that HMG had power to dispose of the leased territory after the term specified in the convention; probable provocation of Chinese propagandists; the expense and bother of claims for compensation if rights granted in such leases could not be secured. But Clementi's motive was thought sound, and the conference hoped some other way out of the difficulty would be devised. Thus another meeting was held in Hong Kong. The policy of granting normal leases renewable beyond 1997 at the lessor's option was rejected as little better than the original suggestion, which was in fact confirmed. But the practice then followed should continue until Sino-British relations were either more stable or worse, unless application for a longer lease was made by someone dissatisfied with the current term. The prospective lessee would then, if he inquired, be informed verbally that HMG intended to try and protect his rights in any negotiations with China, and that Hong Kong was, anyway, acting within its legal powers.[49]

The Foreign Office recommended, as an alternative, that 'when the question of renewing the 75 years' lease comes up for consideration in the year 1973 every effort will be made, possibly by means of some arrangement with the Chinese Government, to give the lessees greater security of tenure than could be afforded under the normal extension of 24 years less 3 days'.[50] Amery requested reconsideration of Clementi's proposals, but to no avail. Eight months earlier he had recognized that from a strictly legal point of view the grant of leases purporting to endure beyond 1997 was improper; to prevent 'an atmosphere of uncertainty and dismay' he had unsuccessfully sought, however, to give Clementi full rein.[51]

Thus the form of title to New Territories land was, and is, vastly different in one vital respect from the form of title to land in Kowloon and Hong Kong island. If the issue of security of tenure was raised with the Chinese government in 1973, as the Foreign Office had suggested in 1929, there was no public announcement of the fact, and title to land in the 'extension' remains due to expire in June 1997.

Land Resumption in the 1920s

It has been shown that decisions of great importance for the administration of the New Territories were affected by the form in which the leasehold was acquired: not only was it politically expedient to assert that Britain had full sovereignty in the area, but paradoxically, HMG's freedom of action was recognized to be restricted by the terms of the convention. This can be further illustrated by reference to land resumption and compensation, a very sensitive matter which first became a political problem in the 1920s.

New Kowloon, a part of the New Territories whose inhabitants were thought well acquainted with the more sophisticated laws and customs of Hong Kong and to which all of the colony's ordinances and regulations were therefore applied,[52] provided convenient land for the necessary expansion of old British Kowloon following the influx of numerous refugees from disorder in Kwangtung after the republican revolution. In the 1920s development took place there on an unprecedented scale: hills were levelled, valleys raised, water-courses diverted, drainage laid, and large areas were reclaimed from the adjacent bay.[53] There were two important effects of this development: private land had to be resumed by the government for the implementation of town-planning principles, and a wild speculative land boom occurred. In January 1922 a town planning committee was appointed; it recommended filling in the cultivated swamps and tidal flats by cutting down the foothills, a work which could be undertaken only by the government because of the minute sub-divisions of holdings. Yet in resuming the land the government could simply not afford to pay the prices for land existing during the boom, and boards of arbitration awarded compensation on cultivated land according to its value as agricultural land, though it was required, of course, for the erection of buildings and the execution of Public Works Department plans and was worth far more on the speculative open market.

Consequently, aggrieved land developers initiated action in the Supreme Court, submitting that the Crown Lands Resumption Ordinance 1900 and the New Territories Regulation Ordinance 1910 were *ultra vires* as in conflict with the requirements of the royal instructions. Gollan CJ, however, dismissed the application, holding that section 4 of the Colonial Laws Validity Act ensured the validity of the ordinances.[54] A petition was therefore addressed to the secretary of state by 671 signatories praying that the government's legislative action was inconsistent with both equity and the convention.

This is an interesting document raising important questions. The submission that the convention was violated is considered in a subsequent chapter,[55] but complaint was also made that the resumption system was 'inconsistent with the British Government's solemn engagements'. It is significant that this was answered, though not very satisfactorily, by reference to Chinese land law in 1898. The petitioners had noted that the block crown leases provided for such rent on buildings erected on agricultural land as was specified in the building licence; that this provision was not intended to prevent landholders from building on agricultural land (although, by refusing to issue licences, the government had so prevented them); and that landholders under Chinese jurisdiction would have been free to use their land as building land if they so desired. Stubbs and Clementi admitted that Chinese law, if not expressly permitting it, did not actually forbid the conversion of agricultural land into building land, though landholders were in duty bound to report any change in the nature of their holdings so that tax could be re-assessed; but, wrote Stubbs, 'local custom usually required that they should get permission from the Village Elders—who in some cases made a charge, in the nature of a fine or premium, for grant of such permission'.[56] Clementi put forward *fung shui* as tightly fettering the freedom to build. 'Here,' he disingenuously submitted, 'there is ... at least an embryonic form of the town-planning idea and of the limitations which it must impose upon private rights and wishes ... and it is entirely untrue that at that time [1898] a landowner could build upon his land when, where, and how he personally chose.'[57]

This was tantamount to arguing that, if resort to official Manchu law could not absolve Hong Kong of the accusation that a breach of faith had been committed, local customary law would do the trick. Yet, in Clementi's words, during the Ch'ing dynasty 'a rural landowner could erect buildings on agricultural or waste land without official permission';[58] under the British régime he could not. With regard to compensation, however, the position was more satisfactory from the government's point of view; the Manchu code made no provision for it, and if a Chinese officer undertook systematic town development 'the amount of compensation paid to expropriated owners would have varied inversely as the confidence of the officer in his ability to suppress forcibly any expressions of dissatis-faction'.[59] The Hong Kong practice of paying no more than the value of the land when devoted to the purpose for which it was in fact used was 'undoubtedly in accordance with Chinese law and custom which do not recognise any potential value in land apart from its immediate value assessed according to user, and assessed moreover according to tax paid'.[60]

The Colonial Office doubted whether the policy of the Hong Kong government did not infringe the convention, and wrote to Clementi that a more fair and generous method of assessing compensation might still the controversy. The governor disagreed, but Amery ordered an inquiry to be made in Hong Kong. He hoped that the resulting report would convince the Chinese community that they were enjoying fair treatment.[61] No such report has been discovered, and the Chinese community (or, at least, that part of the Chinese land-owning community as is spoken for by the Heung Yee Kuk) has never admitted that it has been fairly treated.[62]

6

BOUNDARIES OF THE NEW TERRITORIES

Introduction

THE previous chapter has indicated how the Convention of Peking 1898 influenced the policy adopted in establishing an administrative system for the New Territories. There were other effects as well, and in continuing to explore the history of the convention it is necessary to consider particular problems to which it gave rise and recurrent issues which it exacerbated. That is the task of this and the next two chapters. A study of these aspects—the consequences of a poorly-drafted unequal treaty—provides further material for an analysis of the convention's meaning.

In one respect the convention was necessarily vague: the exact limits of the leased territory could not be known until precise geographical information was available and the lines 'indicated generally on the annexed map' were much more closely defined. Yet the process of boundary-making subsequent to signing of the convention has been so confused that even now it is impossible to ascertain with certainty the limits of the New Territories.

The making and maintaining of an international boundary generally involves four main stages: allocation (the agreement to divide territory and to settle the appropriate line of division); delimitation (the determination of the boundary and its definition in a treaty, statement of arbitration or boundary commission's report); demarcation (the actual physical construction by a fence, stones, pegs, etc. on the ground); and administration (involving maintenance, political arrangements regarding visas, rights of access and so on).[1] The northern New Territories boundary was allocated in the 1898 convention, delimited and partially demarcated by Stewart Lockhart and deputy Wang in March 1899, and has, of course, been administered by Great Britain and China ever since. The other boundaries have been allocated but not properly delimited or demarcated. All these processes imply consultation and agreement between two sovereign entities, though China's sovereignty was limited during and after the Ch'ing dynasty by the rights of foreign powers.

The present situation regarding the New Territories boundaries is, without exaggeration, extraordinary. The convention was based on almost total ignorance of geographical conditions and on a most inadequate sketch-map; the delimitation commissioners' memorandum has apparently remained unratified; proper demarcation of all boundaries has apparently never been carried out; and the demarcation report regarding the northern border seems not to have been formally and officially ratified by either of the two governments concerned. Yet boundary disputes, except in so far as the Walled City may be considered a boundary dispute, are virtually unknown.

In 1910 the contemporary state of the boundaries was brought to the attention of the Colonial Office by the governor, Sir Frederick Lugard. A resultant minute by J. R. W. Robinson, clerk in the Eastern Department, summarized it in these words:

The whole position appears to be as follows, assuming that the Foreign Office did not inform the Chinese Government of the modification of the Western boundary (I think this is a fair assumption).

The land portion of the Northern boundary has been delimited by properly appointed officers in accordance with the convention; the point from which the Eastern boundary starts has been fixed by British officers alone; the southern boundary differs from the line shown in the Convention map since latitude 22° 9'N does not touch Tai A Chau but is to the south of it. The authorised [Intelligence Division] map shows the line: unauthorised maps show a different line: the western boundary has been modified from the line shown in the convention map. Great Britain claims territorial powers within the three mile limit of the islands included in the leased area; and claims the whole foreshore, within the limits of the territory, of Mirs Bay and Deep Bay. The Chinese Government have not been asked to agree to any one of these points, though by the terms of the Convention, the exact boundaries are to be fixed when proper surveys have been made by officials appointed by the two Governments.[2]

Twelve years after the treaty its provisions remained unsatisfied; even now it is doubtful if proper agreement on any of the boundary alterations unilaterally carried out by the British authorities has been reached with China.

British Revisions prior to 1911

Apart from the delimitation talks between Stewart Lockhart and Wang Tsun-shan, the records do not reveal any initiative by either Britain or China before the take-over to settle the New Territories boundaries. It may have been thought that no further discussions were necessary; in any event, relations between Hong Kong and Canton in 1899 were probably so bad that continued co-operation would have been impossible. But several matters had been left outstanding and an attempt was made to sort them out during the first decade of this century.

One problem was whether the foreshores (the land between low-water and high-water marks) of the two bays had been included within the 'extension'. This was of considerable importance, for a large area of land in Mirs Bay and Deep Bay is exposed at low tide and numerous proposals to erect wharves and jetties there were expected.

The question was first raised in 1899 when the Land Office in Hong Kong received an application from one Pun Sik-man, who ran a launch service, to build a pier on the Mirs Bay foreshore. Stewart Lockhart asked the acting attorney-general, Henry Pollock, whether the foreshore could be regarded as within British territory, and Pollock replied that Britain could only claim rights conferred by the convention: these included the right of navigating up to the high-water mark when the tide was up but did not confer any title to the land beneath. Blake tentatively agreed, but Bruce Shepherd of the Land Office argued that the term 'waters' includes the shore to high-water mark and Stewart Lockhart noted that a contrary ruling would seriously hamper the prosperity and development of the leased territory. Shepherd and Pollock gave second opinions; Shepherd's was based largely on admiralty jurisdiction at common law, the governor being vice-admiral of the colony. The two bays, he said, are

... within the flow of the sea, and, as there is no exception to the grant of the waters, admiralty jurisdiction would extend to high water mark and thus include all the shore within the flow of the sea....

The shore between high and low water marks has always been held to be prima facie extra-parochial and cannot be held by any individual or corporation except by direct grant from the Sovereign, who controls the waters, or by ancient prescription. There appears to be no difference in the common law of China on this subject. One of the heads of the Clan [owning

Cheung Chau] told me they held sovereign rights over the whole island, and on inquiring how far over the sea he claimed these sovereign rights to extend he admitted that they stopped at high water mark and that they had no claim to the foreshore.

By implication the general rights of Her Majesty's subjects to use of the foreshore applied to the extension, for there was no exception stated in the treaty. (The correctness of this view need not be assessed here, but it should be noted that the argument assumes British acquisition of full sovereignty over the New Territories.) Pollock, meanwhile, maintained his earlier opinion and advised that it would be safer to assume no rights to the soil between high-water and low-water marks.[3]

Blake asked that the issue be settled by the law officers of the crown. Their report, written on the first day of the new century, agreed with Shepherd's conclusion but was based on the convention, the memorandum of the delimitation commissioners, and Blake's Chinese proclamation.

It appears to us that the term 'the waters of Mirs Bay and Deep Bay' must include the ground covered by the waters of these Bays, and that no distinction can be drawn between the foreshore and the soil of the bays below low-water mark. This appears to us to follow from the fact that the boundary is traced along high-water mark. British sovereignty under the lease extends to high-water mark in these bays.[4]

They added that there might be rights of private property, and perhaps rights of access over the Chinese territory above high-water mark, which would require consideration before the granting of new rights. Edward Wingfield, permanent under-secretary in the Colonial Office, minuted that control over the foreshore might be an embarrassing advantage to Great Britain and lead to difficulties with the Chinese government.[5] When the question was referred to the lords commissioners of the Admiralty, however, they considered it essential that Great Britain claim the foreshore as of right.[6]

Chamberlain now decided, with Salisbury's concurrence, to inform Hong Kong of the law officers' report and state that the Chinese government had no power to grant leases on any part of the foreshore.[7] The matter was bound up with discussions concerning the publication of an Intelligence Division (War Office) map of the colony. The map had originally borne no indication of the northern boundary and the Colonial Office was asked to provide the necessary particulars; Chamberlain considered that it should show the extreme limit of British territory, including the fore-shores.[8]

The British records do not indicate that any further action was taken on this matter. From a Chinese source, however, it appears that official correspondence passed between Hong Kong and Canton in 1900–1. The British consul is quoted as follows:

> In response to your communication on the limits of British territorial waters in the New Territories, the governor of Hong Kong states, in his letter, that the Hong Kong government does not regard British territorial waters to extend to riverine ports on the bays or on the Sham Chun river in the New Territories, but does hold that it reaches the high-water mark in each bay, and covers the entire Sham Chun river up to its northern bank.[9]

The viceroy, writing to the Tsungli Yamen, did not dispute Blake's claim to the foreshores of the bays. In the meantime, Hong Kong enacted the Foreshores and Sea Bed Ordinance empowering the governor to grant leases of foreshore and seabed 'within the limits of the territorial waters of the Colony'.[10]

Much of the uncertainty in respect of the New Territories bound-aries was the result of sub-standard cartography. A map sent by Blake in January 1900 seemed to the Colonial Office clearly wrong, showing the northern boundary south of the Sham Chun River and excluding Lo Wu. Its inaccuracy was common to all maps of the area, for no proper survey had been conducted; reliance was largely placed, it seems, on the 1866 map of an Italian priest, Father Simeone Volonteri. But, however commendable Volonteri's efforts, the result was not precise enough for the making of compli-cated and exact boundaries. Latitudes were out of place and the coastline of Deep Bay was misrepresented;[11] yet the Hong Kong director of public works in 1899 considered that it correctly showed the coastline,[12] though he thought the map attached to the conven-tion extremely inaccurate. Despite a survey of the northern bound-ary made for the Chinese Imperial Maritime Customs, the acting governor, Gascoigne, stated in June 1900 that no correct map of the leased territory was possible until the survey then begun by the Hong Kong authorities was completed.[13]

Then the western boundary as it appeared on the convention map was discovered to be erroneously marked; the meridian of 113° 52′E longitude did not meet the Nam Tau promontory to the west of Deep Bay but passed to the west of the promontory. This, of course, affected the northern boundary, for the governor's Chinese proclamation had stated: 'From the mouth of the Sham Chun river the boundary follows the high water mark along the coast of Deep Bay till the point where the meridian of 113° 52'E bisects the land.'[14] Lucas minuted that the intention was to acquire the waters of Deep Bay; no more land was wanted.[15] The Colonial Office thereupon suggested a significant alteration of the western boundary:

10. The longitude of the extreme south western point of the peninsula to the West of Deep Bay is now found to be 113° 53' 29'' 7E. [*sic*] The adoption of this meridian is however objectionable in that . . . it passes Eastward of, and would exclude from British territory, an island which lies about midway between the Island of Lantao and the point at which the meridian cuts the mainland.

11. Mr Chamberlain therefore proposes, if Lord Salisbury concurs, to request the Intelligence Department to make the Western boundary northward from Lantao follow the Meridian originally selected (113° 52') to a point . . . immediately to the west of the south-westernmost point of the peninsula, and thence to turn it directly East till it meets that peninsula.[16]

Salisbury did indeed concur, and considered it unnecessary in the circumstances then existing to invite the agreement of the Chinese government to the proposed modification; instead, the British minister at Peking would be instructed to inform the Tsungli Yamen of the actual modification when affairs in China had resumed a 'more normal' condition.[17] Sir Ernest Satow, MacDonald's successor at the Manchu court, stated at the end of October that publication of a change in the boundary, even though in China's favour, seemed inopportune, and the Intelligence Division map was therefore not issued until considerable time had elapsed. The new western boundary was sketched in, but the Colonial Office informed the director of military intelligence that there was to be no publication until Satow had negotiated with the Chinese; the northern boundary was to remain provisional until completion of the on-going survey.[18]

Another problem requiring decision was noted by Blake in July 1901. Numerous islands were included within the leased territory; did possession of them include territorial rights over the waters within their three-mile limit? The point was generally important, of course, and specifically so in the case of Lantau, for Peaked Hill on the south-west was shown on existing maps as an island outside the

limits of the territory. In fact it was joined to Lantau by a causeway
120 yards long and 50 yards wide and was surrounded by water
only at full tide; could it be considered as belonging to Britain?[19]
Lucas treated the map representation of Peaked Hill as a mistake
which merely required correction by the Intelligence Division car-
tographers, and the question of the three-mile limit was referred to
the Foreign Office. Without, apparently, seeking the opinion of the
law officers Lord Lansdowne (then secretary of state for foreign
affairs) agreed with Chamberlain that territorial rights around the
islands had been conferred by the lease: the delimitation commissioners' memorandum of 19 March 1899 had included the whole of
Lantau as leased territory, and the extension had, in the submission
of the law officers, become British territory.[20] If there was any
doubt, however, as to British rights in the waters west of Lantau
(required for the suppression of piracy and smuggling) Bertie
quoted article 52 of the Treaty of Tientsin; this gave British ships
not hostile to China the liberty to visit all ports within the dominions of China.[21]

It is one of the curious aspects of the common law system that
matters of great import are sometimes without authoritative determination for many years. The outer limits of colonial territory is
one example, and there continues to be judicial disagreement as to
whether British colonies included a three-mile sea and its subjacent
land.[22] Administrative and legislative practice, however, has long
assumed that territorial waters and their sea-bed and subsoil were
within colonial boundaries.[23] In 1867 the law officers reported that
one marine league of open sea passed to Her Majesty on the cession
of Hong Kong,[24] and if the lease of the New Territories was to be
assimilated to the cession of Hong Kong and Kowloon it followed
logically that land in the leasehold had its own territorial sea.

With regard to the western boundary and Lantau, two other
points require mention. The police station at Tai O (at the western
end of the island) was constructed on Po Chue Tam, a promontory
half a mile north of Tai O town, at first sight connected to Lantau
but in fact separated from it at all tides by a very narrow creek. If
the three-mile limit did not apply, could this small island be considered British territory? Two boundary stones were erected on Lantau in 1902, one on the north and one on the south side; part of the
inscription on each read: 'From a point at High water mark due
[North/South] of this stone, the boundary follows the shore of Lantao to the Westward.' As the governor, Lugard, pointed out in

1910, these words ignore the three-mile limit and, if correct, place Po Chue Tam in Chinese territory.[25] Moreover, the southern stone proclaimed that the boundary 'runs due South to the parallel of 22° 9′ 0″N', whereas the convention map drew a diagonal south-western line from Lantau to Tai A Chau. Po Chue Tam was some-how considered by one Colonial Office official to be covered by the terms of the 1898 convention.[26] The northern stone declared the original western boundary, despite prior unilateral alteration.

The eastern boundary, meanwhile, was marked at its conjunction with the coast of Mirs Bay by another stone, set up in 1902 by Lieutenant F. M. Leake, RN, of HMS *Bramble* and placed in Chinese territory. Its inscription was correct but in 1910 there was no record of Chinese knowledge of or acquiescence in the stone's position. The southern boundary, however, had subtly and unoffi-cially changed its direction. It was shown on the treaty map as 22° 9′N latitude from the eastern boundary to a small island in the west (Tai A Chau) and thence diagonally to the south-western tip of Lantau. Here another error in the convention map was dis-covered, for 22° 9′N does not in fact touch Tai A Chau but passes to the south of it, as was recorded in the unpublished Intelligence Division map. A map reproduced from one prepared in Hong Kong by the Public Works Department and appearing in the *Colonial Office List, 1909* showed a quite different line from Tai A Chau to Lan-tau. 'Still,' minuted Robinson, 'as the line [on the Intelligence Division map] runs from the SW tip of Lantao through the SW tip of Tai A Chau to the Latitude 22° 9′N it carries out the intention of the convention map.'[27]

By the first month of 1902, therefore, Britain had claimed ter-ritorial rights to the foreshores of Mirs Bay and Deep Bay and ter-ritorial rights within an arc of radius three miles from each island; she had made a unilateral revision of the western boundary; and she was still not able to publish a map showing the exact northern boundary. This line was demarcated with stones by British officials alone in 1905, and by 1909 the southern limit was confused. China had been consulted on none of these points, except at the provincial level in respect of the foreshores, and had not once asked the Brit-ish authorities for clarification of the leased territory's boundaries; the dynasty was apparently too concerned with self-preservation to bother with legal niceties. Yet it was a surprising situation to exist years after a convention which stated that 'exact boundaries shall be hereafter fixed when proper surveys have been made by officials appointed by the two governments', and Lugard, raising these matters in 1910, was mildly astonished to discover it. He thought it undesirable to take action prior to the successful negotiation of the working agreement for the Kowloon-Canton railway, and Lord Crewe (then secretary of state for the colonies) concurred. A long letter to the Foreign Office was drafted, asking Sir Edward Grey, after the settlement of the railway agreement, to invite the Chinese government to appoint a commissioner to verify demarcation of the northern boundary and the northern tip of the eastern boundary and to accept the modified western and southern boundaries. Further, explicit Chinese recognition of the British claims to foreshores and the three-mile limit should be obtained; should the Chinese prove reluctant, Great Britain could demand the western boundary as stated in the convention map, that is, 113° 52′E longitude extended to the mainland and thus including most of Tai A Chau and the whole foreshore opposite the district city of Nam Tau. Finally, if the waters within three miles of Lantau were not subject to HMG's territorial rights they must be considered *mare liberum*; the Chinese government could not claim territorial rights over these waters since they were not within three miles of any Chinese territory.[28] This reinforcement of the primary argument was necessary because Lugard had reported that officials of the Chinese customs and the salt commissioner had occasionally acted as if Tai O harbour and all waters west of meridian 113° 52′E were subject to China.

Grey concurred generally, and it was noted that the Tsungli Yamen had not in fact been informed of any boundary changes in 1900. 'This omission was no doubt due to the disturbed state of China at the time.' But China was still disturbed in 1910:

I am at the same time to point out that having regard to the very strong feeling now prevailing throughout China as to the so-called 'recovery of rights' over all foreign concessions and [settlements], and nowhere more strongly entertained than at Canton, the present moment would seem far from opportune for approaching the Chinese Government on the subject. Sir E. Grey, therefore, entirely agrees with the suggestion that action should be postponed until the settlement of the Kowloon Canton Railway question, by which time the existing agitation may possibly have subsided.[29]

W. G. Max Muller, chargé at Peking, was sent copies of the correspondence, and he also expressed agreement with postponement:

The strength of the 'sovereign rights' feeling now ... prevailing throughout China, has never been shown so clearly as it was in Canton in regard to the proposal to delimit the frontiers of the neighbouring Colony of Macao, and there is no reason to believe that proposals in regard to delimiting the frontiers of Hong Kong, however just and harmless, would meet with a better reception at the hands of the Self Government and other kindred Societies in Canton, whose enmity it is certainly not advisable in the interests of British trade generally and of Hong Kong trade in particular to stir up.[30]

Further, at a time when Great Britain was virtually refusing the Chinese request to delimit the boundary between Burma and Yunnan it would be hopeless to expect Chinese co-operation regarding Hong Kong boundaries.

A further element was introduced into this intriguing boundary situation by May's confidential despatch of 8 October 1910. Swallow Rock, a small island lying off Tai O village and within the three-mile limit, was excellent for fishing at certain times of the year; a fisherman, Ch'an Kung-po, claimed fishing rights on and around it and produced a 'red' deed, which would probably have satisfied the San On magistrate, in respect of these rights. Cecil Clementi of the New Territories Land Court recommended in 1904 the granting of an annual licence for a fee of 10 dollars. But it was then brought to the notice of the governor, Sir Matthew Nathan, that Swallow Rock was not included in the leased territory and that IMC officials denied Hong Kong's right to license junks at Tai O, the waters of Tai O harbour being under Chinese jurisdiction. Nathan accordingly granted no licence for fishing rights on the rock (though he continued to license boats at Tai O as if the right existed), and in 1910 a percentage of profits on the catch was still being paid to the Chinese authorities at Nam Tau. May, as acting governor, mentioned this matter in order to place HMG in possession of all the facts when the question of the New Territories boundaries should come up for 'final settlement'.[31]

Since 1910 there has been no public agreement between Great Britain and China settling the boundaries of the New Territories. The available records indicate that all four boundaries remain as delimited or demarcated by Britain without Chinese approval. But there are several more documents relating to this issue which must be considered, and one more alteration (or, at least, correction) of the northern boundary which must be mentioned.

Further Developments

In 1912 the acting governor, Claude Severn, wrote that press rumours indicated British recognition of the new Chinese government on condition that the leased territory was further extended. Such a proceeding seems highly unlikely, and of course nothing of the sort actually occurred; Robinson minuted his preference for conversion of the lease to a cession if any amendment of the convention was to be arranged.[32]

After the first world war there was a proposal to lease for reclamation a small area in British territory near the northern boundary; but the project would alter the high-water mark. The Foreign Office thought that the reclamation would involve a further acquisition of territory, and the lease was not granted.[33]

The Po On magistrate was of the opinion, in 1928, that as Po On (previously San On) district was 'closely connected, geographically speaking, with Hong Kong, it is not unusual to find serious disputes and unavoidable misunderstandings between the Chinese and British Governments, if and when the boundaries are not clearly demarcated'. His memorandum, suggesting that a special deputy of the Canton government be appointed to re-demarcate the New Territories boundaries, is both confused and confusing, and the proposal itself is the only matter of interest it contains. It was presented to a 'rehabilitation conference of the western region'. The British records do not mention it again, so it is probable that the proposal was rejected or that no action was taken on it.[34]

Clementi, now governor of Hong Kong, discovered in 1929 that the northern boundary at the western extremity was not clear. Arrangements had been made to take aerial photographs as soon as a suitable tide occurred in April. Caine, clerk in the Far Eastern Department of the Colonial Office, minuted:

It is rather startling to find that the boundary between the Hong Kong leased territories and China is so indeterminate and it is rather surprising that there have not been any disputes about it. It is not very clear how the aerial photographs are going to assist in determining the proper boundary but I suppose we can only wait until they have been taken.[35]

Again, however, there is no further correspondence on this matter, unless the appropriate file in the Public Record Office is still closed.

The issue of jurisdiction over the waters included within the boundaries arose in a most interesting communication from the

Admiralty in 1935. The Hong Kong commodore, C. G. Sedgwick, had observed that Hong Kong claimed jurisdiction 'against all Nations over all waters embraced by the definition in the Interpretation Ordinance whether within three miles of British soil or not', though subject to the reservation in the convention of the use by Chinese warships of Mirs Bay and Deep Bay. This was not, however, consonant with international law: those waters outside the three-mile limit were high seas beyond the power of China to lease to Great Britain and beyond the interests of Great Britain to claim. Sedgwick noted that open claim to such an extent from the land might prejudice the British government's usual refusal to recognize more than a three-mile limit. The Admiralty therefore proposed to authorize the insertion in the China station order book of a note to the effect that HMG did not claim jurisdiction over all parts of the sea area included in the definition, but claimed the usual territorial rights over the waters bordering the land territories of the colony. Thus territorial waters would in some places extend beyond the limits defined in the ordinance and in others fall considerably short of them.[36]

The Colonial Office concurred, though with a rider that any islands included in the defined area were 'ceded' to Hong Kong and were therefore territories of the colony.[37] It seemed to G. E. J. Gent that the purpose of enclosing the waters surrounding Hong Kong in the lease was to cripple the action of the Chinese customs; the 'blockade' being no longer a problem, there was no sufficient reason now to attempt to maintain jurisdiction over the high seas for the purpose. The lords commissioners of the Admiralty had presumed 'that the limits of the colony were described in the Convention by roughly rectangular co-ordinates mainly as a matter of convenience, and not for the purpose of claiming jurisdiction over any portions of high sea enclosed by these co-ordinates'. But C. Y. Carstairs believed that the intention of the definition clause in the ordinance was to make clear the claim of the Hong Kong government to the areas within the treaty limits of the colony.

Further discussion of the waters included in the convention map took place in 1937, though the records are incomplete: many files on such sensitive topics from this period are still closed ('not to be opened until 1988'). The 1937 issue concerned the neutrality of Hong Kong waters during the Sino-Japanese conflict, and a memorandum by Fitzmaurice of the Foreign Office posed three questions: the status of leased territory in war (which is discussed elsewhere);[38] the extent and status of the waters leased in the convention; and the position regarding use of the two bays by Chinese vessels of war.

On information from the Admiralty Fitzmaurice drew an analogy with Great Britain's Antarctic dependencies: what is intended by straight lines drawn across high seas is merely to delimit the areas within which any dry land which may exist is considered to be British, and any portions of the sea claimed would be merely the territorial waters round any such land. There remained the third question: 'Both these bays being less than ten miles at the mouth can be considered as territorial bays, and the Chinese consequently had the right to lease to us the whole waters of these bays, as they did.' Sir John Pratt referred to correspondence in 1916 with the local authorities at Canton, where the Hong Kong government maintained that the waters of Mirs Bay were 'territorial waters of Hong Kong and spoke of British territorial rights'. Pratt and Fitzmaurice agreed that Great Britain had exclusive jurisdiction over the waters of both Mirs Bay and Deep Bay.[39]

Thus, by 1937, it seems that HMG had decided to claim any islands within the sea boundaries (those boundaries as unilaterally altered by Britain) as included within the leasehold, with the appropriate three-mile limit around each; in addition, the whole of the waters of the two bays were territorial waters of the colony.

In 1964 a United States Department of State intelligence bulletin stated:

Since early 1958, occasional incidents have occurred over attempts by the Chinese Communists to extend the offshore limits of territorial waters from the 3 miles recognised by the British to 12 miles and also over the use of certain fishing grounds by residents of Hong Kong. For the most part, the incidents have been of minor importance and they have been played down by the United Kingdom Government. A strenuous pressing for a 12-mile territorial sea, however, could seriously restrict shipping corridors, air approaches, and fishing grounds in the Hong Kong area.[40]

The author considered the sea boundary as an exception to the ordinary recommendation that international boundaries not be shown in the oceans, since the 1898 convention 'specifically delineates the water boundary and, as a result, it has almost the same validity as the terrestrial frontier. Furthermore, the boundary should be shown on official maps as an established and accepted boundary'.[41]

Clearly the sea boundaries are *not* 'established and accepted', nor does either party consider them as having the validity of the terrestrial boundary. As there has been no proper bilateral delimitation of the sea boundaries their inclusion on an official map as 'international boundaries' could only be misleading. Although the law relating to territorial sea is at present fluid and changing, if one assumes a three-mile limit the true boundaries of the leasehold's territorial sea are quite different from those appearing on the convention map.

Until 1968 the northern boundary marked in the end-paper map of the Hong Kong government's annual report followed the Sham Chun River towards the west but, instead of proceeding 'down to Deep Bay' as the delimitation commissioners' report required, it curved to the north for about two miles and terminated at the coast a mile or so above the conjunction of river and sea. An apparently official publication noted that the boundary in fact took a wide sweep north of the existing channel near its estuary in Deep Bay.[42] But the annual report for 1968 subtly inserted, without comment of any kind, a correction of this erroneous line and the new map indicated the boundary as following the Sham Chun River along its entire length.

Administration

In 1948 Chinese and British officials met at Sha Tau Kok and replaced in their original position a number of boundary stones which had been disturbed during the Japanese occupation.[43] Any documents which might exist relative to this event are not yet in the public domain.

Administration of the sea boundaries of the New Territories is virtually restricted to the occasional arrest by Chinese boats of Hong Kong shipping which inadvertently strays outside colonial waters. The Chinese customs, by virtue of an agreement signed in 1948, are permitted to patrol a 'prohibited area' within Deep Bay and Mirs Bay and to stop any vessel found there.[44] It seems that administration of the northern boundary until 1949 was mainly concerned with the supression of smuggling and the supervision of Hong Kong gamblers crossing over to Sham Chun. But with the establishment of the People's Republic the border became much more important as a political line of division between China and the colony, and a more thorough-going boundary policy was required.

The original fence was erected by Britain along the south bank of the Sham Chun River, designed to protect Hong Kong against large-scale immigration. After the April-May influx of immigrants in 1962 a new barrier was built south of the first, and a third fence has since been constructed approximately along the limits of the border's closed area. British border administration now involves supervision of farmers from both sides of the boundary who work land inside the closed area, customs and immigration procedures at Lo Wu, police control of illegal immigrants and maintenance of the curfew, and military arrangements for the defence of the boundary.

There are four main points of contact between China and Hong Kong along the northern boundary. The Kowloon-Canton railway crosses the river at Lo Wu by a Bailey bridge destroyed in 1941 to discourage the Japanese invaders, rebuilt after the war and fitted with its unattractive corrugated iron roof in 1963. There is a Hong Kong immigration office and a police post at Lo Wu, and railway yards for the shunting of goods trains from Chinese locomotives for the short journey to Tsim Sha Tsui. A road bridge, carrying goods traffic and Chinese farmers working land across the border, was built at Man Kam To in 1940, and there is a footbridge at Lo Fang-Ta Kwu Ling. Ta Kwu Ling is the main police post along the frontier. The village of Sha Tau Kok straddles the boundary, though most of its residents live in Chinese territory; locals freely shop on both sides of the two streets bearing the demarcation signs (stones along Chung Ying Street, a nullah flanking San Lau Street).[45]

In the days of relatively unsophisticated warfare the northern land boundary was crucial for Hong Kong's defences, for the British fleet was considered powerful enough to deter a naval attack upon the colony. The boundary's fortifications, however, were never more than minimal, and the first effective line of defence against the Japanese in December 1941 was the more southern Gindrinker's Line. 1967 saw some belligerent action by Chinese red guards across the boundary, resulting in the deaths of several Hong Kong police,[46] but this is the only reported incident of hostilities at this primary line of division between Chinese and British territory. It is in the interests of both countries to secure the border and maintain an effective boundary policy.

Conclusion

Three of the New Territories boundaries are relatively unimportant; they are artificial, geometrical boundaries superimposed upon an inadequate map, two of them being subsequently discovered as incorrect and altered accordingly by one party alone. The western boundary was demarcated at the points where it touches Lantau, and the obelisks erected by British naval officers in 1902, bearing statements no longer honoured by Britain, remain in position. The eastern boundary is unchanged though its demarcation on the coast was unilaterally performed; the southern line, being a sea boundary after its erroneous description was corrected, has not been demarcated, and has not, apparently, been the subject of Sino-British discussion. Only the northern border, a natural or physical boundary, has undergone thorough (though defective) demarcation and proper administration, yet as recently as 1968 official British maps purported to modify portions of it.

The sea boundaries indicate the lack of proper topographical information at the time they were delimited; the northern line was more accurately defined by the delimitation commissioners and demarcation work was carried out. Yet it has never been a good boundary for the purposes of Hong Kong defence, and its bisection of Sha Tau Kok and of land owned by local peasants has complicated its administration. Being about twenty-two miles in length (from the mouth of the Sham Chun River to Sha Tau Kok) it facilitated the smuggling which Great Britain promised to control in return for the leased territory. The portion which follows the river was perhaps unwisely drawn, for riparian interests on the Chinese side no doubt suffered from sole British 'sovereignty' over the waters; one scholar notes that a boundary line giving an entire river to one state 'may be the result of unequal treaty or power politics',[47] which is clearly the case in this instance.

The history of the leased territory's boundaries confirms the peculiar failure of HMG to prepare its claim for an extension of the colony. The Hong Kong authorities should have been able to supply a more accurate and detailed map; the exact area and limits of the extra territory required should have been made known to Sir Claude MacDonald well before he began his negotiations. In fact, however, no major dispute has arisen, probably because important economic and other interests have not been affected by the confusion and because of ideological complications: China is not concerned with boundary details regarding territory acquired under unequal treaty. Peace has generally prevailed along colonial borders. With the emergence and success of modern Chinese nationalism it became impossible for Britain to raise boundary matters for negotiation, and China seems to have tacitly acquiesced in the various modifications to New Territories boundaries since 1898. If a dispute should arise and be submitted to an international judicial body, the doctrine of estoppel could probably be invoked by Great Britain in powerful support of a claim to the present boundaries.[48]

The Hong Kong ordinance governing the interpretation of legislation did not, prior to the lease of the New Territories, attempt to lay down what were the waters of the colony; presumably it was thought that the courts would recognize and accept the view of the law officers in 1867. No amendment was made to accommodate the New Territories until 1911, when the new Interpretation Ordinance defined 'colonial waters' as all waters, whether navigable or not, included within a specified area. The definition of the western boundary at its northern end followed the changes made in 1900; at its southern end, however, the boundary did not follow the convention map or the Intelligence Division map but repeated the view inscribed on the southern Lantau stone and thus enclosed a larger area of sea than seemed justified. The line followed the western coast of Lantau between the points to the north and south where the meridian of 113° 52′E intersected the island, and it was expressed to include 'the waters appertaining thereto'. In 1950 the colony's waters were defined as all those included within the colony, and the definition of the colony, being 'the whole area of land and water lying between' scheduled boundaries, adopted a similar formula for the south-western corner as had been promulgated in 1911.[49] The western boundary was not brought into line with the Intelligence Division map until 1966. Its southern end was then described thus:

The boundary then follows the western coast line of Lantau Island including the waters appertaining thereto to the extreme south-west point thereof and thence runs in a south-easterly direction to the extreme south-west point of Tai A Chau Island in the Soko Island Group and continues in the same straight line to the point at which it intersects the parallel of latitude 22° 09′ north.[50]

Also in 1966 the interpretation ordinance became a little more sophisticated in its definitions. Where they occur in local legislation, the expressions 'Colony' and 'Hong Kong' now mean both the area of land within certain boundaries (specified in the second schedule) and the area of the two bays similarly enclosed, as well as the 'territorial waters appertaining thereto'. This emphasizes Hong

Kong's claim to exclusive jurisdiction over Mirs Bay and Deep Bay. There was in addition an amendment to the definition of 'Colonial waters'; these consist of territorial waters and 'all waters, whether navigable or not, included in the Colony'. Since the 'Colony' is land, bays and territorial sea, 'all waters ... included in the Colony' can only refer to Mirs Bay and Deep Bay and any other internal waters; that is, 'Colonial waters' does not refer to sea which, though embraced by the boundaries laid down in the second schedule, is outside territorial waters. 'Territorial waters', meanwhile, are 'such part of the sea adjacent to the Colony as is deemed by international law to constitute the territorial waters of Hong Kong...'. The Hong Kong legislature has therefore proclaimed the views of Her Majesty's advisers in respect of the bays while permitting international law (though as decided by the Hong Kong courts) to settle the question of a territorial sea.

It is surprising to note that in recent practice the Hong Kong government has apparently denied that the territorial waters include a three-mile belt of sea around land in the New Territories. The occasion was the arrival late in 1978 of the refugee ship *Huey Fong* from Vietnam, which was required to anchor at a point about one and a half miles off Po Toi. This island is at the edge of the southern 'sea boundary' as defined in the second schedule of the interpretation ordinance. The government claimed that the ship was outside Hong Kong. Yet if international law grants a three-mile territorial sea, and if the definition of 'Hong Kong' as including a territorial sea is accepted, the ship must have been within the colony.

As a matter of general common law, it can be doubted whether the territory of British colonies ever included a territorial sea: it has often been asserted that the outer limit of the realm was low-water mark, although of course the British crown always claimed a three-mile zone of coastal waters in which it had special interests.[51] If this is so, it is problematical whether Hong Kong's legislature can assert that the colony includes territorial waters. Two legal principles are here in conflict. One is that a colonial legislature, like that of Hong Kong, is restricted in its competence to legislate with extraterritorial consequences. If such a restriction exists, it would be meaningless if that legislature could define 'colony' in any way it pleased. The second principle is that the acquisition of territory by the crown is an act of state which cannot be enquired into by the courts. In a case from Nigeria the Privy Council regarded a local ordinance as authoritatively determining the effect of a treaty;[52] the Hong Kong interpretation ordinance could be seen as conclusively declaring the limits of Hong Kong territory.

If the principle of extraterritoriality is selected, the colony of Hong Kong must be as indicated by the New Territories order in council of 20 October 1898:[53] there is no doubt that such purely prerogative legislation is conclusive.[54] Yet the order in council merely referred to 'the limits ... described in the said Convention', and therefore it is those vague and erroneous borders (as further defined by the memorandum of the delimitation commissioners) which must prevail. This absurd result could be avoided by denying Hong Kong's legislative incompetence in the area and accepting the ordinance as a superseding determination of the extent of territory acquired by the crown at Hong Kong. Alternatively, a new order in council incorporating the unilateral revisions made by Britain and adopted by the Hong Kong legislature could be issued. If this course was followed, section 1(1) of the Colonial Boundaries Act 1895 would operate to confirm the revised boundaries for the purposes of municipal law. Perhaps that course was originally eschewed in order to avoid giving public notice to the Chinese government of the various boundary amendments made by the British. That reason is hardly likely to be cogent now.

7

THE WALLED CITY
OF KOWLOON

Introduction

WHILE China, at the official level, seems to have been unperturbed about Britain's unilateral revisions of the Convention of Peking 1898 in respect of boundaries, she has consistently opposed British expulsion of Chinese jurisdiction from the Walled City of Kowloon. Protests in 1899 were unavailing, but although HMG has proved intransigent in its interpretation of the Walled City clause the Hong Kong government does not in fact exercise full jurisdiction in the area. Hong Kong officials were even quoted in 1975 as saying that the Walled City is not under the jurisdiction of the government.[1]

The Walled City no longer has walls and in no way resembles a separate city: it is now a foetid, high-rise slum, in stark contrast to the area of wide streets, dignified buildings and pleasant trees which the Volunteers occupied in May 1899. It is a squalid reminder and tangible evidence of the inadequacies of the convention and of China's determination to maintain her own interpretation of the Kowloon City clause.

The early history of the city, its fate during convention negotiations and its farewell to Chinese officialdom have already been explained.[2] In the present chapter it is intended to examine various developments affecting the place and its role in Sino-British relations in the period from 1899 to 1971, and then to present a static portrait of the city as it was in 1972. From this picture one can see to what extent the Walled City became a special area administratively distinct from the rest of the colony. Subsequent developments show a gradual trend towards integration of the city with the surrounding Kowloon City district, but it will probably be a long time before the Walled City loses its peculiar character as a haven from certain aspects of Hong Kong law.

The Walled City, 1899-1971

The order in council of 27 December 1899[3] confirmed, so far as the Hong Kong legal system is concerned, the complete incorporation of the Walled City into the New Territories and thus into the general colony. But no special steps were taken to show the flag of government inside the walls. In 1904 there was nothing but desolation there, the city being virtually unoccupied except for a couple of schools and a home for the aged.[4] Plague was prevalent around it: the local Chinese maintained a plague hospital until the epidemic died out, and in 1925 the secretary of state approved a crown lease for a dispensary and hospital on the same site. The governor, Sir Reginald E. Stubbs, noted that 'it would not, on account of its associations, be well to make use of or to sell this site for other than a public purpose such as this',[5] and it is clear from the fact that he sought approval for the grant of the lease that government policy did not envisage development of the area. The walls, in fact, were to be preserved, and in 1930 one could still see the remains of old official residences and yamen, and several old cannon.[6] But squatters had probably been drifting in during the rapid development of the Kowloon City district in the twenties.[7] The 1921 census reported that a large reclamation scheme in front of the suburbs had been under way for some years and that a road joining Kowloon City to Yau Ma Tei and Mong Kok was being built.[8] The Kowloon Tong residential estate was completed in 1930 and the nearby villages were soon absorbed by modern suburbia.[9] But plans to evacuate residents and build a park inside the Walled City initiated the first of many re-assertions by China of rights over the area.

The governor, Sir William Peel, stated that four lots held on short-term lease by the Church Missionary Society and one by the secretary for Chinese affairs (for a free school) would be renewed after expiration of the leases on 31 December 1934; but residents of other lots, mainly Chinese pig-breeders, were to be removed for sanitary reasons at the end of 1934. Their dwellings would be demolished and the city preserved as 'a place of popular resort and antiquarian interest'.[10] On 10 June 1933 the Hong Kong government issued a notice to inhabitants stipulating resumption of land by the end of 1934 and offering compensation (money and land) for those who registered before September. There were at that time 436 people living in sixty-four houses inside the walls, and they

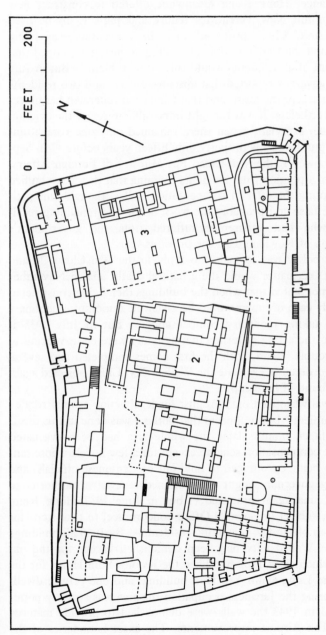

0   FEET   200

N

3. THE WALLED CITY OF KOWLOON, 1902

The following can be identified with a fair degree of confidence:
1 Lung Chun Yee Hok, 1847–99; New Territories Land Court, 1900–5
2 Deputy Magistrate's Yamen until 1899; Kwong Yum Home for the Aged, 1902–71; Grace Light School
3 Plague Hospital; Kowloon City Public Dispensary, 1925–33
4 Main gate

The boundaries are at present approximately indicated by Sai Shing Road on the left of the plan, Lung Shing Road on the right, Tung Tau Tsuen Road at the top, and Lung Chun Road at the bottom.

Source: 1900–2 Survey, District No. 1, Sheet No. 2; enclosure in Stubbs to Amery, 26 June 1925: CO129/488.

appealed to the national and Kwangtung provincial governments for assistance; Hong Kong meanwhile offered to construct new houses on full New Territories tenure and pig-sties to be used under permit. China protested that the convention was being ignored, and the Foreign Office, unwilling to negotiate, hoped that the consent of all residents would solve the problem.[11] But in July 1934 the governor reported that absentee owners and two residents refused to accept the terms and that China had reiterated her objections; nevertheless, it was thought impossible to revise the eviction programme, especially when there remained only one recalcitrant who had purchased his property only fifteen years before.[12] In September, however, the Wai Chiao Pu (Ministry of Foreign Affairs) referred to a petition from residents claiming that they were bullied into accepting the offer of compensation.[13] Peel thought this petition quite false and probably the work of the one remaining recalcitrant, who had apparently suffered from the government's resumption of Kowloon Tsai the previous year.[14]

British policy was to make no reply to the Wai Chiao Pu and hope that the matter would die a natural death, and in November the governor stated that when the buildings then being constructed were ready each occupier would be given the option of accepting a house or taking monetary compensation.[15] But in July 1935 it seemed to the acting governor that agitators were endeavouring to stir up trouble,[16] and, with the first homes completed and several residents ordered to evacuate the Walled City, China objected again on the ground of hardship.[17]

Approval was given on 9 August for legal action against recalcitrant occupiers[18] but it appears that nothing was done in this direction. Eighteen months later the whole area had been evacuated under the compensation scheme except for a few hovels whose tenants were being encouraged to hold out by Cantonese officials, and the acting governor sought and obtained renewal of authority to evict.[19] China again protested,[20] but in June 1937 Hong Kong proposed, subject to Colonial Office concurrence, to take steps for the eviction of the few remaining residents.[21] By 1940 all buildings inside the Walled City had been demolished except for the old yamen (which since 1902 had been the Kwong Yum Home for the Aged), the Lung Chun Yee Hok building, and one private dwelling.[22] During the Japanese occupation the area was sparsely populated, and in 1943 the walls were demolished to provide material for Kai Tak Airport improvements. The exact boundaries of the

Walled City cannot now be determined. After the war the Chinese government planned to restore her administration and the provincial authorities announced an intention to establish Chinese civil courts there.[23]

With the re-establishment of the old order after the Japanese surrender there was a large and rapid influx to Hong Kong of returnees and Chinese refugees from the civil war, and the resulting pressure on war-damaged accommodation was such that the Walled City became occupied once again by squatters. About two thousand inhabitants were to be relocated at the end of 1947. Armed with a court order,[24] police and Public Works Department employees expelled the reluctant squatters on 5 January 1948 and demolished their huts, and a week later several people were injured in a riot resulting from police efforts to deal with those who had returned. Sympathy with the resisters was widespread: a crowd fired the British consulate in Canton, students in Shanghai declared a two-day protest strike, the Po On magistrate addressed residents in the Walled City under the Chinese flag to encourage their militancy, while a 'comfort mission' from the Kwangtung provincial government distributed largesse among them, and the Nanking government officially protested to Great Britain.[25] On 19 January the squatters were still squatting, children were playing football and a police squad merely stood by as British and Chinese diplomats sought an amicable solution to the dispute.[26] 'The Chinese Government', said Hong Kong's *Annual Report 1948*, 'considered that they had cause to intervene in this matter since according to their interpretation of the Peking Convention ... jurisdiction in Kowloon City was reserved to China. His Majesty's Government have been unable to accept this interpretation.'[27] Nevertheless HMG did not care to exacerbate Anglo-Chinese relations by continuing the eviction programme and the city became, in the governor's words, 'a cesspool of iniquity, with heroin divans, brothels and everything unsavoury':[28] just what its suburbs had been, in fact, in 1898. The government cautiously began to send in police, initially deporting rather than prosecuting offenders lest the defence raise the issue of jurisdiction, but by 1959, at least, suspects were arrested and charged and their defence lawyers' arguments found unacceptable by the courts.[29]

The next incident, this time involving the government of the People's Republic, occurred in January 1963 when the local authorities attempted to resettle occupants of the Walled City and demolish a corner of it for the Tung Tau resettlement estate. A 'Kowloon City anti-demolition committee' was formed and China supported its aims, protesting to the British chargé d'affaires in Peking on 17 January that 'the City of Kowloon is China's territory, and within China's jurisdiction and that this has all along been so in history'. According to reports from the mainland press, plans for the general development of the area were published in Hong Kong in May 1960 and were immediately opposed by local residents; but in March 1962 resettlement notices were posted and by the end of the year 'resettlement notifications' were 'forcibly issued'. 'Local residents expressed great indignation at this truculent act by the British authorities in Hong Kong.' The British chargé, T. W. Garvey, was asked in Peking on the first day of 1963 to tell Hong Kong to give serious consideration to the matter, and when specific times for demolition of premises were given a week later China protested the 'gross violation of China's sovereignty'.[30] The official reply denied the validity of the Chinese claim, yet agreed to defer, 'for the time being, action in the Kowloon "Walled City" confident that in the interval discussions with the Chinese Government on the plan will make it possible to dispel their concern'.[31] In fact the Tung Tau resettlement scheme was amended and occupants of the Walled City left undisturbed.[32] They played no major part in the riots of 1967, but in July of that year a police raid brought forth a protest in an official Chinese news release, and a statement issued by the 'anti-persecution struggle committee' of the city's residents 'demanded immediate release of the kidnapped school headmaster, apologies and admissions of guilt to the Walled City residents, and assurances that no similar incident would occur in the future'.[33]

The Hong Kong government is clearly not concerned to provoke another international incident, and did not insist on the removal from the Walled City of two old cannon discovered in 1970 when residents claimed possession of them.[34] Also, as Jones points out, Peking

... could not ignore an appeal from Kowloon City landlords, but can hardly have enjoyed taking up the cudgels on their behalf. Moreover it probably does not like to claim sovereignty over Kowloon City, for fear of implicitly abandoning its claim to the rest of Hong Kong at the same time.[35]

Apparently, however, China has not intimated to Great Britain any fundamental change of attitude regarding the Walled City, though when leftist elements attempted to occupy the old folks' home in 1971 their plans were frustrated by a large body of Hong Kong police. According to informants involved in the affair, the valuable property was handed over to the Christian Nationals' Evangelism Commission for use as a school after government efforts to persuade the previous tenants to stay on had failed; the schoolchildren moved in with their desks under police protection as the aged and infirm moved out. Chinese representatives in Hong Kong did not on this occasion object.

The Walled City in 1972

Incidents giving rise to Sino-British controversy provide one means of documenting the consequences of the Convention of Peking. Another method, appropriate when discussing the Walled City of Kowloon, is to turn from historical events and look instead at geographical and political or legal considerations. The material presented in this section was collected in 1972; it attempts to portray the city at rest, so to speak, and at one moment in time. It seeks to demonstrate that one important effect of the convention can be seen at the mundane level of urban development.

Once the observer on the ground has located the Walled City—a conglomeration of high, narrow concrete buildings clustered in a parallelogram next door to Sai Tau Tsuen on one side and Tung Tau Tsuen on another—an immediate impression is that the suburbs so abhorred by Hong Kong residents in the nineteenth century have moved into the fort and taken it over. The mandarin's yamen building is still there, and a temple, but the sense of spaciousness and almost solitude which must have existed before the second world war is now crowded out by twisting lanes, dark alleyways, malodorous open drains, clattering factories, brothels, gambling halls and drug dens, mangy dogs and dubious citizens. The city has character, perhaps, and one might even detect a certain sense of community amongst the people of the area; but it is a vile place, noisy, dingy, filthy, unkempt, unhealthy, unsightly.

The 1971 census reported that 10,004 people from 2,161 households occupied 2,185 living quarters in the Walled City. Observation, and common opinion, suggest that these figures are far too low. One informant doubted that the enumerators would have dared to knock on every door, though the Census and Statistics Department reports that residents were very co-operative; lay estimates often include the nearby village of Sai Tau which is frequently mistaken for the Walled City. Accurate information of the population's size is therefore unobtainable.

The people are engaged in a variety of occupations: the majority of them go outside the city to work, and live there merely because they have always lived there and see no reason to move out. Work inside is provided by the factories, ordinary food shops and restaurants, and by the current spate of rebuilding. Some residents are engaged in one or other of the illegal enterprises: they are unregistered doctors (with thriving abortion practices) or dentists, common criminals, prostitutes, drug-pushers, and operators, spies, touts or 'militia' of gambling dens, blue-movie parlours, and dog-meat restaurants. These are the lucrative businesses, though the major outlet for drugs is in fact outside the boundaries of the city and the prostitutes do not look particularly enticing.

There are several missions operating clinics and churches in the Walled City and they are suspected by some of exaggerating the iniquities of the place in order to elicit funds. A Tin Hau temple and two shrines large enough to be indicated on the map cater to non-Christian spiritual needs; several schools, including the large Grace Light school, provide some sort of education. Though tempting, it is not accurate to see the Walled City as a self-contained, independent community. It is an integral part of the wider Kowloon City district and relies on its contacts with the outside world.

Occupants suffer the same lack of general facilities as occupants of other squatter areas: standpipes and illegal tapping rather than proper piped water (the Christian Nationals' Evangelism Commission has the only metered supply), and no sewerage system. Electricity is provided but the wiring arrangements are beyond belief; street-lighting is almost non-existent; drainage is poor and flooding common. So-called 'streets' are often no more than five or six feet wide, while new buildings reach a height of ten storeys or more without lifts or, one suspects, proper foundations.

Apart from these admittedly rather superficial geographical observations, it is pertinent to consider the degree of government control, of ordinary law enforcement, in the Walled City. It must at the outset be noted that the government of the People's

Republic of China does not appear to attempt the exercise of any jurisdiction there at all: the residents appeal to Peking when it is convenient to do so but are not subject to its dictates. The *kaifong* (neighbourhood association) is left-wing but apparently has little real power other than moral suasion. Numerous mainland Chinese flags were flying on 1 October 1972, but there were several Nationalist flags up nine days later during 'double tenth' celebrations.

Although by municipal law the Walled City is as much a part of Hong Kong as Queen's Road, Central, the colonial government does not in fact exercise full jurisdiction over it. The Rating and Valuation Department has not assessed premises to rates; six lots have been registered in the name of a mission body which pays a nominal crown rent on a short-term basis, and all other occupants are technically squatters. But the Squatter Control Unit does not go inside the city. Unregistered doctors and dentists operate modern and completely open clinics, and are not harassed by medical authorities; schools are not supervised by the Education Department; the Public Works Department does not usually enforce buildings regulations.

Some government departments, however, do exercise some control. The Fire Services Department has served fire hazard abatement notices, prosecuted offenders, and seized illegally stored dangerous goods. Nevertheless the Walled City is an obvious fire hazard; no one has objected, naturally, to the department's firefighting there.

Residents, whether born in the Walled City or not, are theoretically required to apply for registration with the Registration of Persons Office and will normally be given an identity card; they qualify for a Hong Kong British passport and may (and do) seek legal aid without reference to their origin or place of residence. The GPO has no post-box within the boundaries of the city but delivers mail to resident addressees; the Social Welfare Department provides social services; the Labour Department enforces its safety and employment regulations; prosecutions would be launched against income-tax defaulters though known evasion is not common. The Urban Services Department sends in a team four times a day to chlorinate the four wells, collect night-soil and rubbish, and to campaign for cleanliness. Warning notices are issued, though offenders are not prosecuted, and health regulations are not enforced.

Police regularly patrol the Walled City, and the police visiting book is the only physical evidence there of Hong Kong government presence. The Kowloon City division of the uniform branch sends in regular patrols; other police units also enter the area, though no ordinary policeman is allowed over the boundary without prior approval from above. Police make some arrests each day yet are rarely seen; sundry sources allege that special 'arrangements' exist between police and the vicelords though there is, of course, no real evidence. The general rationale seems to be the isolation of the various rackets inside the Walled City where they can be controlled to some extent and gradually eliminated; the topography of the place and the racketeers' early-warning system successfully prevent large-scale raids.

Real political power seems to be exercised mainly by the secret societies, of which five are based in the city; the King Yee and Sun Yee On are the most influential, but the 14K, Wo Shing Wo, and Tai Ho Choi are also represented. These groups co-exist peacefully, in the main, though there will be occasional skirmishes by their young troops over minor matters. The King Yee, Sun Yee On, and Tai Ho Choi are Chiu Chow triads, the last-named being an independent splinter group of the Fuk Yee Hing. Organization is primarily 'quasi-triad' rather than conventional triad, and it is estimated that about 900 members of the former and 200 of the latter are either resident in or closely connected with the Walled City. There is no 'Mister Big', but one man above others, a middle-aged non-active member of the Sun Yee On, is spoken of with respect by younger members. He is a principal landlord in the Walled City, deported to Macao in 1964 but since allowed to return. He functions now only in an advisory capacity. Triad power, which is considerable and lucrative, is exercised by violence or the promise of it.

The position is, therefore, that for fear of inciting official Chinese protest there are some government regulations which are not enforced; some relatively minor ones *are* enforced; and police operations are limited for various reasons. The legal lacuna that results is filled partly by the secret societies and partly by various civil organizations.[36]

The Walled City in 1972 was therefore a special area, distinguished in certain geographical aspects from the urban landscape around it and by the unique political considerations affecting law enforcement. This state of affairs is a direct consequence of failure by Britain and China to agree on an interpretation of the convention's Kowloon City clause. The point is confirmed by Frank Leeming, a geographer whose basic data was collected in 1970–1; his chapter on Kowloon City concludes that poverty and filth are responsible for the physical appearance of the district. 'Both of these things arise from the underlying anomaly of status which is the walled city's distinguishing mark, and which in some degree extends to the villages.'[37]

Subsequent Developments

In 1973–5 the Walled City was frequently mentioned in the columns of the local press. From these reports it appeared that the government of Hong Kong was taking a renewed interest in the place, and it may be that some initiative towards an agreement with China was about to be taken.

One multi-storey building, nearly completed, was demolished in January 1973 when it was found not to comply with Public Works Department regulations and to be situated just outside the Walled City.[38] The owner complained that it was inside the boundaries, though his claim was clearly untenable. In 1975, however, two new buildings unarguably sited within the city were the subjects of closure orders under the Hong Kong Airport (Control of Obstructions) Ordinance[39] and their tops were lopped off.[40] Since then, staff of the Buildings Ordinance Office have regularly inspected construction work to ensure that flight paths to Kai Tak Airport are not obstructed.

Another development has been an increase in police action against triads, illegal drugs, and vice.[41] One newspaper claimed in 1973 that China approves.[42]

The Walled City and its living conditions were debated in the House of Lords in 1974.[43] Earl Cowley seemed to accept that China's claim to the place was valid and he was not contradicted when he said: 'China's sovereignty rights could be protected by the so called "sovereignty umbrella" and remain unaffected or unrestricted by any agreement arrived at, or by the negotiations themselves.'[44] Lord Goronwy-Roberts, speaking for the Foreign and Commonwealth Office, said:

The Governor's aim is to build up a working relationship with the inhabitants of the Walled City itself which will enable specific problems to be discussed on the local level, for there to be acceptance and co-operation in ameliorative policies which in turn will have their effect upon the attitude and reaction of the great People's Republic of China which, understandably, is watching everything that is happening in Hong Kong and in the Walled City....

I have recently consulted the Governor. He intends to continue to improve the areas around the Walled City, so far as possible, in such a way as to avoid friction, and gradually to expand urban services within it, as he and his Government are now doing. It is his and our hope that this policy will generate confidence among the city's inhabitants and, there-fore, beyond the boundaries of the city and the boundaries of the Colony, and will produce an acceptance of this policy of social reform and a posi-tive desire to help over the improvement of conditions within the city.[45]

He indicated that 'the attractive and sensible suggestion' of a posi-tive approach to the government of the People's Republic would be discussed at the highest levels.

Although the publicity created by the House of Lords debate was said to have caused postponement of an official investigation into living conditions in the Walled City, the government is likely to continue their gradual improvement. In late 1978 it seemed that the place had already improved. Three trends could be identified. First, the residents were much less suspicious of gov-ernment representatives and facilities: the District Office in Kow-loon City is often asked to mediate in their quarrels, and it organ-izes an annual children's fair and other activities. The atmosphere was more relaxed, less foreboding. Apart from ensuring that new buildings did not exceed height restrictions, however, the gov-ernment did not overtly extend its control beyond the limits noted in 1972. The one lift in the city had not been inspected under the Lifts and Escalators (Safety) Ordinance! Some unlicensed dentists, though, were reported to be sending their children to get proper dental qualifications because they feared that the government would sooner or later take action against them.[46] Secondly, there was apparently less poverty, indicated by the declining business of the several welfare agencies inside the boundaries.[47] Thirdly, poli-tics was not so much in command: there was talk of sending a delegation to Canton when the buildings on the periphery were demolished in 1973, but nothing eventuated and there seem to have been no appeals to China since then. The *kaifong* was less active and probably less influential.

One government official suggested that rebuilding in the 1970s provided homes for many people from outside who were not imbued with the traditional attitudes of long-time residents. They were nevertheless pleased to be left alone by the government, provided they could claim public assistance if need arose. Although technically squatters, they were rent-paying tenement dwellers or even owners of the flats they lived in, and they had acquired attitudes more familiar to lower middle-class districts than to squatter areas. They were as anxious as concerned outsiders to see improvements to the city's environment.

If such demographic and social changes continue, and if China follows a hands-off policy, it will be just a matter of time before the arid treaty dispute represented by the Walled City is finally resolved.

8

CUSTOMS, CABLES,
NATIONALITY, AND NEUTRALITY

The Chinese Maritime Customs

THE customs issue was not dealt with in the convention: the Tsungli Yamen preferred to rely on a British promise to ensure that China's revenue was not prejudiced by the extension of colonial boundaries. As has been shown, however, the Chinese belief that the IMC would be allowed to continue operations in the leased territory and its waters was rudely shattered by the IMC's expulsion in 1899.[1] The British compromise was a scheme whereby the Hong Kong government was to collect duty on opium and hand it over to China. A bill to implement this proposal was prepared and introduced in the Legislative Council. But before it went to a second reading viceroy Li Hung-chang passed through Hong Kong and, on being informed that the duty received by the IMC on opium had recently increased, he wanted no further steps taken in the matter.[2]

Hong Kong had, indeed, gone some way towards partial fulfilment of MacDonald's promise to the Yamen in 1898. A condition was placed in the opium farmer's contract limiting him to only one boiling house, for the maintenance of two separate boiling establishments had afforded him easy facilities for smuggling by providing an excuse for the presence of raw opium on his junks. A stringent ordinance to prevent the smuggling of arms was passed.[3] Nevertheless the value of the opium farm rose steeply: in 1898 it was worth $372,000; in 1901 the farmer paid $678,000, a tender he was able almost to treble three years later. In 1914 he invested $3,741,500.[4] It is unlikely, therefore, that smugglers were discouraged by removal of the customs houses.

This comment is borne out by the new arrangements undertaken by the customs. The Kap Shui Mun station was replaced by two collectorates at Taishan and Lintin, while stations at Shauchang and Samun took over from Fat Tau Chau. Cheung Chau was

137

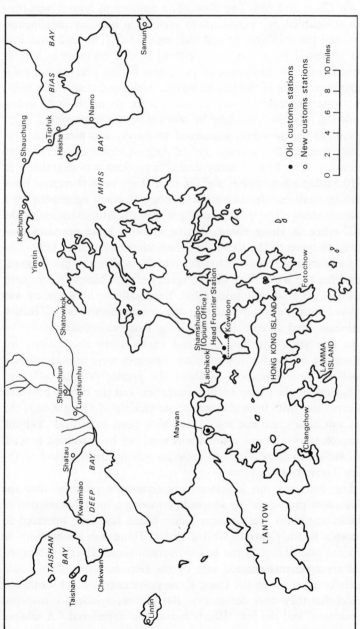

4. CHINESE CUSTOMS STATIONS AROUND HONG KONG

The 'old' stations were established prior to 1899 and were replaced, soon after the occupation of the New Territories, by the 'new' stations. The spelling of the names is that used by the source material.

Source: Adapted from Stanley F. Wright, *Hong Kong and the Chinese Customs* (Shanghai: Statistical Department of the Inspectorate General of Customs, 1930), between pp. 1 and 2.

replaced by Tungho. In 1901 collectorates were in operation at Sham Chun and Sha Tau Kok. The number of houses was thus almost doubled, with consequent expense in building, administration, and the employment and training of staff. The land boundary was increased from two and one-third to over 60 miles in length, requiring the establishment of eight new border posts and a great expansion in size of the border guard. Additional roads were built. The water boundaries were extended from about 20 to 80 miles, rendering effective patrolling by revenue vessels impossible.[5]

Smuggling, therefore, continued to thrive, and numerous proposals were made for some sort of Anglo-Chinese co-operation to control it. The first of many draft conventions was negotiated in 1910.[6] It lapsed, however, and for nearly forty years thereafter there were intermittent discussions attempting to reach agreement on a customs treaty. The greatest obstacle was official recognition of the IMC office in Hong Kong, for the Queen's Road premises continued to be let to the Kowloon commissioner even after 1899. The *de facto* arrangement was too convenient to disturb, but to grant this office the status of an official agency of the Chinese government was deemed politically intolerable. Eventually such an agency was allowed only on condition that the commissioner be of British nationality and acceptable to the Hong Kong authorities.[7]

In one sense the extended and exasperating negotiations for agreement on joint anti-smuggling measures were almost solely a result of the convention. Without the greater facilities afforded smugglers by the extension of boundaries, and the excuse provided to expel the IMC from the immediate vicinity of Hong Kong, the loss to China's revenue would not have been so critical. Yet the complex story of these negotiations need not be examined here; it will suffice to emphasize two episodes which directly relate to the New Territories.

The first was the Kowloon commissioner's proposal that the 'Kiaochow procedure' be adopted, involving a formal admission of official status for the customs house which had long operated in Queen's Road, Central. Well aware of Hong Kong's hostility to Chinese officialdom in the colony, commissioner Harris submitted that arrangements entered into by the German government could easily be accepted by the Hong Kong government, which could not object that they were derogatory. But they were indeed considered derogatory, and the first 'Harris convention' foundered.[8] A scheme which envisaged customs operations in the leased waters of the colony was therefore rejected, the implications being that what may have been good enough for one leased territory was not good enough for another and that the New Territories was an integral part of ceded Hong Kong in which an official Chinese customs house could not be tolerated.

Secondly, after much further negotiation there were hopes that a new agreement, this time permitting the Chinese Maritime Customs to establish a head office and sub-office in Hong Kong and CMC revenue vessels to patrol colonial waters, would be reached in 1930. But when Sir William Peel succeeded Clementi as governor he denounced the idea of a Chinese preventive service in the colony because it would encourage the irredentist tendencies of the southern Chinese.[9] Thus the customs houses, originally removed from the New Territories in 1899 for the ostensible purpose of avoiding administrative difficulties there, were not allowed to return for fear of promoting the abolition of British administration altogether.

A treaty was finally concluded in 1948 which explicitly granted the CMC the right to establish offices in Hong Kong and to patrol Mirs Bay and Deep Bay.[10]

The Chinese Telegraph Administration

While the extension of Hong Kong's boundaries complicated the question of Chinese customs administration, it also inflamed another long-standing colonial grievance: the operation of telegraph lines in Hong Kong by the Chinese government. Just as the leased territory included customs houses, it also included wires belonging to the Chinese Telegraph Administration.

The background to this affair is that a Danish company, the Great Northern Telegraph Company of Copenhagen, and its British rival, the Eastern Extension Australasia and China Telegraph Company Limited, which were the first commercial concerns to lay telegraph lines in China, amalgamated their interests and signed agreements in 1883–4 with the newly-formed Chinese Telegraph Administration. They undertook to provide facilities for the CTA's line to Hong Kong, including the establishment of a CTA office in Victoria, while China granted similar facilities with respect to the companies' lines at Shanghai. The British government supported the companies and, despite opposition from the colony, extended the Chinese right to an office in Hong Kong until 1910. The two Chinese wires from Canton were joined in a house at the border of

British Kowloon to the wires of the Eastern Extension Company running to Hong Kong.[11]

The convention, of course, removed the Hong Kong-China border, but not the house where the wires were connected, some twenty miles to the north. The section of the telegraph line in the leased territory continued to be owned and maintained by a company apparently controlled by the Chinese government, and this, to a colonial administration intent on asserting virtually plenary rights in the leasehold, was unacceptable. Sir Henry Blake therefore proposed that the CTA transfer ownership of the New Territories section to the Eastern Extension Company. The director general of the imperial CTA, however, replied that the line was privately owned, and nothing was done until Blake raised the matter again in 1903. This time the same reply was received—but another reason for rejecting Hong Kong's time limit for the removal of station, wires and poles was put forward:

> The [Sham Shui Po] office is, however, in the Kowloon Extension, which, as stated in the Treaty of 1898, is leased for a period of ninety-nine years, and is accordingly not on the same footing as the British Territory of Hong Kong. The [Sham Shui Po] telegraphs in the Kowloon Extension are in identically the same situation as the telegraphs in Shanghai and Tientsin Concessions, and also those of [Weihaiwei] and Ch'ing-tao, where the Chinese Telegraph Administration has established offices and set up poles for many years without the slightest opposition. It seems only natural that the precedent established in other concessions should be followed in this.[12]

Hong Kong countered, of course, with a denial of the analogy with mere 'concessions', since the New Territories was in every respect British territory and wholly subject to British administration for the ninety-nine year term. China again demurred, and sought extra time pending full discussion.

Sir Matthew Nathan, Blake's successor, sought in October 1904 to settle the matter by legislation making illegal the construction and working of telegraph lines without a licence from the Hong Kong authorities. The CTA would be granted a licence on various conditions, including payment of an annual sum and the vesting of the line's ownership in the colonial government. It was recognized, however, that such action might lead to Chinese retaliation regarding the Eastern Extension Company's operations in Shanghai and Foochow. Passage of the bill was postponed lest Kowloon-Canton railway negotiations broke down as a result.[13]

Meanwhile, title to the Sham Shui Po office had been upheld by the New Territories Land Court, either upon the claim of the CTA superintendent in Hong Kong[14] or upon the claim of the Eastern Extension Company.[15] Despatches contradict each other as to the identity of the claimant, though it is more likely that the company, rather than the CTA, was successful. It is also probable, though neither of the relevant despatches referred to this point, that the governor issued title to the company subsequent to the Land Court's decision. But no claim was upheld in respect of the poles carrying the wires. Then, without reference to Hong Kong, HMG signed an extension of the 1883–4 agreements in 1904, carrying them forward to 1930. Colonial hands were thus tied by what amounted to an international treaty.

Although the CTA was managed by a Chinese official it was not strictly subservient to the Chinese government. The superintendent had, however, on various occasions interfered in Hong Kong matters quite unconnected with telegraphs. The colonial government therefore viewed with alarm an attempt by the Chinese Board of Communication in 1908 to buy out shareholders in the CTA, and the governor, Sir Frederick Lugard, revived the question of removing the CTA from Hong Kong.[16] Again the fear of reciprocal action against the Eastern Extension Company urged caution. Sir John Jordan, British minister in Peking, thought that, with pressure, the Chinese government might be induced to remove the terminal station from Sham Shui Po to the new border; but the Wai Wu Pu had already expressed reluctance:

They pointed out that a similar state of things existed at [Weihaiwei], where they had a telegraph line running through the leased territory and a telegraph station on the mainland, opposite to the island; and that at Kiao-chow they had a Chinese telegraph line of some 30 miles passing through territory leased to Germany, a Chinese telegraph station at Tsing-tau and the frontier of the leased territory, and that Germany had never raised any objection to these arrangements. Why, therefore, should the Hong Kong Government make such difficulties at the present moment?[17]

On the one hand, China had admitted the sovereignty of Britain over the ceded areas of Hong Kong by placing the station at Sham Shui Po; on the other hand, a clear parallel was drawn between the New Territories and other foreign leaseholds, and a clear distinction was made between ceded and leased territory. Unable to rely on any unambiguous convention clause supporting her point of view, Great Britain was in no position to insist on removal of the terminal station from the New Territories. As Lugard complained, the telegraph line was a continual trespass on crown land,[18] but the precedents set in the other leased territories were largely instrumental in preventing HMG from enforcing the British interpretation of the convention. The problem of the Sham Shui Po station was only solved by the construction of a new telegraph line along the Kowloon-Canton railway,[19] but the line continued to be controlled by China until 1930.[20]

In 1911 R. E. Stubbs, then a clerk in the Eastern Department of the Colonial Office but later governor of Hong Kong, thought the removal of the terminal station a very trivial matter.[21] On the contrary, however, it was of some theoretical and legal importance, for the station was originally placed at Sham Shui Po because it could not justifiably be erected inside ceded Kowloon. To allow it to remain within the leased territory implied recognition of a different status for the New Territories and acceptance of China's analogy with concessions in the treaty ports. Yet such factors did not seem so important in respect of the Opium Office, also at Sham Shui Po, maintained by the IMC under the opium agreement of 1886. According to the treaty the office was to be established 'on Chinese territory, at a convenient spot on the Kowloon side'. According to the commissioner, the site was too advantageous for Hong Kong merchants dealing in opium; although it was moved to another house a few streets away, the Opium Office remained within the newly British territory.[22]

The Nationality of New Territories Inhabitants

Sir Claude MacDonald was aware of the customs complication when he negotiated the lease of the New Territories, but there is no evidence that he knew of the difficulties likely to arise concerning the telegraph line. Similarly, it did not, apparently, occur to anyone in the British government to settle the question of the nationality of Chinese who were resident in the leased territory.

Traditionally, China regarded all persons of pure Chinese race as Chinese nationals; Chinese nationality was indelible, even if its holders and their ancestors had been born outside the Middle Kingdom. In the case of Chinese born in British territory, however, the Chinese government agreed to allow them the status of British subjects on condition that they did not wear Chinese dress.

The 'costume regulations', issued in 1868 by Sir Rutherford Alcock, embodied this scheme. In 1867 it was advised by the law officers that children born in a British possession of immigrant Chinese who were Chinese subjects could not validly claim the protection of HMG; but in 1882 the crown decided to accept as British nationals all Chinese persons in possession of a passport issued by the governor of any British colony. Such persons were thence entitled to register with consuls in China and receive protection so long as they complied with the costume regulations.[23]

There were several classes of 'Anglo-Chinese' (persons of Chinese race who might claim British nationality). By 1885 the following classes were recognized: Chinese domiciled in Hong Kong or Kowloon at the time of cession, and their children; Chinese born in a British possession of parents also born in a British possession; and Chinese born in a British possession of naturalized British subjects. Naturalized British subjects themselves received no protection in China because their rights as British subjects extended no further than the possession in which they were naturalized. Chinese born in a British possession of immigrant parents subjects of China were originally beyond the scope of British protection but were eventually merged with the other classes. From 1892, at Sir William Robinson's suggestion, birth certificates were issued to all Anglo-Chinese except naturalized subjects.[24] These certificates were amended in 1904 and the costume regulations were withdrawn.

What was to be the position of New Territories inhabitants? In 1899 a resident of Sai Kung applied for a certificate from the registrar-general entitling him, as a British subject, to enter British Columbia without payment of the fee required from Chinese nationals. W. M. Goodman, acting chief justice, posed the problem: 'does the cession of the new territory and its incorporation with this Colony act as a *naturalisation* of all the Chinese then resident, so as to confer upon them all the rights of duly naturalised British subjects, as well as the duties and obligations of such subjects?'[25] The law officers reported that, from 16 April 1899, all Chinese inhabitants of the New Territories were to be regarded as British subjects for all purposes, as were all persons born there during the continuance of the lease.[26] Chamberlain instructed Hong Kong accordingly.

Not only, therefore, had the New Territories been integrated into the colony of Hong Kong, but its inhabitants were placed in the same position as inhabitants domiciled in the ceded colony itself. As such they were incorporated into the certificate system tacitly accepted by the Chinese government. But, as with the question of boundaries, no representations on the subject had been officially made to China: the Yamen was unaware, until 1909, of the status in British law of New Territories residents and continued to regard them as Chinese subjects.

Liang Tou's case provided the occasion for further consideration of the problem. Liang Tou was born in the New Territories and had resided there since birth. On 20 August 1909 he joined with others in attacking and robbing two police constables, both of whom subsequently died; he then fled across the border where he was arrested by the San On magistrate. J. W. Jamieson, consul-general at Canton, applied to the acting viceroy, Yuan, for the fugitive's extradition. But His Excellency refused, observing that 'the territories are merely held on lease and are not on the same footing as lands belonging to the British Crown. All Chinese residents of these territories, therefore, still retain their status of Chinese subjects and cannot be dealt with as if they were British subjects.'[27]

Jamieson protested, again demanding extradition, and Yuan again refused. Sir John Jordan noted that inhabitants of Weihaiwei received no British protection outside that territory and owed allegiance solely to the emperor of China; the situation was the same in Kiaochow; and the Liaotung lease specifically provided for trial of Chinese by Chinese officials.[28] It was decided by the Foreign Office that the viceroy was within his rights in refusing to extradite. As Yuan had explained, if Liang Tou had been arrested in the colony he could have been tried by a British court; but within the limits of the Chinese empire, the Foreign Office stated, he could reasonably be deemed by the Chinese government to be a Chinese subject amenable solely to Chinese jurisdiction. The application for extradition amounted to an admission of that principle, since if he was a British subject for all purposes the fugitive could have been dealt with by the consular court under the Fugitive Offenders Act.[29] Hong Kong therefore had no option but to cooperate with the authorities in Canton, who tortured Liang Tou into confessing and executed him.[30]

The Foreign Office decision meant that inhabitants of the New Territories must be deemed to be Chinese subjects when in Chinese territory, and must be placed on a different footing from Anglo-Chinese in Hong Kong.[31] They were not, apparently, to be considered British subjects for all purposes. But the Foreign Office concurred in the Colonial Office suggestion that the matter be allowed to drop 'in the manner least prejudicial to any contention' which HMG might wish to uphold in the future, indicating that no final ruling had been given.[32]

The confusion regarding nationality resulted directly from the inadequacy of the convention, for not only did it fail to define clearly the status of the leased territory, it made no mention at all of the national status of inhabitants. Sir Ernest Satow remarked in 1905 that it was the modern practice in treaties of cession to allow the natives to emigrate if they wished; he went on to say that the natural inference from the non-expulsion provision was that inhabitants did *not* lose their Chinese nationality.[33] Sir W. E. Davidson, legal adviser to the Foreign Office, commented: 'To hold that the very day after the cession every Chinaman in [the New Territories] without any choice, or knowledge even, on his part of the antecedent circumstances became a British subject seems to me unreasonable and unusual although it may in strict law be technically arguable and defensible.'[34] Apparently, however, MacDonald did not imagine such a repercussion at the time of the lease.

Admittedly, the whole question of national status was particularly complex, and in fact the further complication added by the convention has not been of much importance. Since the Liang Tou affair, China has not insisted on the distinction drawn between residents of ceded and leased portions of the colony. British diplomatic energies were devoted to clarifying the position while in China of Anglo-Chinese generally, and the eventual policy adopted was more in compliance with China's than with British wishes. The acting attorney-general of Hong Kong in 1911, C. G. Alabaster, stated that Chinese resident in the New Territories at the time of the lease became of dual nationality; Sir Frederick Lugard insisted that they be considered British subjects for all purposes,[35] but following a slight Chinese compromise permitting 'denationalization' only those Anglo-Chinese who possessed denationalization certificates were to be protected in China by HMG.

This position was reached after much complex negotiation. Although China had admitted in 1893 that if the name of a man's ancestor had been expunged from his district register his allegiance might be dissolved, it was not until the promulgation of a new Chinese law of nationality towards the end of the Manchu dynasty that the possibility of renouncing Chinese nationality was formally recognized.[36] There were practical difficulties in arranging for the granting of denationalization certificates: the matter was complicated by the Chinese view of the issue as submerged in the question of extraterritoriality and by the Foreign Office determination in 1930 to treat China as a free and equal country. It was 1935 before British colonies were informed of the final decision to treat all non-denationalized Anglo-Chinese in China as Chinese subjects only.[37]

The conflicts between Chinese and British concepts of nationality have in practice been resolved. By municipal law, all residents of the New Territories at the time of the take-over and all persons born there since 16 April 1899, formerly citizens of the United Kingdom and colonies, are now British Dependent Territory citizens under the 1981 Act.[38] In international law there is uncertainty respecting the right of a state to represent its nationals against another state which regards the same individuals as its own subjects, but in practice Great Britain does not pursue claims on behalf of British subjects in such cases.[39] This is confirmed by the notes in the regular Hong Kong British passport. China, meanwhile, seems content to forgo her rights in respect of the people of the New Territories: Hong Kong Chinese generally, whether born in the ceded portion of the colony or in the New Territories and whether residing in the leased area before 1899 or born there since, find it very difficult to obtain Chinese travel documents. Their British passports are recognized by China as sufficient for the purposes of travel within China. The problem of New Territories residents in China will not therefore arise if the respective policies of China and Great Britain are consistently followed.

Neutrality

Another important issue left undetermined by the convention was the status of the leased territory during war. By the ordinary law of neutrality, belligerent states are severely restricted in the use they can make of the territory of a neutral state. The territory of Her Majesty, in international law, clearly includes territory which has been ceded to the British crown, but whether it includes the New Territories depends on the true effect of the Convention of Peking: did full sovereignty over the leasehold pass to Great Britain for the period of the lease, or did the New Territories remain part of the territory of China? If the former question is answered in the affirmative, there would be no doubt that the status of the New Territories for the purposes of neutrality law follows that of Great Britain and ceded Hong Kong.

In 1898 it was assumed that, once the New Territories had been occupied by the authorities in Hong Kong, the district took on the neutrality of Great Britain *vis-à-vis* the Spanish-American war.[40] In 1905, Japan took action against Russia in the Liaotung peninsula, and Japan and Great Britain attacked German forces in Kiaochow during the first world war; in both cases Chinese protests that her neutrality was breached went unheeded.[41] At no time did HM's advisers consider in detail the theoretical position: British action in respect of Kiaochow was dictated by military and political factors, and was not affected by any conscious decision that China had no interest in the matter because of the lease of Kiaochow to what was then a belligerent state. The possibility that leased territory might remain Chinese and thus be neutral in any conflict in which China remained neutral, regardless of the status of the lessee state, was apparently not recognized until 1937, when the whole issue became of considerable potential importance.

The question arose in the context of the Sino-Japanese war: if China and Japan fought a sea battle within the area indicated on the convention map, what should the British attitude be? Fitzmaurice of the Foreign Office stated the argument that leased territories remained Chinese territory, and continued:

> The result of this view would be that, in theory, the status of the leased territory during a war ought to depend on the position of the Chinese Government, and not on that of the lessee government. If the territory is, strictly speaking, Chinese territory, then, if China is at war, it ought to be treated as belligerent territory, even though the lessee is neutral. Similarly, if the lessee is at war and China neutral, it should be treated as neutral territory.[42]

In practice, however, Fitzmaurice noted, the status of the lessee state was the governing factor for determining whether leased territory during a war was belligerent or neutral. But a complication arose from the provision in the Convention of Peking which reserved the right of Chinese warships, whether neutral or otherwise, to use the waters of Mirs Bay and Deep Bay. Assuming that the neutrality of Great Britain in the Sino-Japanese conflict was the determining factor, HMG was confronted with a contradiction between its obligations to China under the convention and its obligations to Japan under the ordinary law of neutrality. As a neutral cannot justify a departure from neutrality on the basis of a previous treaty with one of the belligerents, the contradiction could not in theory be reconciled.

The policy suggested by Fitzmaurice was to prevent by some means the use of the bays by Chinese vessels of war. 'Should the Chinese refuse, probably the only course which will not involve either hostilities between us and the Japanese or hostilities in the bays between Chinese and Japanese, with resultant damage and inconvenience to British leased territory, would be to involve ourselves in a breach of the Convention by telling the Chinese that we cannot allow them to use the bays.'[43] But a threat to allow the same facilities to the Japanese under neutrality rules as afforded to the Chinese under treaty obligation would, it was hoped, secure Chinese agreement to refrain from sending ships to those waters.

The Colonial Office did not accept Fitzmaurice's interpretation of the convention but referred to the law officers' opinion of 27 September 1899 and denied that any element of sovereignty over the New Territories remained vested in China.[44] In practical terms the disagreement did not matter, for the Foreign Office confirmed that 'for the purposes of the present situation' the leasehold was being treated as the actual property of the lessee.[45]

9

THE QUESTION OF RENDITION

China's Reaction to
the Scramble for Concessions

FOREIGN imperialist rivalry at China's expense, most vividly represented by the territorial leases of 1898, prompted in the Chinese people a sense of shock and extreme crisis. The consequence was a rapid development of nationalism amongst Chinese who feared the dismemberment of their country and loss of their independent identity. The retrieval and defence of Chinese sovereignty became the common goal of all classes and political groups, and the traditional 'mainstream approach' of Middle Kingdom officials to international affairs, a pragmatic policy designed to control foreigners and minimize their impact, was destroyed. Despite the temporary set-back when the dowager empress brought the 'hundred days of reform' to an end, the scramble for concessions at the end of the nineteenth century ensured the eventual predominance of the reformers' ardent nationalism. The most important component of that nationalism was exhibited in the campaign for the recovery of sovereign rights and the termination of unequal treaties.[1]

Apart from the Boxer movement, whose aim was said at the time to be the wresting back of leased territories,[2] demands for the return of British acquisitions were 'curiously muted' before the establishment of the republic. 'Here,' comments Mary Wright, 'the effort seems to have been to contain rather than to expel for a variety of tactical reasons...'[3] As will be seen in the next chapter, the Ch'ing dynasty interpretation of the Convention of Peking 1898 sought to restrict British authority over the New Territories and maintain some form of Chinese influence, and the Nationalist régime adopted a similar approach: it was some years before abrogation of the convention became a regular demand. Without a full study of Chinese foreign affairs documents the 'variety of tactical reasons' for this lapse can only be surmised. At the end of the first world war, however, the Chinese case for the rendition of all leased territories was clearly enunciated before an international audience for the first time.

The Paris Peace Congress, 1919

The stimulus to nationalism provided by the scramble for concessions was reinforced and even magnified by Japan's presentation in 1915 of the notorious 'twenty-one demands'. Yuan Shih-k'ai's submission to the Japanese threat provoked another upsurge of nationalist indignation and determination to win back sovereign rights.[4] Japan had entered the world war in furtherance of her designs on China; by 1918 Japanese imperialism had triumphed in Eastern Asia, having succeeded in adding Shantung, Eastern Mongolia, Northern Manchuria, and Fukien to Japan's spheres of influence. Secret assurances from Great Britain, France, and Italy in support of claims to Shantung and the Pacific islands had been negotiated in 1917, and the Lansing-Ishii agreement won for Japan American recognition that 'territorial propinquity' gave her 'special interests in China, particularly in the part to which her possessions are contiguous'. China, meanwhile, had entered the war with high hopes that a respectable slice of the cake would be handed over at the peace table, and much rejoicing in Peking and elsewhere greeted the cessation of hostilities. The peace conference, it was hoped, would restore all German interests in China, readjust Sino-German agreements, and give teeth to Wilson's 'fourteen points'.

Chinese internal politics were at this time in confusion, with an indecisive battle raging between northern warlords, who dominated parliament in Peking and relied on Japanese financial support, and Sun Yat-sen's party in the south. The delegation to the Paris congress reflected this split.[5] But although the militarists supported Japan's exertion of pressure on the moderates to withdraw Chinese claims in regard to Kiaochow[6] the general optimism in 1919 prompted hopes for a reconciliation between north and south, and the Paris mission was instructed to put forward an ambitious programme of proposals. Included was the demand that any territory leased to a foreign power be returned to China or made into an international settlement.[7]

The consequence of Britain's most regrettable assurance of support for Japanese claims to Kiaochow was that, in fairness to Japan,

HMG could only assist China's just request for a favourable settlement of the 'Shantung question' by acceding to a general programme for the restoration of all leased territories.[8] Sir John Jordan in Peking promoted such a scheme:

I have carefully considered the question of the Hong Kong extension and fully realize that its retrocession would entail a considerable sacrifice for us; but without sacrifices on the part of all Powers who acquired or inherited the leased territories of 1898 no solution of China's problem seems possible. If United States policy has not changed I venture to think that we should now revert to our former attitudes and endeavour to come to some arrangement for neutralization or internationalization of all leased territories under conditions which will secure immunity from attack and render such terms as 'open door' and 'China's integrity' realities and not the meaningless expressions they too often are at present.[9]

Rendition of the New Territories could only, however, be allowed if the absolute security of Hong Kong was not jeopardized. Lord Cecil of the Colonial Office section at Paris agreed, but the Colonial Office and the Foreign Office were united in rejecting even the possibility of surrendering the New Territories. Earl Curzon, who staunchly opposed even the rendition of Weihaiwei, wondered 'how far we have encouraged these altruistic speculations on the part of Sir J. Jordan'; to give back the Kowloon extension was out of the question.[10]

Should the conference agree to some general settlement regarding foreign leaseholds it was hoped to elicit American support for exclusion of the New Territories, on the basis of Secretary Hay's 'open door' note of 1899. Hay had asked each power claiming spheres of interest in China for a pledge of commercial equality to all foreign nationals within each sphere; at Salisbury's insistence he had altered the wording of the declaration in recognition of the administrative incorporation of the New Territories into the existing colony.[11] Ronald Macleay (Foreign Office) minuted: 'Supposing the Chinese Delegates should put forward a claim to the restoration of the Hong Kong Extension (Kowloon), we ought to have no difficulty in securing the support of the United States Government in resisting such a demand in the view of their attitude in 1899.'[12]

In April 1919 the Chinese representatives presented a lengthy memorandum which sought to raise before the conference the whole range of Chinese grievances. 'As the Peace Conference seeks to base the structure of a new world upon the principles of justice, equality, and respect for the sovereignty of nations ... its work would remain incomplete if it should allow the germs of future conflicts to subsist in the Far East.'[13] Since discredited Germany had, by its aggression in Shantung, disturbed the Far Eastern balance of power and initiated the demands for leased territories, there was now no need to maintain the foreign leasehold system. Yet the delegation did not expect a specific settlement at Paris; its major hope was for a general declaration in the Versailles treaty recognizing China's rights and laying a basis for future progress towards sovereignty.[14]

Only President Wilson was sympathetic, and on 14 May 1919, Clemençeau, chairman of the conference, wrote to the Chinese minister of foreign affairs:

... while the Supreme Council of the Principal Allied and Associated Powers fully recognize the importance of the questions raised they do not consider that they fall within the province of the Peace Conference and they suggest that these matters should be brought to the attention of the Council of the League of Nations as soon as that body is able to function.[15]

Japan's succession to Germany in Kiaochow was confirmed at the conference, though under an obligation to restore the place to China in full sovereignty at some unspecified future date. This led to another outburst of Chinese nationalism and anti-foreignism and must have intensified the determination to recover leased territories.[16]

While the first demand for rendition of the New Territories was a failure, as an exercise in public relations the Chinese statement of her brief against foreign domination was relatively successful; within three years the arguments were put again to the world, this time with more effect. The New Territories, of course, remained with Great Britain: the conference at Paris had given the Foreign Office the chance to rehearse the justifications of its claim and to work out a defensive policy to meet a more sustained attack.

The Washington Conference, 1921–1922[17]

The nine-power conference which opened in Washington on 11 November 1921 had two general objects: the limitation of naval armaments and the removal of sources of international misunderstanding in the Pacific and the Far East. The major nations had differing objects in view; China, of course, hoped for specific agreements leading towards full sovereignty, and she particularly sought the implementation of Japan's promise at Paris to restore Kiaochow. The United States in general supported Chinese aims, and wanted a reduction of Sino-Japanese hostility. Japan and Great Britain, however, were more circumspect. They were the two powers with most to lose in China; yet while the Anglo-Japanese alliance had benefited both nations in the post-war years it was becoming of decreasing importance to Great Britain, whose growing friendship with and reliance on America were jeopardized by loyalty to the aggressors of Shantung. Unless renewed, the alliance would lapse in 1922, and HMG feared the isolation of a potentially hostile Japan if no definite promise of American support for Great Britain's weakened Far Eastern position could be obtained.[18] British policy thus had to follow simultaneously two contradictory aims. Japan's general interests counselled avoidance of seeming to go it alone in the East:

There were two Japans, one militant, the other liberal. Like the thin man inside the fat man crying to get out, Japan's thin little liberal alter ego emerged in the 1920s for a brief beleaguered heyday before it was regorged. The victory of the democracies in the war had impressed Japan and had endowed her parliamentary parties and moderate leaders with new prestige. They had no great appetite for a naval race or for aggressive militarism and they advocated a settlement of goodwill with China. They were anxious about the alliance with Britain and they wanted to obtain American recognition of Japan's mandate of the Pacific islands. Japan came to the Washington Conference for these reasons.[19]

Affairs in China were no less chaotic than they had been in 1919. There was a financial crisis in Peking; the premier had resigned over the issue of the delegation to Washington; Sun Yat-sen had declared himself president from Canton and, when his government was unable to secure separate representation at the conference, refused to recognize any agreements made. The three leaders of the delegation, however, were southern in sympathy and they resolutely presented the views of Chinese nationalism.[20]

In August 1921, Curzon requested Colonial Office advice regarding the precise grounds upon which the exclusion of the New Territories from any policy of rendition at the conference could be justified when China would herself be represented, possibly supported by America.[21] One minute stated: 'The FO are far too anxious to please America and China by abandoning the vital interests of the British Empire',[22] and the secretary of state, Winston Churchill, expressed great objection to the surrender of either Weihaiwei or the New Territories. The rendition of the latter, especially, would be a shattering blow to British prestige in the Far East, and HMG's representative at Washington should avoid as far as possible any declaration on proposals to restore leased territories to China. The fundamental reason was defence, but others were suggested: the birth of a new generation of British subjects since 1898, who should not be abandoned by a sudden reversal of policy; the expansion of Hong Kong; capital investment in the New Territories; and the Kowloon-Canton railway.[23]

China's initial statement of her aims made no specific mention of leased territories, though she referred to the removal of 'existing limitations upon China's political, jurisdictional, and administrative freedom of action', while resolutions by the powers on 21 November agreed to respect China's sovereignty.[24] Perhaps in frustration at the failure of earlier attempts to expel Japanese troops from Manchuria,[25] but probably because the matter was on the Chinese agenda anyway, Wellington Koo, on 3 December, asked for the annulment and early termination of all territorial leases. France immediately agreed to evacuate Kwangchow Wan and Balfour announced on 2 February 1922 that Britain would give up Weihaiwei in the collective restitution of foreign leaseholds. Japan noted her undertaking in Paris to restore Kiaochow and the negotiations then going on to achieve rendition, though Hanihara of the Japanese delegation stated that his government had no intention at that time of relinquishing the rights she had lawfully acquired with great sacrifice in Port Arthur and Dairen. The British decision was designed to encourage a ready solution of the Shantung question,[26] despite earlier opinion in the Foreign Office against using Weihaiwei in this fashion for fear of raising the general question of leaseholds in China and putting the New Territories at risk.[27] But Balfour was careful to exclude the New Territories, which should remain under Hong Kong's administration because, he said, 'without the leased territory, Hong Kong is perfectly indefensible and would be at the mercy of any enemy possessing modern artillery'; and the safeguarding of Hong Kong was an interest in which the whole world was concerned. 'The lease of the Kowloon Extension had been obtained for no other reason except to give security to the port of Hong Kong, and it would be a great misfortune if anything should occur which was calculated to shake the confidence of the nations, using this great open port, in its security.'[28] The Chinese reaction was to suggest that the retention of the New Territories was not necessarily the sole solution to the problem of protecting Hong Kong.[29]

In relation to Weihaiwei, Lugard had suggested in 1909 that 'permanent cession' of the New Territories be a condition of its return to China, and careful consideration of that idea had been promised by the Colonial Office when the time came.[30] But Balfour's decision to restore Weihaiwei was taken on his own initiative amidst the give-and-take atmosphere of the conference; circumstances precluded even the possibility of bargaining for an improvement of the British position in the New Territories.

There was little further discussion of leased territories at Washington. Arrangements for the restoration of Kiaochow to China were completed in 1922; Weihaiwei became fully China's once more in 1930; France finally surrendered Kwangchow Wan in 1945. Not until ten years later did the Soviet Union, successor to Japan in Port Arthur and Dairen, return these territories to China. But the New Territories remained under British control.

One critic holds that Great Britain's position at Washington was tenuous because China was willing to neutralize the New Territories and thus prevent its use in time of war.[31] It is doubtful whether then, or at any time before 1949, China had the capacity to enforce neutrality, and any such arrangement could only have weakened the security of Hong Kong. Even when fully defended (although, it must be said, the Washington conference itself forbade further fortifications of the colony), the New Territories provided slight impediment to the invading Japanese in 1941. But, although Balfour rested the British case on the needs of Hong Kong defence, he must have borne in mind the other reasons put forward by the Colonial Office to justify retention; from the colony's point of view the exclusion of the New Territories from any general scheme of rendition was vital.

The question of the leaseholds in China was minor in comparison with arms limitation and future relations between, in particular, Britain, Japan, and the United States. Nevertheless one commentator, taking a long view, points out that the less dramatic achievements of the Washington conference in relation to the Far East were of great consequence;[32] it is certainly significant as far as the future of Hong Kong was concerned that Britain, before the world at large, was able to secure recognition of the sole characteristic— contiguity to an established colony—which distinguished the New Territories from the other leaseholds.

Proposals prior to the Pacific War

China does not seem to have made any other formal request for return of the New Territories before the Japanese attack on Hong Kong in 1941, although, said a British official in 1930, it had 'long been included in the list of leaseholds which are to be recovered "according to plan" in the near future'.[33] The Kuomintang's first national convention in 1924 urged the cancellation of all unequal treaties, and the 1898 leasehold agreements came into this category.[34] HMG was concerned to prepare a suitable policy in advance of irredentist demands.

Several governors of Hong Kong had already proposed the outright cession or extension of years of the leased area.[35] Sir Cecil Clementi, governor from 1925 to 1930, was a fervid advocate of annexation, even suggesting picking a quarrel with China to provide the opportunity.[36] In January 1926 he wrote a secret despatch concerning the tenure of the New Territories,[37] and a year later he telegraphed that it was then, in view of the China-wide agitation for rendition of all leased territories and concessions, very important to make the leased area a permanent acquisition as soon as possible. Specifically, cession could be obtained as a *quid pro quo* for the restoration in fact of Weihaiwei, or for a 'very generous' revision of treaties, or as a condition of resumption of friendly relations if Great Britain were 'eventually compelled to take warlike action against the South'.[38] Lampson in Peking, however, thought that Clementi's suggestions 'would merely intensify charges of Imperialism against us which I am doing my best to stifle as ungrounded',[39] and the Foreign Office considered it necessary to follow an utterly quiescent policy and to avoid raising the matter.[40]

But the governor was not daunted, and he asked in March 1927 if the District Watch Committee could be given an explicit assurance that HMG did not intend to return the colony or its leased territory to China.[41] Such a statement was thought unnecessarily provocative, though Clementi was authorized to give this statement:

His Majesty's Government will give the fullest protection to Hong Kong and its mainland territories during the civil war now unhappily raging in China, and they have no intention whatever of surrendering Hong Kong or of abandoning or diminishing in any way its rights or authority in any part of the adjacent mainland territories under British administration, to the

maintenance of which His Majesty's Government attach the highest impor-
ance.[42]

When in London in June 1928, Clementi asked if he could
assume that the New Territories would never be returned to China.
Was he to devote large sums from the colonial exchequer for the
development of an area which would remain British for, at the
most, a further sixty-nine years, and could he issue ordinary crown
leases for the usual seventy-five years? The Colonial Office wished
to answer both questions in the affirmative, 'on the assumption that
the future Government of the New Territories, whether British or
Chinese, will always be such as will administer the Territories in a
business-like spirit'.[43] (When Clementi continued to press the
issue in 1929 it was minuted: 'In the present state of Chinese feeling it is no use asking for application of practical business-like
methods.')[44] The Foreign Office disagreed on the matter of crown
leases: to appear to grant title until some time after 1997 would lead
to embarrassing suggestions that Britain proposed to ignore the
convention:

> In view of the great development ... of international arbitration and of
> the extent to which international relationships are governed by the League
> of Nations and the provisions of the Convention, it is hardly conceivable
> that His Majesty's Government would be able to keep possession by force
> of the New Territories under the plea of economic necessity. The solution
> of Hong Kong's difficulty and the ultimate future of the New Territories
> would appear both to be matters for negotiation with China, and until a
> favourable opportunity for initiating such negotiations has arisen it seems
> essential to avoid any action which could be construed as an intention on
> our part to violate our obligations towards China.[45]

But inability to assume long-term possession of the New Territories
was an obvious exasperation for the colonial authorities, who had
not yet adopted the view that, when planning the development of
the district, 1997 must be ignored. In Clementi's time construction
of the Shing Mun reservoir was temporarily halted because of the
government's unwillingness to spend its own funds on work which
would soon enure to the benefit of China rather than of Hong
Kong.[46]

In 1929 a set-back in negotiations for the rendition of Weihaiwei
prompted hopes that a satisfactory agreement regarding the New
Territories might be arranged in return for British acceptance of
Chinese demands on Weihaiwei.[47] Nothing resulted, however. Yet

R. F. Johnston, the last commissioner at Weihaiwei, feared that its rendition would 'merely encourage the Chinese to open their mouths wider' and attempt to swallow the New Territories as well. 'Already kites are being flown in the Chinese press ... as a preliminary advertisement of what is eventually to become a nationwide demand (emphasised by strikes and boycotts) for the surrender of Hong Kong itself.'[48] Weihaiwei was duly returned to China and C. T. Wang duly cited its 'retrocession' as 'the first step towards the retrocession of all leased territories held by foreigners in China.'[49]

During the first few years of the 1930s departmental opinions were being gradually formulated. The Colonial Office, of course, frequently pressured by Hong Kong, wanted to secure a more permanent title to the New Territories as soon as an opportunity arose.[50] But the Foreign Office was thinking along entirely different lines. In 1928 Sir John T. Pratt had mentioned 'letting in a certain amount of Chinese control in Hong Kong in return for being allowed to continue to exercise a certain amount of British control in the New Territories';[51] he believed such an arrangement would be ultimately unavoidable if Hong Kong and the New Territories were to remain as one economic unit. Eighteen months later his views were unchanged. The colony could become a special area under joint Anglo-Chinese protection, and if a workable constitution was devised 'Hong Kong would prosper greatly and the question of her relations with China would no longer constitute an obstacle to her becoming a real base for British influence in China.'[52] The Foreign Office embarked on a campaign for 'softening the CO mind': the question of leased territories was expected to be raised comparatively soon and it was well that Downing Street should become accustomed to the loss of exclusive control over Hong Kong.[53]

It had been feared that failure to obtain a satisfactory customs agreement between Hong Kong and China in 1930 would so distress China that retaliation might take the form of a demand for the return of the New Territories. When accord was apparently reached, however, the Foreign Office was sanguine that such a demand had been averted for the time being.[54] Yet the suggestion had been made to Lampson that the customs agreement be used as a lever to secure China's consent to British retention of the New Territories after 1997. Lampson replied that there was not the remotest chance of striking a bargain on the subject:

An opportunity might occur for dealing with the matter during the next 60 years, but in the meantime it would be most unwise to risk stirring up trouble by raising the question now. I did not think that failure to reach an agreement would lead to an agitation for the recovery of the leased territories, which would probably come, if it came at all, irrespective of the Customs question.[55]

Meanwhile, fundamental questions of policy were being examined, just in case China aimed irredentist objectives at the Hong Kong extension.

Clementi's successor, Sir William Peel, contributed a memorandum in which he examined in some detail the value to the colony of the leased portion (Pratt, on first reading it, remarked that 'Sir C. Clementi's suggestion that forcible annexation is the right solution becomes more fantastic than ever').[56] Peel's considered opinion was that the greater part, if not the whole, of the New Territories was absolutely necessary to Hong Kong, for both economic and strategic reasons: trade, residence, water supply, the government building programme, and the armed services' requirements supported a policy of retention. Pratt drew the conclusion that it was not worth paying a very high price for permanent title to the New Territories:

Our aim should be *not* annexation but the preservation of the water supply and possibly other minor amenities and conveniences. Our method of accomplishing this aim should be to grant the Chinese every possible facility and advantage in Hong Kong ... and thus build up a strong bargaining position against the time when rendition ... becomes a burning issue.

Military considerations should be brushed aside: 'As usual our generals urge that we should garrison the moon in order to guard ourselves against a possible attack from Mars.' Chinese heavy artillery was no problem, Japanese would be unpleasant but, he added unprophetically, 'what real chance is there of Japan attacking Great Britain? And if Japan did declare war would we make any attempt to defend Hong Kong *in Hong Kong*?'[57]

The Foreign Office had no intention of raising the question of the New Territories,[58] but wanted to be prepared if trouble in this respect were caused 'not only by the Chinese but by Governors like Sir C. Clementi'.[59] Press reports in 1933 that Kan Chieh-hou, the Cantonese inspector-general for foreign affairs, had been instructed to negotiate for the return of the New Territories were denied by Great Britain and withdrawn from the Canton official gazette.[60] The whole matter remained dormant until a new governor of Hong

Kong, Sir Geoffrey Northcote, declared in 1938 that the New Territories was essentially necessary to Hong Kong, that Hong Kong was essentially necessary to Great Britain, and that the time might be ripe for purchasing a cession or an extension of the lease.[61]

There was, initially, considerable support for Northcote's proposal, although the idea of cession was immediately ruled out as chimerical while China's war slogan was 'no alienation of sovereignty of territory'. China was in desperate need of a foreign loan in order to support its currency, and extension of the lease might appeal as a suitable consideration for a large capital sum. 'Today, I believe,' the governor wrote in August, 'the Chinese Government would come in on the deal: once the present hostilities cease that attitude on their part is much less probable; and if Japan is victorious outright she might also be able to block it and in another ten [years'] time China and Japan might—and I think very probably would—unite in opposing it.'[62] An inter-departmental meeting was called to discuss the matter, and Northcote's plan was rejected.

Three major reasons were adduced. It was impossible to calculate the value of the New Territories and to foresee what conditions might prevail in 1997; from the defence point of view the existing tenure was satisfactory, especially considering the recent Committee of Imperial Defence decision that there were to be no further military commitments on the mainland. HMG had received no suggestion from the Chinese authorities that the lease be extended, though they had put forward many other schemes, some of them 'quite fantastic', for giving Britain some return for a loan or grant. Relations with Japan would be jeopardized, and a Japanese puppet government in south China would repudiate any agreement made with the current Chinese government. Finally, the Cabinet had recently overruled a scheme for a Chinese loan for fear of antagonizing Japan.[63]

There were lingering hopes that the proposal might be salvaged, but the occupation of Canton by Japanese forces put an end to it.[64] Cabinet had, in fact, discussed it but were told that, although an extension of the duration of the lease was being examined, the present was not a favourable moment for opening the question.[65]

During this period it could almost be said that the greater threat to the territorial integrity of Hong Kong came rather from the Foreign Office than from the Chinese. Sir John Pratt, in particular, was opposed to British retention of a territory which had been acquired during a period of 'gross foreign aggression on China'.[66] His war-time book vigorously denounced the New Territories lease: it was 'a most indefensible demand' and 'an example of the discredit that commonly results when a government allows a political question to be decided on military grounds'.[67] Fortunately for Hong Kong, the occasion for implementing his proposals never arose.

The Position after 1941

British policy in the thirties had wavered between sympathy for China and conciliation of Japan. Some endeavour had been made to assist the Chinese economy, yet Japanese aggression in China continued with scarcely a word of protest from Britain; Whitehall was content so long as British commercial interests were not greatly endangered. But when the Sino-Japanese conflict merged with the second world war relations between China and Britain improved.[68] At an Institute of Pacific Relations conference at Mont Tremblant in December 1942 the Chinese delegation admitted that China had no legal claim to the colony,[69] though Pratt had publicly declared that the Chinese would be completely satisfied when the time came to deal with Hong Kong.[70] During the negotiations for the relinquishment of extraterritoriality the Chinese reply to the first British draft insisted upon rendition of the New Territories. Sir Anthony Eden declared the matter outside the scope of the treaty but said he was willing to discuss it after victory in the war,[71] and, although it seemed for a time that Chiang Kai-shek would make rendition a *sine qua non* of the agreement, the Chinese government unexpectedly relented at the end of 1942. After the treaty was signed, however, T. V. Soong, the Chinese minister for foreign affairs, wrote to the British minister in Chungking:

The early termination of the Treaty of June 9, 1898, by which the said lease was granted, is one of the long cherished desires of the Chinese people and, if effected on the present occasion, would go far, in the opinion of the Chinese Government, to emphasise the spirit of the new era which the Treaty concluded today is intended to inaugurate in the relations of our two countries.[72]

Earlier in the war against Japan there had been general approval in the Foreign Office of a Colonial Office memorandum advocating return of the whole colony 'on terms', but after 1942 the policy of retention became more firmly entrenched.[73]

At Cairo in 1943 HMG stated that it did not contemplate any 'modification of sovereignty' in British Far Eastern territories. Hong Kong, to President Roosevelt's mind, had become a symbol of old-fashioned and unwanted British imperialism, and Roosevelt and Chiang Kai-shek agreed that post-war Hong Kong should be an internationalized free port under Chinese sovereignty.[74] But Churchill was adamant in his refusal to contemplate the surrender of territory: '"Hands off the British Empire" is our maxim and it must not be weakened or smirched to please sob-stuff merchants at home or foreigners of any hue.'[75] Chiang Kai-shek was almost as determined to recover all leased territories. Although he stated in his book *China's Destiny* that the New Territories and Hong Kong were 'geographically interdependent and their status must be settled simultaneously',[76] there were repeated calls after 1943 for the return of the New Territories alone. It was rumoured that British and Chinese forces were racing each other to take over from the Japanese. On 24 August 1945, however, the generalissimo announced that 'China would not send troops to accept the surrender of Hong Kong lest this should arouse allied misunderstanding'—and it was a British naval commander who replaced the rising sun with his nation's flag in Hong Kong. Yet Chiang had declared in August his hope that the New Territories would not remain the exception, now that other leased territories had been returned.[77]

The New Territories did, of course, remain the exception. The Nationalist government was not strong enough to press its claims and had vowed, anyway, to achieve the object of rendition by diplomatic negotiation rather than unilateral abrogation.[78] The communist government has apparently not made any forceful representations on the subject, though it has clearly enunciated its view that Hong Kong will be recovered in due course. Its pronouncements have not distinguished between the Treaty of Nanking 1842, which ceded the island, the Convention of Peking 1860, which ceded Kowloon and Stonecutters, and the Convention of Peking 1898: all are considered unequal treaties to be dealt with in the same fashion. This was implied in the first public reference to the position of the colony when the *People's Daily* editorialized in 1963:

With regard to the outstanding issues, which are a legacy from the past, we have always held that, when conditions are ripe, they should be settled peacefully through negotiations and that, pending a settlement, the status quo should be maintained. Within this category are the questions of Hong Kong, Kowloon, and Macao...[79]

Eighteen months later the Chinese delegate to a world youth forum sponsored by the Soviet Union pointed out that Hong Kong was Chinese territory occupied by British imperialism through the device of unequal treaties; it would be restored to China at an appropriate time.[80] A less restrained statement was made during the riots of 1967:

> We must tell the British imperialists that not only have the Chinese peasants the rights to till the land in the 'New Territories', but the whole of Hong Kong must return to the domain of the motherland... How can it be imagined that Hong Kong will always be under the rule of British imperialism? Of course it can't; it is absolutely unthinkable... Hong Kong is an inalienable part of Chinese territory...[81]

And in 1972, for the purpose of removing Hong Kong from the agenda of the United Nations General Assembly's Special Committee on Colonialism, the Chinese ambassador said that the settlement of the 'question' of Hong Kong 'is entirely within China's sovereign right' and would take place 'in an appropriate way when conditions are ripe'.[82]

Meanwhile, of course, the Korean war brought the ruin of the colony's entrepôt economy and industrialization became essential. The lament of the *China Mail* in 1895—that there was 'a lack of space on this tiny precipitous rock for building big factories and populous artizan colonies to work them'[83]—had been dealt with in the Peking Convention of 1898, and in the 1950s the New Territories became more indispensable to Hong Kong than ever before. If not the case in the 1930s it certainly became true two decades later that without the leasehold the colony could not exist.

10

THE MEANING OF THE CONVENTION

British and Chinese Interpretations

THE lease of territory for a specified term from one state to another was virtually unknown before 1898, and no precedent or doctrine in international law provided guidance in the matter of interpretation. What was the legal effect of what may be called a 'public international lease'?[1] What rights did lessor and lessee retain and acquire to the leased territory?

The interpretation of an international treaty depends on such factors as the intention of the parties at the time of making the agreement, their subsequent practice and declared position as to the treaty's meaning, and the rules of treaty interpretation adopted by many states as part of international law. In regard to the Convention of Peking 1898 it has been shown in some detail how the demand for a lease came about and how China reacted; if one thing is apparent from this study, it is that on the fundamental question of what the lease meant in international law there was no agreement between the parties. There was not even any discussion of the issue, and British officials did not concern themselves with it until some time after the convention was signed and ratified. Assumptions were apparently made, but it is not possible to talk of a common intention as to the broad effect of the convention. Subsequent practice, as has been seen, indicated many points which were unclear and upon which China and Great Britain disagreed. In this chapter it is intended, first, to summarize the conflicting Chinese and British interpretations of the convention as a whole, then to see how particular clauses have fared, and finally to examine the convention in the context of theoretical aspects of treaty interpretation.

As a matter of policy, the Colonial Office determined from the outset that the New Territories should be integrated with the ceded colony of Hong Kong.[2] Chamberlain instructed Blake that the district was to be regarded as a British possession.[3] The Foreign

Office stated that the viceroy's attempt to treat the leased territory as a 'settlement' at a Chinese treaty port was inadmissible.[4] The draft order in council was prepared for the purpose of *annexing* the New Territories to Hong Kong, a term which in international law implied a transfer or assumption of full sovereignty, and the law officers considered it sufficient and proper for that purpose.[5] In the original Colonial Office version of the draft order no mention was made of the limitation in time; further, it was based on an order for the incorporation of territory which had been ceded, not leased.[6] The official published version declared the leased territories to be 'part and parcel of Her Majesty's Colony of Hong Kong, in like manner and for all intents and purposes as if they had originally formed part of the said Colony.'[7] A suggestion that crown leases in the New Territories be renewable for a further seventy-five years 'if the Hong Kong Government is then competent to grant such renewal' was rejected partly because it would involve 'a dangerous admission in a formal document that renewal of the lease of the New Territories is doubtful. The renewal is of course an open question but [it] seems desirable to avoid any formal admission that it is so.'[8]

Every attempt was made, therefore, to imply that the rights of Great Britain in the New Territories were co-extensive with the rights of Great Britain in Hong Kong; that is, that the empire had acquired another possession, upon which the sun would not set for at least ninety-nine years. It was clearly in the British interest that such an idea should gain currency, and the American 'open door' note of 1899, which recognized a distinction between the New Territories and the other 1898 Chinese leaseholds, seemed to confirm it.[9] But, pragmatic considerations aside, could HMG justify it in law? The attorney-general, Pollock, maintained in July 1899 that the New Territories was leased, not ceded, and that the convention in no way affected the nationality of the region's residents.[10] A prominent Hong Kong barrister argued on behalf of Tang Cheung-hing's murderers that the word 'jurisdiction' in the convention only conferred power to administer Chinese law, and not to make laws that were inconsistent with the concept of a lease.[11] The chief justice, Sir John Carrington, held in 'the shell case' that 'the Crown has only a limited or qualified Sovereignty in the leased District'.[12]

The law officers were not asked for an opinion on this specific issue, but they had no doubts as to the correct answer. The leased territory, they said, became British territory; it was ceded, and the fact that the cession was for a term of years did not affect the conclusion that by the cession the inhabitants became for that term British subjects.[13] Elsewhere the law officers referred to 'British sovereignty under the lease . . .'.[14] This is the view which seems to have prevailed in the Colonial Office mind ever since. For instance, Sir Cecil Clementi and his legal advisers submitted in 1929 that the convention conferred full sovereign rights on HMG for ninety-nine years and that 'those sovereign rights include the right to dispose of land and grant leases even beyond the period in question'.[15] The secretary of state, Amery, believed such an interpretation only reasonable and practical.[16] The governor of Hong Kong stated in 1916 that 'no limitation of the absolute jurisdiction of Great Britain had been made in the Convention . . .'.[17]

The official Ch'ing dynasty interpretation, however, in so far as it can be discovered from British sources of the period, was quite different from that of the law officers. Perhaps the clearest example is in the viceroy's 'regulations'. One of these read: 'Land owned by Chinese subjects within the new settlement must pay the land tax to the Chinese authorities'; another stipulated that the expression 'Boundary of the Colony' must not appear on boundary stones.[18] One of the Tsungli Yamen ministers claimed that MacDonald had been told the lease would be 'like the leaseholds of the settlements at the Ports',[19] and approved of the viceroy's initiative. In Stewart Lockhart's papers there is a translation of a memorandum, apparently from deputy Wang or viceroy T'an, which contains 'regulations' similar to but not the same as those available from official sources. One of them reads: 'In communications between the two Governments the new territory shall be styled "San Tso K'ai"— newly leased territory.' Another is as follows: 'Whether any officer of the Chinese Government shall be appointed to co-operate with the British officials on matters affecting the relations between the two Governments in the newly leased area must be decided by the high officers of both countries.'[20] The implications were clearly that China was to remain suzerain even during the ninety-nine years and that Chinese residents were to remain Chinese subjects.

The latter point is confirmed by acting viceroy Yuan's response to HMG's demand for the extradition of Liang Tou: 'the territories are merely held on lease and are not on the same footing as lands belonging to the British Crown'.[21] A Chinese could not therefore be extradited as though he were a British subject. China in fact remained ignorant of the law officers' opinion that Chinese inhabitants of the New Territories became British subjects from 16 April 1899 until carelessly informed by consul-general Jamieson in 1909. Yuan replied that he could not accept this opinion, as it had never been agreed to by China.[22]

Again, China objected to removal of the telegraph station and line from the New Territories because they were 'in identically the same situation as the telegraphs in Shanghai and Tientsin Concessions, and also those of [Weihaiwei] and Ch'ing-tao'.[23] In the Chinese view, Hong Kong's leased territory had the same status as concessions or 'settlements' in the treaty ports, which Salisbury had previously recognized and rejected.

After the collapse of the Ch'ing dynasty a similar attitude was maintained. The Kowloon commissioner of customs urged in 1916 that his vessels be allowed to use Deep Bay and Mirs Bay and the Sham Chun River, 'inasmuch as those waters had been placed under the jurisdiction of Great Britain for defence purposes only and that it had never been contemplated that by such transfer of jurisdiction facilities should be afforded for smuggling to the detriment of Chinese revenue.'[24] In the 1930s Dr Philip Tyau, special delegate for foreign affairs for Kwangtung and Kwangsi, wished to grant mining licences in the New Territories and fishing licences in the waters of the colony. His contention was that mining and fishing rights in the New Territories were not ceded by the Chinese government, which therefore retained the power to grant licences. In general, reported HM's consul-general at Canton, Tyau's line was 'that the New Territories, and Kowloon City in particular, are no part of the Colony proper of Hong Kong, and that China has by no means forfeited all her rights, as ground landlord, in these territories, and the adjoining waters under the lease agreement.'[25]

Tyau was reiterating T'an's interpretation, for the viceroy had told Sir Henry Blake in 1899 that the New Territories was only leased; 'it is China', he remarked. Blake replied with the British view which, with the exception of a Foreign Office opinion in 1937, has since been consistently maintained by HMG: 'Whether leased, lent, or ceded, as soon as the British flag is hoisted it becomes for the time as effectually British territory as Government House, Hong Kong.'[26]

Chinese Nationalist leaders and scholars were hostile towards what they termed unequal treaties, including the New Territories lease, but they did not assert that such treaties were devoid of effect or capable of unilateral abrogation.[27] The 1898 convention was unequal but not illegal, and the only fundamental disagreement with Britain related to its proper interpretation. The Chinese communist régime, however, has poured scorn on the very notion that territory can be legitimately acquired by one state from another. The cession or lease of territory, formally achieved by unequal treaty, is merely a disguise for the plunder of a weak or small country by imperialist force.[28] The concluding section of this chapter will examine the communist theory in more detail; but it must be noted here that what immediately follows assumes that the Convention of Peking 1898 is still valid as a binding treaty, albeit a controversial one, between Britain and China.

The British concept of a 'cession for a term of years' raises some difficulties. What does it mean, and is it validly applied to the New Territories? Such questions, while perhaps of more theoretical than practical interest, are nevertheless important, for both Chinese and British policy in respect of the New Territories has been guided by what was claimed to be legally sound analyses of the lease concept. These analyses themselves deserve analysis. First, however, it is useful to consider how particular clauses of the convention have been affected by developments since British occupation of the New Territories in 1899.

The Kowloon City Clause

It is at the same time agreed that within the city of Kowloon the Chinese officials now stationed there shall continue to exercise jurisdiction except so far as may be inconsistent with the military requirements for the defence of Hong Kong. Within the remainder of the newly-leased territory Great Britain shall have sole jurisdiction.

On 30 May 1899 China was officially informed of the reason for expulsion of her officials from the Walled City. After the recent experience which HMG had had, wrote Lord Salisbury, of the danger posed by the Chinese garrison at Kowloon, it was impossible to permit the resumption of Chinese authority there.[29] This was scarcely satisfactory: as Stewart Lockhart had pointed out,[30] the convention itself impliedly barred Chinese troops from the Walled City, and the necessity of their removal was a poor excuse for denying the exercise of a purely civil jurisdiction. Nevertheless, in 1934 the Colonial Office rejected the notion that China could base a claim on the Kowloon City clause.[31] Less tersely, the Foreign Office rehearsed three possible arguments to meet any Chinese request for resumption of jurisdiction. No one in HMG doubted that the original occupation of the Walled City was justified by military realities at the time, and it might be possible to establish that China's exercise of jurisdiction was still inconsistent with military requirements for the defence of Hong Kong, a view certainly held by the lords of the Admiralty and by the War Office. Sir John Pratt minuted: 'We must of course accept this but I hope the Chinese don't take us into Court!'[32] Secondly, it might be argued in the alternative that a continuing state of necessity was not required by the convention and that Hong Kong had every right to remain in occupation of the city once having reasonably assumed jurisdiction in 1899; but this was doubtful on the strict wording of the clause. The third device was resort to the idea of prescriptive right. Unhappily, however, the case for continued exercise of British jurisdiction in the future was not considered a strong one unless military requirements remained in favour.[33]

Great Britain has never admitted the Chinese position and China has never renounced her claim to jurisdiction; no international tribunal has ever been asked to adjudicate. But the question of jurisdiction has been judicially considered in Hong Kong. It was first raised in the colony's courts in early 1948. The chairman of the Walled City residents' association and another were brought before a magistrate, Blair-Kerr, who dismissed as frivolous initial arguments as to jurisdiction. The issues were not, therefore, roundly debated, though the prosecutor summarized the British point of view. The defendants did not appeal.[34]

But in 1959 the Full Court, in *Re Wong Hon*,[35] heard an application for habeas corpus made on behalf of a Chinese accused of murder. Counsel argued that Wong Hon was an alien whose alleged offence, committed inside the Walled City, was beyond British jurisdiction. The attorney-general submitted that Chinese jurisdiction in Kowloon under the convention was temporary, limited, and not exclusive, and was terminated by the order in council of 27 December 1899; further, that the two orders in council were prerogative acts of state and therefore conclusive declarations of the jurisdiction conferred on the local courts. This latter ground was accepted by the Full Court, and the case therefore merely applies municipal law.[36] But some interesting dicta by the chief justice, relating to Wong Hon's claim that the Queen's writ did not run in the Walled City, are worthy of mention.

Chinese jurisdiction was, he said, restricted to the jurisdiction of officials stationed within the city at the time of the convention; use of the word 'now' seemed to suggest that the authority pertained to an individual rather than to an established office. The parties to the convention were concerned 'not with the reservation of some measure of sovereignty, but simply with the safeguarding of the rights of the existing officials'.[37] The jurisdiction granted to the mandarins was not defined and cannot be considered exclusive. On the issue of unilateral decision by Britain:

> It is legitimate to infer that in such a vital matter as the defence of the Colony it was to be understood, under the terms of the Convention, that the decision was one to be taken by the British authorities; in the realm of national defence, clearly, the authorities most competent to make such a decision would be the authorities concerned with the defence of the Colony.[38]

A persuasive contrary argument, however, can be put forward. If the convention did seek merely to protect certain officials from unemployment, and this was certainly not the contemporary Chinese or even the British interpretation, it was violated when the mandarin was expelled after occupation of the Walled City on 16 May 1899. It is equally legitimate to infer that in such a vital matter as the modification of an international treaty it was to be understood that the parties would confer and come to some agreement. It is surely reasonable to assume that the jurisdiction which 'the Chinese officials now stationed there shall continue to exercise' is the jurisdiction which they have always exercised, so long as it is not inconsistent with the military requirements for the defence of Hong Kong, that it is exclusive to that extent, and that it should devolve upon successors in office. Only that behaviour which is barred by the convention should be legally proscribed, not the performance of all official duties. Finally, if we are 'to pay regard to the principle of *contemporanea expositio* in dealing with events of more than half a century ago in a part of the world where so many changes have occurred',[39] as the chief justice suggests we should, the failure of the colonial authorities to exercise jurisdiction in the Walled City as though it were part and parcel of Hong Kong would seem to vindicate rather the Chinese than the British interpretation. On the other hand, however, there is no evidence that the present mainland government attempts to treat the Walled City as administratively belonging to China.

Re Wong Hon settled the matter as far as the Hong Kong courts are concerned. When, in 1975, the government sought closure orders on two Walled City buildings, a magistrate referred to this case as justifying his assumption of jurisdiction.[40]

The Non-expropriation Clause

It is further understood that there will be no expropriation or expulsion of the inhabitants of the district included within the extension, and that if land is required for public offices, fortifications, or the like official purposes, it shall be bought at a fair price.

In 1898 the law relating to the 'expulsion' of Hong Kong inhabitants was governed primarily by the Banishment and Conditional Pardons Ordinance 1882 and the Peace Preservation Ordinance 1886. By section 3 of the former ordinance, the governor in council had the power to prohibit any person, not being a natural born or naturalized subject of Her Majesty, from residing in or being within the colony for any period of time up to five years. The latter ordinance provided for the making of a proclamation by the governor in council whenever it appeared necessary for the preservation of public peace; during the existence of such a proclamation any person, not being a natural born subject of Her Majesty (whether such person had been naturalized under any colonial ordinance or not), could be banished by order of the governor in council. Neither ordinance was exempted from operation in the New Territories.[41]

A banishment order under one or other of these ordinances made against a New Territories resident would seem to conflict with the convention's prohibition against expulsion. There is no reported case of any such order, however. Ironically, British acceptance *in toto* of the Chinese position respecting the nationality of New Territories inhabitants would have had the consequence of allowing the governor in council to expel Chinese residents without regard to the convention; the British interpretation ensured that Chinese residents of the New Territories were, if not 'natural born', at least naturalized British subjects.[42]

The expulsion of inhabitants is now regulated by the Immigration Ordinance.[43] While, in certain circumstances, the deportation of 'Chinese residents', 'United Kingdom belongers', and 'resident

United Kingdom belongers' is permitted, there is no authority for the deportation or removal of 'Hong Kong belongers'. This category includes British subjects by birth, naturalization, registration, or marriage. It seems, therefore, that municipal law no longer allows the 'expulsion of the inhabitants of the district included within the extension'.

The land survey and settlement secured, as was their object,[44] the non-expropriation of New Territories inhabitants, and every care was taken to determine proper owners and to compensate those whose claims were upheld but whose lands were acquired by the crown. The promises made in the convention were thus fulfilled, and no complainants came forward. But in the mid-1920s the petitioners objecting to land resumption policy specifically raised the issue of expropriation and the fidelity of the Hong Kong government to this clause of the convention.

They claimed that resumption for the development of building land and its subsequent sale was not an official purpose under the convention, which 'contemplated only such permanent official purposes as roads, fortifications, Government buildings etc, and ... free purchase of lands required for such purposes, and not compulsory resumption'.[45] The governor, R. E. Stubbs, merely countered with the statement that full value was given; and he thought it was a matter to be settled with the Chinese government rather than with the petitioners. On the latter point he was rebuffed by Amery: 'If people are usually treated in Hong Kong in this offhand fashion, it cannot be wondered at that agitation results.'[46] The petitioners' complaint received close attention: the secretary of state informed the next governor that the question was not at all frivolous, and 'it does appear that the views of the Hong Kong Government as to the rights of the holders of land under Chinese law have become less sympathetic as time progressed and the Convention and the promises made under it receded into the past.'[47]

Amery's despatch on this issue is worth quoting at some length:

I find great difficulty in agreeing with Sir R. E. Stubbs that the compulsory purchase of land is not expropriation, or that town planning, carried on in the way which he describes, is an official purpose within the meaning of the Convention. The wording of the Convention is very precise, and it will be observed that the expression 'official purposes' is not used generally, but with reference to public offices and fortifications. . . .

I am advised that the relevant clause in the Convention means that there will be no expropriation or expulsion of the inhabitants of the district, unless the land is required for public offices, fortifications, or for official purposes of a like nature to public offices and fortifications, in which case it shall be bought at a fair price.... A fair price must mean a fair market price, and a fair market price is the price which, having regard to its actual and potential value, the land would fetch in the open market. This seems to me to be a very different thing from the artificial method adopted by the Colonial Government of ascertaining the value of land for compensation. ... I note that Sir R. E. Stubbs states that the amount of compensation which is granted is in accordance with Chinese law and custom. This may be so, but it is surely not the point, which is, whether or not it is in accordance with the Convention.[48]

Clementi offered an alternative construction: the non-expropriation clause really meant that there was to be no confiscation without compensation of inhabitants' property, even where land was required for official purposes. A fair price must always be paid. Reading 'expropriation' *ejusdem generis* the drastic term 'expulsion', Clementi argued, suggests the more drastic meaning of 'confiscation without compensation' for the ambiguous 'expropriation'. The railway clause indicated that the convention contemplated the compulsory acquisition of land. Further, a fair price means no less than would be granted under Chinese law and custom.[49]

Amery decided, as a matter of policy, to ignore his own strict construction of the non-expropriation clause. He informed Clementi that to adopt the governor's version would be to risk accusations of violating the convention; nevertheless, he was prepared to do just that. He did not, however, concur with Clementi's proposals regarding fair price: 'The Convention was drawn up in English, and the term "fair price" can only bear the interpretation that is placed upon it in this country.'[50]

The secretary of state for the colonies thus believed that Hong Kong could not acquire land compulsorily, even on payment of full value, except where land was required for public offices, fortifications, or the like official purposes, in which case a fair price must be paid.[51] China has apparently not objected to British policy in defiance of strict law as the Colonial Office saw it. Such a situation, from the point of view of New Territories development, is fortunate indeed.

In more recent years the Heung Yee Kuk, the statutory New Territories advisory body, has revived the essentials of the petitioners' complaint,[52] and in 1977 it sought a legal opinion on the conformity of the government's land policy with the letter and spirit of the convention. Two local Queen's Counsel and their junior stated their opinion that the Crown Lands Resumption Ordinance conflicted with the convention in respect of both the purpose of land resumption and the fair price provision. The chief secretary's reply declined to comment on this aspect of their opinion.

The non-expropriation provision was again discussed in relation to Walled City evictions in 1934. China herself did not raise the issue, no doubt because she did not wish to imply acceptance of Britain's assertion of authority over the city; but HMG reviewed the position just in case. The Colonial Office maintained its former stand: construction of a public park could not come within the words 'like official purposes' but Hong Kong was justified in expropriating residents in the interests of the good government of the colony.[53] And the Foreign Office hoped to establish, if necessary, tacit Chinese acceptance of the status quo that the terms of the convention permitted any public work or development scheme which was to the general benefit of the area.

Other Clauses

Chinese officials and people shall be allowed as heretofore to use the road from Kowloon to Hsinan.

This provision was inserted at the request of the Tsungli Yamen and little comment is required. Hong Kong places no restriction on Chinese or others who may wish to enter China from the New Territories. Both Hong Kong and China, however, restrict use of the road in the other direction.[54]

It is further agreed that the existing landing-place near Kowloon City shall be reserved for the convenience of Chinese men-of-war, merchant and passenger vessels, which may come and go and lie there at their pleasure; and for the convenience of movement of the officials and people within the city.

MacDonald accepted the reservation of the landing-place with reluctance and in order to obtain the main demand without resort to diplomatic threats. He hoped that the inconvenience, if any, would be tolerated as long as possible. The meaning of the clause is far from clear: was the Kowloon City pier to remain there for ninety-nine years, and did 'reserved' mean that only *Chinese* shipping and residents of the Walled City could use it?

One of the first tasks of the Public Works Department in the New Territories was repair of the pier; timber-work was renewed at a cost of almost $6,000 and the work was completed in 1900.[55] It was not long, however, before the landing-place disappeared upon reclamation of part of Kowloon Bay. The Kai Tak Land Investment Company began development of the area in 1917, and in the 1920s most of the reclaimed land was taken over by the government for construction of the airport.[56] It was no longer possible for Chinese ships or Walled City officials (of whom, anyway, there was none) or Walled City residents to use the pier which had existed in 1898; the landing-place was no longer 'reserved' for their convenience.

This clause was the basis of a fruitless appeal before the Supreme Court in 1975 on behalf of an illegal immigrant from China. It was argued, rather imaginatively and desperately, that the float used by the 'freedom swimmer' was a Chinese passenger vessel and the reclamation of the bay gave such a vessel the right to come and go from any convenient place in the New Territories.[57]

When hereafter China constructs a railway to the boundary of the Kowloon territory under British control, arrangements shall be discussed.

'It is so vague as to be almost grotesque,' reflected MacDonald,[58] with much justification, but he thought the vagueness was not without advantage, since it would deter any foreign syndicate which might wish to undertake construction of the line, whereas an English syndicate could come to some arrangement with the Hong Kong government.

On 6 September 1898 MacDonald secured a preliminary agreement for a British concession to finance and build the Kowloon-Canton railway, in the name of the British and Chinese Corporation.[59] The concession was granted following similar concessions to Belgium, despite earlier plans and surveys by a Chinese syndicate.[60] Although work did not begin until 1905, China was no longer building the line and the railway clause of the convention was rendered meaningless. It was probably never of much importance, for Britain (or, more particularly, Hong Kong) was anxious to join the colony to the Yangtze valley.

The phrase 'under British control' requires emphasis: does it imply that China surrendered something less than full sovereignty during the term of the lease?

If cases of extradition of criminals occur, they shall be dealt with in accordance with the existing Treaties between Great Britain and China and the Hong Kong Regulations.

The relevant treaty provision was article XXI of the 1858 Treaty of Tientsin, which regulated the surrender of Chinese fugitive criminals from Hong Kong to China, and, indeed, still does so (if this particular unequal treaty can be assumed to be still subsisting). The first paragraph reads: 'If criminals, subjects of China, shall take refuge in Hong Kong or on board the British ships there, they shall, upon due requisition by the Chinese authorities, be searched for, and, on proof of their guilt, be delivered up.'[61] The 'Hong Kong Regulations' were presumably the Chinese Extradition Ordinance 1889, which in section 5 laid down various restrictions on surrender and in section 3 restricted the definition of 'fugitive criminal'. Thus the 1898 convention confirmed what was strictly a variation of the Tientsin treaty, at least in so far as Chinese criminals who had taken refuge in the New Territories were concerned. And it is assumed that the customary practice of refusing extradition without an assurance that torture would not be applied to the criminal was continued.[62]

The case of Liang Tou has already been discussed;[63] he was a fugitive, born in the New Territories, who committed a crime in the colony and escaped to China. The Chinese authorities refused Hong Kong's request for his extradition, the Foreign Office admitting the reasonableness of that refusal on the basis of Liang Tou's dual nationality. But what should the position be in respect of a man born in the New Territories who committed a crime in China and was captured in Hong Kong? The acting attorney-general noted in 1911 that the Chinese claimed such fugitives as subjects of China and thus within article XXI of the Treaty of Tientsin. He continued: 'but I do not think we would admit the claim and so the result would be that the offender would go scot free'.[64]

Finally, it is arguable that in this clause of the convention the New Territories was equated with Hong Kong for the purposes of a pre-existing treaty.

The area leased to Great Britain ... includes the waters of Mirs Bay and Deep Bay, but it is agreed that Chinese vessels of war, whether neutral or otherwise, shall retain the right to use those waters.

The Yamen would not have agreed to lease the waters without retaining the use of them; as explained by MacDonald, the ministers had intended Mirs Bay as a base for their proposed southern squadron.[65] Yet it is doubtful whether this reservation has ever been of any real significance, although, as has been seen, it added a theoretical complication to the question of neutrality in the 1930s.[66] Chinese gunboats have often entered Hong Kong waters without any public protest by Great Britain.

Theoretical Considerations

The literature, now rather old-fashioned, in which the meaning of the 1898 China leases was debated is beset by two problems: the shamelessly polemical nature of much of it, and the choice of appropriate terminology. The first problem is indicated when comparing the nationality of contributors to their conclusions: German writers at the turn of the century tended to belong to the 'mailed fist' school, interpreting the transfers of territory as disguised cessions; nationalistic Chinese authors sought by fair logic or foul to uphold the ultimate sovereignty of China over the leaseholds; Americans, in keeping with their country's supposed anti-colonialism, rejected the more strident European claims. Englishmen said very little. Some writers generalized and disregarded the specific terms of each treaty; others examined the actual words and were confused by differences in the texts, or indulged in polemics about particular words like 'sovereignty' or 'jurisdiction'. Some tied their legal reasoning to what they deemed to be political reality; others insisted upon a thorough-going legalism. Disagreements, about both the conclusions reached and the steps in the argument, were common.[67]

Most writers of textbooks on international law nowadays find it necessary to include some mention of the Chinese leases, but they do not consider the subject very important. They generally agree that some sort of transfer of sovereignty took place for the period of the lease.[68]

The second problem—the appropriate terminology—mainly concerns the concept of sovereignty: is the term a useful one in the vocabulary of international law? O'Connell suggests that sovereignty, meaning 'plenitude of legal capacity', should not be abandoned. He sees it in its totality as a combination of residual (or titular) sovereignty and effective sovereignty: the latter passed with the grant of the lease while the grantor retained the reversion.[69] Norem, in his elegant analysis of the status of Kiaochow, prefers to substitute the terms 'territorial right' (retained by China) and 'jurisdictional right' (transferred to the lessee state), although together these rights constitute sovereignty.[70]

By themselves, these various terms do not take the matter very far. The most important question is what capacities the entity under consideration enjoys,[71] or: to what extent does HMG have full legal authority to govern the New Territories and to deal with it so far as sovereign states of the international order are concerned? This is a question of international rather than of municipal law, for it has already been shown that in the domestic Hong Kong legal system the New Territories is part and parcel of a ceded colony over which the crown and parliament have complete authority.

A couple of points seem clear enough. First, complete cession of the New Territories did not take place: the surrender of all other leaseholds and Great Britain's recognition of the ninety-nine year term both indicate that neither in fact nor in law was there any permanent alienation of territory by China. Secondly, the lease can only with difficulty, if at all, be described as a cession for a term of years. Norem argues strongly against the law officers' interpretation: the phrase is a contradiction in terms and the category it supposes cannot exist in international law.[72] A cession involves the transfer of sovereignty, yet the limitation in time allows the grantor to remain residual sovereign. The Colonial Office reply to Fitzmaurice's neutrality memorandum admitted that, unless further arrangements intervened, the New Territories would have to be 're-ceded' at the expiration of the ninety-nine years,[73] yet such an obligation is inconsistent with sovereignty and, in any event, is not mentioned in the convention. It is far simpler to see the reversion of the territory as an automatic process occurring at the precise moment—midnight, 30 June 1997—when British authority ceases. As shown above,[74] Salisbury did not wish to claim full sovereignty over Weihaiwei but found it opportune to do so in the case of the New Territories; this was a decision based on expediency, not law, and Great Britain cannot legitimately claim that the concept of a 'cession for a term of years' necessarily flows from the general words of the leasehold treaty.

If the official British interpretation of the convention does not stand, what can take its place? Clearly, if not a cession, the transfer was a 'lease': but what does that mean in international law? The Sino-German treaty for the lease of Kiaochow was drafted with great care in Berlin, the German government believing they were securing a cession in perpetuity; there was no private-law concept of a lease in Germany (unlike China); and no rent was paid. It therefore seems unlikely that this first of the 1898 Chinese treaties for the temporary disposal of territory was intended, at least by the Germans, to be analogous to a private-law lease. Yet Norem, following Lauterpacht,[75] equates China's 'territorial right' with ownership under the municipal system and the lessee's 'jurisdictional right' with occupancy and use.[76] In so doing he salvages legal significance for the term 'lease' as used in the convention. But, again, however useful as a generalization, such a concept does not much illuminate the particular lease under consideration here. It is necessary to examine more closely the actual words used.

As a matter of political fact, there was no common intention between the parties to the Convention of Peking 1898. Further, the words of the convention itself do not support the notion that the parties were in general agreement about the meaning and consequences of what they were doing: they do not reveal any inherent logic which can be ascertained either from the treaty itself or by matters extrinsic to it. For instance, it is a reasonable supposition that the territory was leased solely to provide Hong Kong with land on which to build defence works for the protection of the colony; defence is the only reason cited in the preamble, and the words 'public offices, fortifications, or the like official purposes' in the non-expropriation clause suggest that government activity is to be restricted to these areas. A Foreign Office minute in 1929 stated that the convention 'does not contemplate the economic development of the territory in any way, but merely its use for the proper protection and defence' of Hong Kong.[77] But, as Clementi pointed out, arrangements for the construction of a railway perhaps appear to contradict such a conclusion. Did China intend to sacrifice all control outside the Walled City? We know from her subsequent behaviour that she did not, and the word 'sovereignty' is not used in the convention; she was content to allow Britain 'sole jurisdiction', but that was all. Yet in the extradition clause, and by the words 'the limits of British territory shall be enlarged', the leased district might be taken as impliedly incorporated into the ceded colony. In the opinion, however, of Sir E. Davidson, legal adviser to the Foreign Office in 1910, the failure of the negotiators to grant Chinese inhabitants a choice of nationality indicated that they 'probably did not regard the cession of Kowloon as an out-and-out transfer of sovereignty even for a term of years'.[78] The 'plain words' of the Kowloon City clause might, standing alone, seem to support the British interpretation of that particular provision, but in context they tend towards absurdity; subsequent practice by the parties, and what *travaux préparatoires* we know anything of, only confirm that there was never any common intention regarding the Walled City (or, for that matter, regarding the lease itself).

One must therefore admit to failure in all attempts to find any sort of logic in this convention. But the so-called rules for treaty interpretation can, perhaps, give some guidance.[79] The presumption against the party which benefits lends support to the thesis that Great Britain did *not* acquire rights approximating to rights under a cession; so does the supposition that the parties intend a result compatible with customary international law. If it is 'permissible to interpret according to a signatory's traditional policy', China's traditional reluctance to part with territory or to grant concessions to other powers suggests that her sacrifices in the New Territories are to be construed as minimal. If we may refer to 'the situation of the parties at the time the treaty was contracted', that is, in the context of the 'scramble for concessions', the result must be the same.[80]

The strongest argument in favour of the 'cession for a term of years' construction relies on the words 'the limits of British territory shall be enlarged under lease'; an obvious implication is that the leased area thereby acquired the character of the ceded colony, that the New Territories was also ceded (though for a limited period).[81] But to adopt this contention is to make nonsense of the lease agreement. When analysed, the crucial words must be considered virtually meaningless, for they cannot impute to a territory a status in law which it cannot possess. Their only function is to underline the purpose of the lease and to recognize the contiguity of Hong Kong.

For convenient shorthand phrases, the terminology of either O'Connell or Norem can be adopted: China, as residual sovereign possessing territorial right, transferred effective sovereignty or jurisdictional right in respect of the New Territories to Great Britain. Some such formulation as this is the only way the lease agreement can be given a sensible meaning. Accordingly, Britain has 'sole jurisdiction' only, does not have full sovereign rights over the New Territories, and cannot legitimately claim that the transfer was a cession for a term of years. And 'effective sovereignty' in this case does not mean absolute authority limited only by China's possession of the reversion: the convention itself restricts British rights and powers. The non-expropriation clause is an obvious example. Hong Kong recognized her duty to confirm the titles of Chinese landholders and clearly would hesitate, by virtue of the convention as much as the need for stable government, to commit out-and-out expropriation, even though policy has not adhered to Amery's strict construction of the clause. In the Walled City, the Hong Kong government has refrained from full exercise of authority, in the face of China's vigorous assertion of rights under the convention. It can hardly be doubted that warships of the Chinese navy would be permitted to use the waters of the bays. Great Britain's effective sovereignty is therefore by no means complete.

This interpretation is supported by a relatively recent contributor to the literature whose rather technical analysis is based on Wesley Hohfeld's 'fundamental legal conceptions':

As in the case of the Weihaiwei lease convention, the municipal legal system is brought under the 'control' and 'sole jurisdiction' of Great Britain, while on the plane of the international legal system, Great Britain assumes certain *in personam* obligations towards China respecting Chinese subjects. Further, ... *in rem* legal relationships are contemplated by the parties as operating on the level of the international legal system.[82]

Two aspects of international practice towards the 1898 leaseholds seem initially to contradict the view that a measure of sovereignty or territorial right remained with China. The first of these is extraterritoriality: all the major powers (except Japan, which adopted the prevailing view when she took possession of Port Arthur) surrendered claims to extraterritorial jurisdiction in the leased territories on the ground that China had relinquished all jurisdiction during the term of the lease. From this it might be inferred that cession had taken place, but the real reason was that the powers did not need to insist upon consular jurisdiction where 'civilized' nations had established their own legal systems in place of China's.[83] The position was governed by sound considerations of policy, not on any determination that leased territories had been ceded.

Secondly, as discussed in a previous chapter,[84] for the purposes of neutrality law the powers assumed that only the status of the lessee state was relevant, not the status of the lessor state. China, as sovereign in reversion, asserted that her non-belligerent status in the Russo-Japanese war and in the first world war at the time of the Kiaochow occupation determined the status of Port Arthur and of Kiaochow respectively, but she was not powerful enough to enforce her claim. Fitzmaurice in the Foreign Office was inclined to agree with the Chinese version in theory but advocated that the practice of relying on the status of the lessee state for determining neutrality be continued;[85] British policy-makers were thus confronted with the dilemma noted above of having conflicting obligations to China and Japan concerning use of the two bays. Yet the dilemma was illusory. As far as the situation in the 1930s was concerned, the precedents relied upon (Port Arthur in 1905 and Kiaochow in 1914) were not true precedents, because in each case the lessee state was a belligerent. Great Britain in 1937 was neutral. It would not have been a matter of pleading a previous treaty with one belligerent against the other belligerent: the only reason Great Britain was concerned at all was the convention by which the territory was acquired in the first place, and which reserved specific rights to China. In any event, if previous practice was regarded as anomalous and the correct theoretical position was maintained, the leasehold would be regarded as Chinese territory and therefore belligerent territory in the Sino-Japanese war whose use by China or Japan would be of no concern to the neutrality of Great Britain. There would then be no conflict with the convention.

But in practice, of course, Great Britain could hardly view with equanimity the waging of war in the New Territories by China and another power, and a more satisfactory theory can be suggested. It is reasonable that the status of a territory for the purposes of neutrality law should depend upon the status of the state exercising effective sovereignty over it, since the residual sovereign is unlikely to possess the means to enforce neutrality in a leased territory. This seems to have been recognized by HM's advisers when dropping the original assumption that neutrality rules ran from the date of the New Territories lease.[86] The law of neutrality could accommodate such a notion, as an exception to the general rule, without implying that full sovereignty has been transferred to the lessee state.

Fitzmaurice, who was later to become senior judge of the International Court of Justice, provided an analysis of the theoretical position of leased territories which summarizes neatly the view taken here, and it deserves extended quotation:

The question which arises with this type of leased territory is where the sovereignty lies during the term of the lease. Strictly speaking, it should be held to remain with the lessor. Otherwise a lease would be indistinguishable from an out-and-out cession. In point of fact, there can be little doubt that the strictly theoretical sovereignty does remain with the lessor. For instance, the Convention of 1898, which effected the Hong Kong lease, made no provision for any re-transfer to Chinese sovereignty at the end of the 99 years term, and it is quite clear on the face of the Convention that the leased territory will automatically revert to China when the term is up, unless some contrary arrangement is arrived at. Therefore, it is not a case of a cession coupled with an obligation to re-transfer, at the end of the period. If it were, there would be no question but that the sovereignty was with the lessee, only he would be obliged to recede the territory at the end of so many years. As it is, there is no question of any re-transfer, there is a genuine lease, at any rate on paper, the residual sovereignty, so to speak, remains in the lessor, and, when the term is up, he automatically resumes full control, without the necessity for any special instrument conferring it upon him.

On this view, these leased territories would, strictly speaking, at all times be and remain Chinese territory. All that the Chinese would have parted with would be the right, during the term of the lease, to exercise effective control....

In actual practice, however, ... it is clear that these pieces of territory have in fact, been treated as amounting to cessions and not leases. According to the practical view adopted concerning them, they are really cessions coupled with an obligation to re-transfer after so many years if no contrary arrangement is come to. But this practical view of the matter is in opposition to the correct theoretical position and to the terms of the leases themselves. Nonetheless, it has prevailed.

Fitzmaurice then quotes from various international law books[87] and briefly discusses Kiaochow and Port Arthur. He goes on:

The assumption made in the above quotations that leases of this kind are merely disguised cessions or at any rate steps intended to lead up to a full cession, has been falsified in the cases of [Kiaochow and Weihaiwei], and, I believe, in certain other cases where the leased territory has duly reverted even before the end of the appointed term of years to the Chinese Government. A position of complete theoretical anomaly is thus created, for, on the one hand, there can be no doubt that these are leases and not cessions; that in strict law, the territory remains Chinese territory under, so to speak, residual Chinese sovereignty; and yet, on the other hand, they are treated during the term of the lease as being the actual territory of the lessee, in the same way in all respects as if the territory had been ceded to him in full sovereignty. It is therefore difficult to find, from the theoretical point of view, any adequate explanation of the position of these territories or any adequate classification of them.[88]

The only reservation one would want to make to these passages is that the New Territories has *not* been treated in all respects as if full sovereignty had been transferred. Great Britain claimed plenary powers, and in municipal law the authority of the Hong Kong government over leased territory is as ample as it is over ceded territory, but in practice things are different. Policy has often been affected by treaty obligations and, where full sovereign rights in defiance of the treaty have been assumed, China has frequently protested. The theoretical position is clear; where the practice seems inconsistent with it, the practice (not the theory) is anomalous or is given respectability by the acquiescence of the residual sovereign.

If this view is accepted, the New Territories cannot reasonably be described as part of 'Her Majesty's dominions': it is Chinese territory, not British. The Judicial Committee of the Privy Council adopted a similar view in relation to a *perpetual* lease of part of Nasirabad to Great Britain by virtue of which, it was said, 'the Sovereign of Kalat made over to the British State the whole of his sovereign rights'[89]—yet the territory did not pass so as to become part of Her Majesty's dominions. If the territory in that case was not transferred to Britain, the New Territories, over which China's full sovereign rights were not surrendered, can scarcely be considered as belonging to the British crown. The New Territories is 'part and parcel' of the colony of Hong Kong by legislative fiat founded on administrative and political convenience rather than on legal logic.[90]

In theory, then, the New Territories can be said to be not ceded but leased, Great Britain possessing effective sovereignty restricted by clauses in the instrument of transfer. That theory, however, assumes that the convention is valid—yet it is one of the unequal treaties China has condemned.

Unequal Treaty[91]

There is no doubt that the Convention of Peking 1898 is an unequal treaty and is so considered by People's China: the circumstances in which it was negotiated were inconsistent with the sovereignty and equality of both contracting parties and its burdens and advantages are non-reciprocal. This does not necessarily mean, however, that it is invalid according to modern international law. Although duress has been recognized, both in the 1969 Vienna convention on the law of treaties and by the International Court of Justice, as a factor which might vitiate a treaty,[92] it is a concept which must be very restrictively interpreted, and it is doubtful that the Convention of Peking 1898, which arguably was not brought about by force or even the explicit threat of force, can be considered invalid on this ground. The doctrine of changed circumstances (*rebus sic stantibus*) was frequently relied upon by nationalistic Chinese polemicists in the first decades of this century,[93] and the Chinese delegation to Paris in 1919 specifically referred to the complete change in the balance of power since 1898 to justify 'retrocession' of leased territories.[94] But this too has been approached cautiously by the international community[95] and is of dubious application to the New Territories convention.

The notion is gradually developing, however, that inequality may itself be a sufficient ground for disputing the validity of a treaty. First, an unequal treaty could be void from the beginning (*ab initio*), without any effect in international law at any time; such a treaty would be incapable of abrogation or repudiation, for it has never subsisted as an agreement between the parties. Secondly, an unequal treaty could be not void but voidable, able to be annulled because of its inherent defects yet effective until annulment. In this second case it must further be determined who may abrogate the voidable unequal treaty, in what circumstances, and how.

Chinese communist doctrine has not clearly stated a position in accordance with such a theoretical framework, and resort must therefore be had to public pronouncements and actual government practice. The 'common programme' of the Chinese People's Political Consultative Conference in 1949 provided that previous treaties between the Kuomintang and foreign governments would be examined and, according to their contents, recognized, abrogated, revised, or renegotiated. This was later extended to embrace all pre-communist Chinese treaties.[96] Since 1949 some prior treaties have been recognized and affirmed, some bilateral treaties have been cancelled after the friendly negotiation of substitutes. Others have been unilaterally repudiated, although no pre-existing treaty affecting territory has been unequivocally abrogated without the agreement of the other party,[97] and the government of People's China has consistently recognized the territorial status quo established by unequal treaties pending negotiations for a fair and just settlement of the issue.[98] Thus, for example, Chou En-lai reported in 1957 that 'the [unequal] treaties signed in the past which concern the boundary between China and Burma must be treated in accordance with general international practice.'[99] Jerome Cohen and Hungdah Chiu suggest that past boundary agreements are therefore considered to retain their validity until renegotiation.[100] Further support for this view can be derived from the statement that 'the treaties relating to the present Sino-Soviet boundary are all unequal treaties [and] they should all be annulled',[101] implying that they are valid until annulment; the same implication is contained in the comment that 'states have the right to abrogate this type of treaty at any time'.[102] Similarly, it could be argued that Chinese support for Walled City residents could not be on the basis of a void treaty, for even the weaker party cannot take advantage of a non-existent agreement, and therefore the Convention of Peking 1898 must be merely voidable.

An alternative interpretation is possible, however. Chou En-lai's reference to the Sino-Burmese boundary dispute explicitly mentioned general international *practice*, not law. Communist Chinese publicists have asserted that 'unequal treaties are in violation of international law and without legal validity'[103] and are 'illegal and void'.[104] At no time has the People's Republic of China publicly relied on the 1898 convention to support her claim to the Walled City.[105] Further, ambassador Huang Hua's letter to the UN Special Committee on Colonialism in 1972[106] was arguably a declaration that the Nanking treaty of 1842 and the Convention of Peking 1860 have always been nullities: the assertion that Hong Kong is Chinese territory occupied by the British authorities is inconsistent with the view that these treaties of cession are valid pending renegotiation, for if they are valid treaties the territory which they ceded to Her Britannic Majesty must be considered British territory, not Chinese. (The Convention of Peking 1898 is not in the same category, for it is legitimate to claim that under the lease agreement the New Territories continues as Chinese territory anyway.) Similarly, deputies from Hong Kong attended the Fourth National People's Congress in 1975[107] and the government of India, following complaints from the Chinese that Hong Kong is part of China, deleted Hong Kong from the list of countries an Indian passport holder is permitted to visit.[108]

All this suggests that China does not recognize unequal treaties as possessing any effect in law, although as a matter of practice and policy in line with the principles of peaceful co-existence the Chinese government prefers to achieve adjustment of the existing situation by negotiation. China recognizes the invalidity of an unequal treaty and 'abrogates' it when she decides to act accordingly; in the meantime her actions *vis-à-vis* the territory are determined not by legal but by political considerations. Affirmation of an unequal treaty or replacement of it by a new agreement between independent and equal sovereign states adds legality to a practical situation not previously governed by rules of international law.

Whatever the true attitude of modern mainland Chinese theorists, it cannot be said that international law yet accepts even the relatively mild position which sees unequal treaties as voidable and capable of annulment by one of the parties. But it is scarcely conceivable that states would oppose unilateral abrogation by People's China of the treaties, including the Convention of Peking 1898, by which Great Britain acquired the colony of Hong Kong, while the popular notion of 'the phone call from Peking' being sufficient for British evacuation from Hong Kong is probably accurate enough. As an American scholar said as long ago as 1927, 'it is quite certain, whatever basis you may place it upon, that a large country will only consent to any unequal treaty which really means a loss of a distinct part of her sovereignty just so long as she is unable and does not have the strength to abrogate it.'[109] And any future development in the international law of treaties obligating the beneficiary of an unequal treaty to revise it if so requested by the inferior party would leave the New Territories and the rest of Hong Kong vulnerable at law, as well as in fact, to Chinese demands for abrogation.

EPILOGUE

THE Convention of Peking 1898 has been of considerable significance in relations between Britain and China and in the politics of the New Territories. The uncertain status of the leasehold, the convention's ambiguities, and the rights and obligations it created have complicated many aspects of the territory's government. These problems are partly the result of the inequality of the contracting parties in 1898: an unequal treaty is not the most reliable and secure basis for the transfer of territory and its subsequent administration. At the same time, the convention permitted colonial expansion at Hong Kong and thus provided the means for economic survival of this last important outpost of British imperialism.

But what of the future?[1] Will the New Territories remain under the 'effective sovereignty' of Great Britain until 1997? If it does, what then?

These questions become more urgent, and are being asked more insistently, as 1997 approaches. Attempts to answer them are primarily based on speculation as to the future policy of the mainland Chinese government, and the most obvious factors put forward for discussion are the success of 'moderate' forces in post-Mao China and the consequent rapid development of China's international trade. Not only does China rely on Hong Kong more than ever as an outlet to the world, an earner of foreign exchange and a source of financial and trading expertise, but direct monetary investment in the colony itself is expanding continually. Hong Kong sleeps easier every time a new multi-million dollar deal is announced which can only show a return for China if the status quo remains undisturbed for many years to come. The economic evidence of a political decision by the People's Republic to maintain Hong Kong's integrity is impressive. And this confirms that no separate action is likely in respect of the leasehold portion of the colony: so long as Hong Kong as a British colony is valuable to China, the New Territories is thought to be safe. Its future is inextricably bound up with the future of the ceded portions not merely because it too was acquired by unequal treaty but for economic reasons.

International law, which is one usual factor in determining future action affecting international affairs, cannot assist here, because the international community would not interfere with the re-absorption of Hong Kong into China even though that would be considered contrary to China's international legal obligations. China's own theoretical attitude to unequal treaties is in any case ambiguous: it is not known whether she considers the Hong Kong treaties to be void or voidable, or whether, if the latter, they can simply be ignored without negotiation and agreement with Britain. Thus legal factors are of no importance in the prognosis of events leading up to 1997. They re-emerge, however, when speculation is focused on what might happen then.

If the Convention of Peking 1898 is void *ab initio*, 1997 is irrelevant; it cannot be the terminal date of a non-existent agreement. On 1 July 1997 China could carry on business as usual, continuing to manage her New Territories investments within the capitalist framework of Hong Kong and continuing to respect the colony's laws and legal system as applying in the 'leasehold'.

If, on the other hand, the convention is voidable, it will lapse in 1997 and China must treat the previously-leased territory as having returned to full Chinese sovereignty. Any remaining British presence could then be considered either unacceptable or tolerable. If unacceptable, Britain would have to go: HMG could scarcely contemplate retaining territory against the will of the residual sovereign after the treaty has expired. If tolerable, the *de facto* status quo could be permitted by China to continue (the New Territories in fact being treated by Britain as part of Hong Kong) although its juridical basis would have changed from voidable treaty to mere practice with the sovereign's acquiescence.

These are the options facing China, but Great Britain is of course in a different position. For the colonizing power, 1997 is crucial: HM ceases to possess any rights over the leasehold from the moment 1 July of that year begins. The British crown cannot ignore the terminal date, for the convention is valid and its terms must be obeyed, and those terms are incorporated (by reference) into the New Territories order in council[2] which confirms British jurisdiction over the area.[3]

What can be done? A new order in council might be issued containing no reference to any treaty but simply defining Hong Kong

as including the land and sea presently claimed by the local legislature; the Hong Kong courts would treat the new order as a conclusive declaration of the extent of their jurisdiction.[4] For the purposes of municipal law, therefore, the present status quo could
remain. Alternatively, and without doubt so far as the domestic
legal system is concerned, the status quo could be preserved by Act
of Parliament.

The last option available to both Britain and China is to reach a
new agreement for the lease or cession of the New Territories. It is
almost unthinkable that the government of the People's Republic
would do so: it would be too much of an affront to socialist ideol-
ogy. A new agreement could perhaps be considered an equal treaty
if freely entered into by both parties and somehow conferring
reciprocal benefits, but the obstacles placed in the way by Chinese
communist theory and by the certain ridicule of the Soviet bloc
would be insurmountable. Renegotiation of the treaty could only be
rendered possible by revisionism carried to remarkable lengths.[5]

If China wants to retain the Hong Kong status quo after 1997 the
practicable solution would be to make very clear that the convention is utterly void, that British administration of the New Territories is simply tolerated despite being without legal foundation,
and that conditions are still not ripe for dealing with this legacy of
British imperialism. Britain must choose a safe device for maintenance of her authority and stoically withstand Chinese protests,
demanded by ideological consistency, at British interference with
China's sovereignty. At the same time, investors must be unoffi-
cially reassured that Hong Kong will remain a bulwark of capitalist
enterprise for the foreseeable future.[6]

No one can say whether such a scenario will take place. In the
meantime, the New Territories remains under the sole jurisdiction
of Great Britain, despite all the difficulties created by the convention and demands for its abrogation. The leasehold is too important
to Hong Kong, and Hong Kong is too important to the general
interests of China, to permit rendition. The unequal treaty has
produced a situation which both parties seek to maintain. Ironically, indeed, that situation is now probably more beneficial to
China, previously the weaker party, than to the imperial power
which dictated the terms of the Convention of Peking 1898.

APPENDIXES

APPENDIX 1
The Convention of Peking, 1898

Note:

(1) The full title is usually rendered as 'Convention respecting an extension of the Hong Kong territory—June 9, 1898'.
(2) The clause headings do not appear in other printed versions (compare LHK 1964 ed., app. IV, pp. 11–12).
(3) Both Li Hung-chang and Hsü Ying-kuei of the Tsungli Yamen signed on behalf of the Chinese government.
(4) Ratifications were exchanged in London on 6 August 1898.
(5) The convention map is reproduced on p. 193, below.

WHEREAS it has for many years past been recognized that an extension of Hong Kong territory is necessary for the proper defence and protection of the Colony.

Territory leased.—It has now been agreed between the Governments of Great Britain and China that the limits of British territory shall be enlarged under lease to the extent indicated generally on the annexed map. The exact boundaries shall be hereafter fixed when proper surveys have been made by officials appointed by the two Governments. The term of this lease shall be ninety-nine years.

Jurisdiction in leased territory.—It is at the same time agreed that within the city of Kowloon the Chinese officials now stationed there shall continue to exercise jurisdiction except so far as may be inconsistent with the military requirements for the defence of Hong Kong. Within the remainder of the newly-leased territory Great Britain shall have sole jurisdiction. Chinese officials and people shall be allowed as heretofore to use the road from Kowloon to Hsinan.

Rights of Chinese ships.—It is further agreed that the existing landing-place near Kowloon city shall be reserved for the convenience of Chinese men-of-war, merchant and passenger vessels, which may come and go and lie there at their pleasure; and for the convenience of movement of the officials and people within the city.

Railway.—When hereafter China constructs a railway to the boundary of the Kowloon territory under British control, arrangements shall be discussed.

Expropriation of natives.—It is further understood that there will be no expropriation or expulsion of the inhabitants of the district included within the extension, and that if land is required for public offices, fortifications, or the like official purposes, it shall be bought at a fair price.

Extradition.—If cases of extradition of criminals occur, they shall be dealt with in accordance with the existing Treaties between Great Britain and China and the Hong Kong Regulations.

Chinese war ships.—The area leased to Great Britain as shown on the annexed map, includes the waters of Mirs Bay and Deep Bay, but it is agreed that Chinese vessels of war, whether neutral or otherwise, shall retain the right to use those waters.

This Convention shall come into force on the first day of July, eighteen hundred and ninety-eight, being the thirteenth day of the fifth moon of the twenty-fourth year of Kuang Hsu. It shall be ratified by the Sovereigns of the two countries, and the ratifications shall be exchanged in London as soon as possible.

In witness whereof the Undersigned, duly authorized thereto by their respective Governments, have signed the present Agreement.

Done at Peking in quadruplicate (four copies in English and four in Chinese) the ninth day of June, in the year of our Lord eighteen hundred and ninety-eight, being the twenty-first day of the fourth moon of the twenty-fourth year of Kuang Hsu.

[LS]   Claude M. MacDonald
[LS]   (Seal of the Chinese
                                                  Plenipotentiary)

Source: MacMurray, *Treaties and Agreements*, vol. i, pp. 130–1.

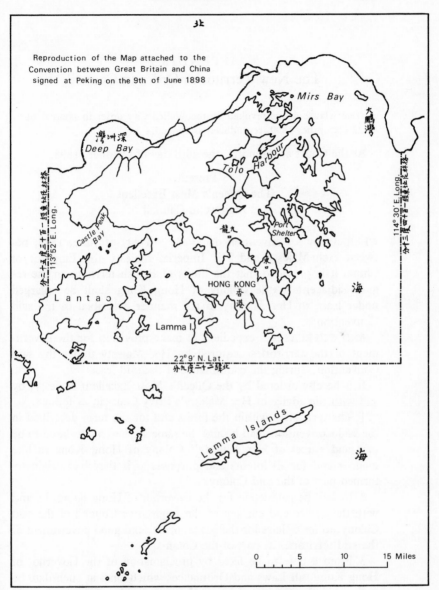

北

Reproduction of the Map attached to the
Convention between Great Britain and China
signed at Peking on the 9th of June 1898

Mirs Bay

大鵬灣

灣洲深
Deep Bay

Tolo Harbour

分二十五度二十一百一提象地形接路
113°52′E.Long.

Castle Peak
Bay

龍九

Port
Shelter

康

HONG KONG
香港

海

L a n t a o

Lamma I.

22°9′N.Lat.
分九度二十二緯北

分十三度四十百一經象住紅林路
114°30′E.Long.

Lemma Islands

海

0   5   10   15 Miles

5. THE CONVENTION MAP

Source: Redrawn from John V. A. MacMurray (comp. and ed.),
Treaties and Agreements With and Concerning China, 1894–1919,
vol. i: *Manchu Period (1894–1911)* (New York: Oxford University
Press, 1921), p. 131.

APPENDIX 2
The New Territories Order in Council

Note: clause 4 was revoked by the Walled City order in council of 27 December 1899, reproduced as appendix 3.

At the Court at Balmoral, the 20th day of October, 1898.

Present,
The Queen's Most Excellent
Majesty in Council

WHEREAS by a Convention dated the 9th day of June, 1898, between Her Majesty and His Imperial Majesty the Emperor of China, it is provided that the limits of British territory in the regions adjacent to the Colony of Hong Kong shall be enlarged under lease to Her Majesty in the manner described in the said Convention:

AND WHEREAS it is expedient to make provision for the government of the territories acquired by Her Majesty under the said Convention, during the continuance of the said lease:

It is hereby ordered by the Queen's Most Excellent Majesty, by and with the advice of Her Majesty's Privy Council, as follows:

1. The territories within the limits and for the term described in the said Convention shall be and the same are hereby declared to be part and parcel of Her Majesty's Colony of Hong Kong in like manner and for all intents and purposes as if they had originally formed part of the said Colony.

2. It shall be competent for the Governor of Hong Kong, by and with the advice and consent of the Legislative Council of the said Colony, to make laws for the peace, order, and good government of the said territories as part of the Colony.

3. From a date to be fixed by proclamation of the Governor of Hong Kong, all Laws and Ordinances which shall at such date be in force in the Colony of Hong Kong shall take effect in the said territories, and shall remain in force therein until the same shall have been altered or repealed by Her Majesty or by the Governor of Hong Kong, by and with the advice or [*sic*] consent of the Legislative Council.

[4. Notwithstanding anything herein contained, the Chinese officials now stationed within the City of Kowloon shall continue to exercise jurisdiction therein except in so far as may be inconsistent with the military requirements for the defence of Hong Kong.]

And the Right Honourable Joseph Chamberlain, one of Her Majesty's Principal Secretaries of State, is to give the necessary directions herein accordingly.

Source: LHK 1964 ed., app. IV, pp. J1–2.

APPENDIX 3
The Walled City Order in Council

At the Court at Windsor, the 27th day of December, 1899.

Present,
The Queen's Most Excellent Majesty

WHEREAS by a Convention dated the 9th day of June, 1898, between Her Majesty and His Imperial Majesty the Emperor of China, it was provided that the limits of British territory in the regions adjacent to the Colony of Hong Kong should be enlarged under lease to Her Majesty in the manner described in the said Convention;

AND WHEREAS by an Order of Her Majesty in Council, dated the 20th day of October, 1898, it was, amongst other things, ordered that the territories within the limits and for the term described in the said Convention should be, and the same were thereby declared to be, part and parcel of Her Majesty's Colony of Hong Kong, in like manner and for all intents and purposes as if they had originally formed part of the said Colony, and it should be competent for the Governor of Hong Kong, by and with the advice and consent of the Legislative Council of the said Colony, to make laws for the peace, order, and good government of the said territories as part of the Colony;

AND WHEREAS by Article 4 of the said Order in Council it was provided that, notwithstanding anything in the said Order in Council contained, the Chinese officials at the date of the said Order in Council stationed within the City of Kowloon should continue to exercise jurisdiction therein except in so far as might be inconsistent with the military requirements for the defence of Hong Kong;

AND WHEREAS, the exercise of jurisdiction by the Chinese officials in the City of Kowloon having been found to be inconsistent with the military requirements for the defence of Hong Kong, it is expedient that Article 4 of the said Order in Council should be revoked, and that the Chinese officials within the City of Kowloon should cease to exercise jurisdiction therein, and that the said City of Kowloon should become part and parcel of Her Majesty's Colony of Hong Kong for all purposes during the continuance of the term of the lease in the said Convention mentioned.

NOW, THEREFORE, Her Majesty is pleased, by and with the advice of Her Privy Council to order, and it is hereby ordered, as follows:

1. Article 4 of the Order of Her Majesty in Council of the 20th day of October, 1898, is hereby revoked, without prejudice to anything lawfully done thereunder.

2. The City of Kowloon shall be, and the same is hereby declared to be, for the term of the lease in the said Convention mentioned, part and parcel of Her Majesty's Colony of Hong Kong, in like manner and for all intents and purposes as if it had originally formed part of the said Colony.

3. The provisions of the said Order in Council of the 20th October, 1898, shall apply to the City of Kowloon in like manner as if the said City had by the said Order in Council been declared to be part and parcel of Her Majesty's Colony of Hong Kong.

And the Right Honourable Joseph Chamberlain, one of Her Majesty's Principal Secretaries of State, is to give the necessary directions herein accordingly.

Source: LHK 1964 ed., app. IV, pp. L1–2.

APPENDIX 4
Memorandum on the Delimitation of the Northern Boundary of the New Territories

The Northern Boundary commences at the point of high water-mark in Mirs Bay where the meridian of 114° 30′ East cuts the land and follows that high water-mark to the point marked with a peg immediately to the West of the market town locally known as Tung Wo Hu and sometimes called Shat'aukok. It then proceeds straight inland for a short distance till it meets a narrow path between fields on the right and a tidal flat on the left. A peg was driven in to the East of the path, and it was agreed that the whole of the path is within British territory but may be used by the inhabitants of both countries. The line follows this path until it reaches a corner of the market town of Tung Wo Hu, where another peg was driven in, and then proceeds until it comes to the bed of a wide stream which is at present dry. It was agreed that the boundary should follow the centre of this river bed. The land to the right of the river, that is, the land on the left bank being within Chinese territory; the land to the left of the river, that is, the land on the right bank being within British territory. This line along the middle of the river's bed continues until a road leading to the village Kang Hau is reached. A peg was driven in at the point where the boundary line leaves the river and follows this road. It was agreed that the whole of the road is within British territory but may be used by the inhabitants of both countries. This road leads up a steep ravine crossing and recrossing the stream. It was agreed that the waters of this stream whether within the British or the Chinese boundary should be available for the inhabitants of both countries. This road passes through a gap about 500 feet above sea level forming the dividing ridge between the Shat'aukok and Sham Chun valleys. The boundary was marked at this point with a peg. It was agreed that the road from this gap should be the boundary and is within British territory but may be used by the inhabitants of both countries. This road passes down the right-hand side of the ravine and has a stream on the left running to Kang T'o. At the foot of the ravine this road crosses a larger stream coming from the direction of Ng Tung Shan and recrosses it within a distance of 100 yards. This road passes

Kang T'o village on the right and reaches the Sham Chun river at a distance of about a quarter of a mile below Kang T'o. It was agreed that up to this point this road is within British territory but may be used by the inhabitants of both countries. It was also agreed that the waters of the stream running from Ng Tung Shan referred to above shall be available for cultivators of land in both countries. A peg was driven in to mark the point where this road as a boundary ended. The boundary then follows the right or northern bank of the river generally known as the Sham Chun river down to Deep Bay, all the river and the land to the south being within British territory. The Western, Eastern, and Southern boundaries are as laid down in the Convention, the whole of the Island of Lantao being within British territory.

The waters of Mirs Bay and Deep Bay are included in the area leased to Great Britain.

Signed in the Council Chamber, Hong Kong, this 19th day of March, 1899.

Source: LHK 1964 ed., app. IV, pp. K1–2.

APPENDIX 5
Proclamation for the Application of Hong Kong Laws in the New Territories

By His Excellency Sir Henry Arthur Blake, Knight Grand Cross of the Most Distinguished Order of Saint Michael and Saint George, Governor and Commander-in-Chief of the Colony of Hong Kong and its Dependencies, and Vice-Admiral of the same.

Whereas by an Order of the Queen's Most Excellent Majesty in Council, made on the 20th day of October, 1898, after reciting that by a Convention dated the 9th day of June, 1898, between Her Majesty and His Imperial Majesty the Emperor of China, it is provided that the limits of British territory in the regions adjacent to the Colony of Hong Kong, shall be enlarged under lease to Her Majesty in the manner described in the said Convention; and after reciting that it is expedient to make provision for the Government of the territories acquired by Her Majesty under the said Convention, during the continuance of the said lease, it was ordered (*inter alia*) as follows:

1. The territories within the limits and for the term described in the said Convention shall be and the same are hereby declared to be part and parcel of Her Majesty's Colony of Hong Kong in like manner and for all intents and purposes as if they had originally formed part of the said Colony.

2. It shall be competent for the Governor of Hong Kong, by and with the advice and consent of the Legislative Council of the said Colony, to make laws for the peace, order and good government of the said territories as part of the Colony.

3. From a date to be fixed by proclamation of the Governor of Hong Kong, all laws and ordinances, which shall at such date be in force in the Colony of Hong Kong, shall take effect in the said territories and shall remain in force therein until the same shall have been altered or repealed by Her Majesty or by the Governor of Hong Kong, by and with the advice and consent of the Legislative Council.

And whereas it is expedient that from the 17th day of April, 1899, all laws and ordinances, which shall at such date be in force in the Colony of Hong Kong, shall take effect in the said territories and shall remain in force therein until the same shall have been altered or repealed by Her Majesty or by the Governor of Hong Kong, by and with the advice and consent of the Legislative Council:

Now, therefore, I, Sir Henry Arthur Blake, do hereby, in pursuance of the powers reserved to me by the said Order of Her Most Excellent Majesty in Council and of every other power (if any) enabling me, by this Proclamation proclaim and direct that from the said 17th day of April, 1899, all laws and ordinances, which shall at such date be in force in the Colony of Hong Kong, shall take effect in the said territories and shall remain in force therein until the same shall have been altered or repealed by Her Majesty or by the Governor of Hong Kong, by and with the advice and consent of the Legislative Council.

By His Excellency's Command,

J. H. Stewart Lockhart
Colonial Secretary

GOD SAVE THE QUEEN
Given at Government House, Victoria, Hong Kong,
this 8th day of April, 1899.

Source: *Hong Kong Government Gazette 1899*, p. 522.

APPENDIX 6

Translation of Proclamations Issued by the San On District Magistrate and the Viceroy of Canton regarding the New Territories

I

CHIU, Magistrate of the San On District, &c, hereby issues this notice for general information. A despatch having been received from His Excellency T'AM [sic], Viceroy of the Two Kwong Provinces, instructing both Civil and Military Officers to attend in person for the purpose of delimiting the Kowloon Extension, the following boundary has been agreed to in accordance with the decision of the Tsung-li Yamen.

From Deep Bay across to Sham Chun and thence to Kang T'o the North side of the river shall be the boundary. From Kang T'o to Kang Hau the mountain path shall be the boundary. From Kang Hau to Tung Wo market town the middle of the small stream shall be the boundary. From the North-East of the Tung Wo market town to the South-West the road shall be the boundary, and then thence to the shore terminating at Mirs Bay. All waterways and roads are included within the leased area but are always to be open to the use of the people of both nations.

You inhabitants are hereby notified that within the leased area as delimited all fields, lands, houses, graves, local customs and usages will remain unchanged. You need not, therefore, be alarmed or suspicious and you must be careful not to create trouble.

Those villages not included in the leased territory will continue to be within Chinese territory and the people living in them are not in any way concerned.

Should any one dare to avail themselves of pretexts to excite or mislead the minds of the people with a view to create trouble, they will most certainly be punished without leniency.

A special notice.

Dated 16th of the 2nd Moon the 25th year
of Kwong Su (27th March, 1899).

II

T'AM [sic], Viceroy of the Two Kwong Provinces, &c, and LUK, Governor of the Kwong Tung Province, &c, issue this notice for general information.

Whereas Kowloon has been leased under the instructions of the Emperor and the boundary has been defined in accordance with the original map forwarded by the Tsungli-Yamen, the following agreement has been come to with the foreign officials:

(1) The people are to be treated with exceptional kindness.

(2) There can be no forced sale of houses and lands.

(3) The graves in the leased territory are never to be removed.

(4) Local customs and habits are to remain unchanged according to the wishes of the inhabitants.

In these respects, therefore the villages and market towns in the leased territory will not differ from those within Chinese territory.

Wherefore this notification is issued to let all know that whatever occurs in the villages and market towns of China has now nothing to do with you (who live in the leased territory). No one must under any pretext excite or mislead the minds of the people. You who live in the villages and market towns of the leased territory should follow your occupations and abide by the law as heretofore.

If in disobedience to the Imperial decree you dare to create strife or avail yourselves of any pretext to stir up trouble, there is now a large military force in the territory which will arrest and deal with the guilty without mercy.

Let every one tremble and obey.

An important special notice.

24th day 2nd Moon 25th year of Kwong Su (4th April, 1899).

Source: Hong Kong Government Gazette 1899, p. 1559.

NOTES

Notes for Prologue

1. MacDonald to Salisbury, treaty no. 2, 10 June 1898: FO17/1347.

2. 'Record Book of Interviews with Yamen, June 1897–November 1899': FO233/44, p. 221.

3. Minute to Sir T. Sanderson, 21 Sept. 1898, on Lo to Salisbury, 5 Aug. 1898: FO17/1335.

4. See appendix 2.

5. The full text is reprinted as appendix 1.

6. See the works cited in note 91 to chapter 10, p. 239, below.

7. See pp. 150–63, above.

8. 'A Comment on the Statement of the Communist Party of the USA' (8 Mar. 1963) in Jerome A. Cohen and Hungdah Chiu, *People's China and International Law: A Documentary Study* (Princeton, New Jersey: Princeton University Press, 1974), pp. 379–81.

9. ibid., p. 384.

10. See pp. 184–7, above.

11. L. K. Young, *British Policy in China, 1895–1902* (Oxford: Clarendon Press, 1970), p. 20.

12. Frank Harris, *My Life and Loves* (Corgi Books, 1966), p. 619.

13. Barbara W. Tuchman, *The Proud Tower: A Portrait of the World Before the War: 1890–1914* (Bantam Books, 1967), p. 12.

14. Young, *British Policy*, p. 66; Tuchman, *The Proud Tower*, p. 62.

15. Denis Judd, *Balfour and the British Empire: A Study in Imperial Evolution, 1874–1932* (London, Melbourne, Toronto: Macmillan, 1968), pp. 17 and 18. See also Blanche E. C. Dugdale, *Arthur James Balfour* (London: Hutchinson, 1936), vol. i, pp. 249–64.

16. See Peter Fraser, *Joseph Chamberlain: Radicalism and Empire, 1868–1914* (London: Cassell, 1966).

17. Quoted by James A. Williamson, *A Short History of British Expansion: The Modern Empire and Commonwealth* (London: Macmillan, 5th ed. 1964), p. 233.

18. Tuchman, *The Proud Tower*, p. 66.

19. Young, *British Policy*, p. 20.

20. Ronald Hyam, *Elgin and Churchill at the Colonial Office, 1905–1908: The Watershed of the Empire-Commonwealth* (London, Melbourne, Toronto: Macmillan, 1968), p. 483.

21. Robert V. Kubicek, *The Administration of Imperialism: Joseph Chamberlain at the Colonial Office* (Durham, NC: Duke University Press, 1969), pp. 17–18. In 1907 Lucas looked forward to the time when he could leave; two years later he thought the Colonial Office was in a chaotic condition with Fiddes the rising man, though he

had not met anyone who had a good word to say for him. See Clementi Smith to Stewart Lockhart, 23 May 1907, and Lucas to Stewart Lockhart, 12 Nov. 1909: vol. xi, *Stewart Lockhart's Papers*.

22. The under-secretaries, the assistant under-secretaries, and the assistant to the legal assistant under-secretary, selected by the secretary of state. The clerks were recruited by competitive examination conducted by the civil service commissioners.

23. See Kubicek, *The Administration of Imperialism*, p. 16: 'The exams were calculated to test those kinds of knowledge and ability fostered by the great public schools and universities. As such they were weighted in favour of the student of the classics.' C. P. Lucas had topped his exam in 1877.

24. ibid., p. 175.

25. Han Su-yin, *The Crippled Tree* (London: Panther Books, 1972), p. 130.

26. *China Mail*, 30 Oct. 1899.

27. Cyril Pearl, *Morrison of Peking* (London: Penguin, 1970), p. 83.

28. ibid., pp. 122, 151, 162.

29. Balfour to Villiers, 17 Nov. 1898: FE/98/14, FO800/162 (*Bertie's Papers*). He was, perhaps, referring to MacDonald's admission that, contrary to instructions, he had left the Kowloon-Canton railway demand on the list of concessions secured in September 1898: MacDonald to Bertie, private, 18 Sept. 1898: FE/98/11, ibid. At the end of August Balfour had considered that, as regards Chinese affairs, Mac-Donald seemed 'very obstinate and not always intelligent': quoted by Edmund S. Wehrle, *Britain, China, and the Antimissionary Riots 1891–1900* (Minneapolis: University of Minnesota Press, 1966), p. 98.

30. Chirol to Foley, 17 May 1898: A/106/13, *Salisbury's Papers*. Young, *British Policy*, p. 21, considers MacDonald's appointment an inspired move by Salisbury. But one critic was reported as saying: 'It would be the best news in the world if Sir Claude MacDonald could be promptly despatched as plenipotentiary to the North Pole': *Hong Kong Daily Press*, 25 Oct. 1898.

31. See *Colonial Office List 1912*, p. 470. Regarding his application for the Ceylon job, see Blake to Chamberlain, 16 Aug. 1901: JC14/2/5/3, *Chamberlain's Papers*; see also his letter of 24 Aug. 1903: JC18/5/3, ibid.

32. He is not mentioned in the *Dictionary of National Biography*. But see Hyam, *Elgin and Churchill*, pp. 230–4.

33. See Harold Z. Schiffrin, *Sun Yat-sen and the Origins of the Chinese Revolution* (Berkeley, Los Angeles and London: University of California Press, 1970), chap. VII.

34. 'It does not seem to occur to the self-satisfied mind of Sir H. Blake that it is a Governor's business to satisfy himself that the estimates are correct, and that we ought to have been told of this [the delays and costs of the land survey in the New Territories] before': minute by Fiddian on Blake to Chamberlain, no. 336, 28 Aug. 1901: CO129/306.

35. Blake to Chamberlain, 16 Aug. 1901: JC14/2/5/3, *Chamberlain's Papers*.

36. Blake to Stewart Lockhart, 28 Aug. 1903: vol. v, *Stewart Lockhart's Papers*.

37. *China Mail*, 20 Nov. 1903. See also *China Mail*, 1 Sept. 1903: 'no one can cavil at the deep human sympathy His Excellency and Lady Blake have displayed whenever any project was advanced for the moral, social and physical elevation of our Chinese fellow-subjects.'

38. Black to Chamberlain, confidential, 27 Aug. 1898: 'Hong Kong: Correspondence (20 June 1898, to 20 Aug. 1900) respecting the Extension of the Boundaries of the Colony': confidential print, Eastern No. 66, serial no. 30, p. 28: CO882/5.

(This confidential print, a valuable source for this study, is hereafter cited as 'CP' and the serial number of the despatch or telegram referred to.) See also minute on Black to Chamberlain, 27 Aug. 1898: CO129/284.

39. Ho Kai and Wei Yuk to Black, 22 Aug. 1898, enclosure in CP30, p. 29.

40. H. J. Lethbridge, 'Sir James Haldane Stewart Lockhart: Colonial Civil Servant and Scholar', in Lethbridge, *Hong Kong: Stability and Change* (Hong Kong: Oxford University Press, 1978), chap. 6.

41. See H. J. Lethbridge, 'Hong Kong Cadets, 1862–1941', in ibid., chap. 2.

42. 'Old Colonial', *Old Hong Kong* (a series of articles published in the *South China Morning Post* between 17 June 1933 and 13 April 1935 and bound together in the library of the University of Hong Kong) notes that he re-organized the district watchmen and had twelve Chinese appointed as a supervising committee and advisory board to the government; he remodelled the Po Leung Kuk; noteworthy improvements in the Tung Wah hospital were largely due to him; he took a large share in the suppression of secret societies; and he 'settled many a strike and quelled many a riot caused by coolies and the labouring classes'.

43. See William Robinson to Stewart Lockhart, 18 Feb. 1896: vol. ii, *Stewart Lockhart's Papers*. Robinson commiserated with Stewart Lockhart, promised to support him if he applied for a better job elsewhere, and expressed his annoyance with Chamberlain.

44. Chamberlain to Robinson, 11 April 1896: ibid.

45. See Gascoigne to Chamberlain, no. 39, 28 Jan. 1902, and the enclosed extract from the *China Mail* of 20 Jan. 1902: CO129/310.

46. Lethbridge, 'Sir James Haldane Stewart Lockhart', pp. 153–4.

47. *Hong Kong Weekly Press*, vol. xlviii, 17 Sept. 1898, p. 239. He was also considered something of a raconteur: see William Ferdinand Tyler, *Pulling Strings in China* (London: Constable, 1929), pp. 181–2.

48. Morrison to Stewart Lockhart, 22 Aug. 1904: vol. v, *Stewart Lockhart's Papers*. See also Lucas to Stewart Lockhart, 9 Sept. 1910: vol. iv, ibid.

49. See Lucas to Stewart Lockhart, 16 Aug. 1897: vol. xi, ibid.

50. See Schiffrin, *Sun Yat-sen*, chap. IV.

51. He was over 80 years old and supposed to be suffering from an acute disease: Bax-Ironside to Salisbury, confidential, 6 July 1899, enclosure in CP238, p. 332.

52. Bax-Ironside to Salisbury, confidential, 12 May 1899, enclosure in CP219, p. 303.

53. *Hong Kong Weekly Press*, vol. xlvi, 18 Aug. 1897, p. 143. MacDonald said in 1896: 'The Central Government are afraid of the Southern provinces and the Viceroy at Canton is getting altogether too big for his boots and he has been most impertinent and obstructive': MacDonald to Salisbury, 17 May 1896: A/106/3, *Salisbury's Papers*.

54. Blake to Chamberlain, confidential, 29 Apr. 1899: CP172, p. 190.

55. *Hong Kong Weekly Press*, vol. xlviii, 8 Oct. 1898, p. 282.

56. Lo Jung-pang (ed.), *K'ang Yu-wei: A Biography and a Symposium* (Tucson: University of Arizona Press, 1967), pp. 114, 163 note 60; William Ayers, *Chang Chih-tung and Educational Reform in China* (Cambridge, Mass.: Harvard University Press, 1971), p. 143.

57. MacDonald to Salisbury, no. 2, 5 Jan. 1900, enclosure 2 in CP303, p. 389.

Notes for Chapter 1

1. See WO to CO, 24 Oct. 1863, quoted by Digby Barker, enclosure in Robinson to Ripon, secret, no. 23, 9 Nov. 1894: CO537/34; Memorandum on the Defences of Hong Kong (23 Dec. 1880): Cab 7/5; Memorandum by the Inspector-General of Fortifications (1882): Cab 7/6; Foreign Intelligence Committee, Admiralty, memorandum no. 110 (July 1886): ibid.; minute no. 10, Committee of Imperial Defence meeting, 26 Feb. 1886: Cab 7/7; Committee of Imperial Defence meeting, 16 Apr. 1886: ibid.; enclosure in Cameron to Holland, secret, no. 329, 22 Apr. 1887, and enclosure in des Voeux to Knutsford, secret, no. 471, 1 June 1889: CO537/34; G. B. Endacott, *A History of Hong Kong* (Hong Kong, London, New York: Oxford University Press, 2nd ed. 1973), pp. 260–1.

2. des Voeux to Knutsford, secret, no. 52, 26 Mar. 1890: CO537/34; enclosure in Fleming to Knutsford, secret, no. 534, 22 Apr. 1890: ibid.; Knutsford to Salisbury, 27 Mar. 1890, and Sanderson to CO, 2 Apr. 1890 and 10 June 1890: ibid.

3. See Fleming to Knutsford, no. 342, 20 Sept. 1890: CO129/246; *China Mail*, 30 Oct. 1895; CO to WO, 16 June 1890 and the WO reply of 25 June: CO537/34. See also *China Mail*, 25 Feb. and 2 Mar. 1891.

4. Robinson to Ripon, secret, no. 23, 9 Nov. 1894: CO537/34.

5. Enclosure in Robinson to Ripon, secret, no. 24, 14 Nov. 1894: ibid.

6. See despatches by Captain W. H. Fawkes and Vice-Admiral E. R. Fremantle in Adm 125/45, pp. 422–4.

7. This caused the Colonial Office some embarrassment: it was the subject of a question in the House of Commons, and Chamberlain issued a circular despatch to all colonies warning colonial service officials, or those recently in that service, of serious consequences should they allow themselves to be interviewed on matters of public policy or on military affairs. See file no. 6103, CO129/286; James William Norton-Kyshe, *The History of the Laws and Courts of Hong Kong* (London: Fisher Unwin, 1898), vol. ii, pp. 530–2.

8. See Colonial Defence Committee memoranda, etc., in Cab 11/57, and reports of the local joint naval and military committee of 1894–5: Cab 18/20.

9. Report no. XVII, 13 May 1895: Cab 18/22A.

10. Lucas minuted that 'from a purely colonial point of view the extension would of course be a gain and so much should be said; apart from whether the extension is thought either practicable or, in other respects, desirable': on WO to CO, secret, no. 36, 12 June 1895: CO537/34.

11. Chater's second letter, endorsed by the committee of the Hong Kong General Chamber of Commerce, was enclosed in Robinson to Chamberlain, secret, no. 43, 25 Sept. 1895: CO537/34. The Ku-t'ien massacre was first reported in the *China Mail*, 5 Apr. 1895; according to the *China Mail* of 1 Oct. 1895, seven of the murderers were executed in the presence of a foreign commission of inquiry, and more executions were to take place. See also Wehrle, *Britain, China, and the Antimissionary Riots*, p. 108.

12. *China Mail*, 30 Oct. 1895; Robinson to Chamberlain, confidential, no. 47, 5 Nov. 1895: CO537/34.

13. WO to CO, secret, no. 45, 25 Nov. 1895: ibid.

14. Bertie to CO, secret, no. 48, 9 Dec. 1895: ibid. Several weeks before, the China Association had pressed for an extension of the Kowloon frontier in Keswick's interview with Salisbury: see Nathan A. Pelcovits, *Old China Hands and the Foreign Office* (New York: King's Crown Press, 1948), p. 187.

15. Schiffrin, *Sun Yat-sen*, pp. 133–4. See also minute by Lucas on Lawson to Chamberlain, secret, no. 67, 17 Aug. 1896: CO537/34.

16. Minute on Bertie to CO, secret, no. 69, 27 Aug. 1896: ibid.

17. Colonial Defence Committee, memorandum no. 74M, secret, 12 Oct. 1896: Cab 8/1.

18. Colonial Defence Committee, memorandum no. 85M, secret, 12 Nov. 1896: ibid.

19. Bertie to CO, confidential, 21 Jan. 1897: ibid.; FO to WO, 23 Dec. 1896: see CDC meeting no. 101, 21 Jan. 1897, para. 17: Cab 7/7.

20. Disorder in Kwangtung suggested to the *Hong Kong Weekly Press* that 'it would be an excellent thing for the British Government to afford the Cantonese an object lesson in the direction of how to administer the rural districts' by acquiring some land behind the Kowloon peninsula: vol. xlvi, 18 Aug. 1897, p. 143. See also 21 Oct. 1897, p. 302. The possibility of Mirs Bay being fortified by the Chinese government aroused further consternation: 2 Dec. 1897, p. 417. At the end of 1897 a false report of agreement having been reached with China (30 Dec. 1897, p. 501; and see vol. xlvii, 13 Jan. 1898, p. 18, and 12 Feb. 1898, p. 91) provided fuel for optimism, and there are numerous references in the press of early 1898 to the necessity of extension.

21. See Robinson to Chamberlain, secret, no. 115, 15 Dec. 1897: CO537/34. See pp. 29 and 31, above.

22. On FO to CO, secret, no. 119, 3 Feb. 1898: CO537/34.

23. MacDonald to Bertie, 29 Apr. 1898: A/106/10, *Salisbury's Papers*.

24. ibid. As to land speculation, see pp. 84–6, above. Advocates of Hong Kong expansion frequently believed that MacDonald's predecessor in Peking, Sir Nicolas O'Conor, had negotiated agreement with the Tsungli Yamen in 1894 or 1895 which was deferred at the time of the Sino-Japanese peace treaty and thereafter allowed to lapse: see, for instance, *Hong Kong Weekly Press*, vol. xlvii, 27 Jan. 1898, p. 63, and Norton Kyshe, *History of the Laws and Courts*, vol. ii, p. 532. There is nothing in the records to indicate any initiative by O'Conor, though it was not far from his mind, and it is possible that he raised it unofficially at some stage during 1895. When the French were demanding ratification of the Tonking frontier convention O'Conor suggested that British acquiescence could be exchanged for a concession: if HMG consent, he remarked, 'we ought to get a suitable *quid pro quo*. An increase of territory round Kowloon and the opening of the West River could not be exaggerated satisfaction to demand from China': O'Conor to Salisbury, 3 July 1895: A/106/1, *Salisbury's Papers*. In fact Great Britain secured other advantages, including a rectification of the Burmese border and a possible railway concession from Burma into Yunnan: see William L. Langer, *The Diplomacy of Imperialism 1890–1902* (New York: Alfred A. Knopf, 2nd ed. 1960), p. 395.

25. Kau Lung Gai is more properly translated as Kowloon Street, and was the name given to the motley assemblage of dwellings and businesses which grew up on either side of the road from the fort to the pier. Foreigners in Hong Kong at the turn of the century referred to the suburbs as Kowloon City, though that was the name given by the Chinese to the fort alone. In modern Hong Kong 'Kowloon City' often means the Walled City, though it is also the name of an administrative district. For an intriguing account of the fort and the town prior to 1899 see James Hayes, *The Hong Kong Region 1850–1911* (Hamden: Archon Books, 1977), chap. 7.

26. See *Hong Kong Telegraph*, 29 Aug. 1881 and 18 Mar. 1890; *Hong Kong Weekly Press*, vol. xlviii, 9 July 1898, p. 26 and 10 Dec. 1898, p. 479; memorandum by Goodman, December 1898: CP51, p. 83; 'Gambling' in *Old Hong Kong*. See also William Mesny (ed.), *Mesny's Chinese Miscellany* (Shanghai, 1899), vol. iii, pp. 96,

117; L. C. Arlington, *Through the Dragon's Eyes* (London: Constable, 1931), pp. 166–8.

27. Enclosure in Robinson to Ripon, secret, 9 Nov. 1894: CO537/34. The report of the joint naval and military committee in April 1894, presided over by Digby Barker, made similar remarks: see Cab 11/57.

28. Colonial Defence Committee memorandum no. 85M, secret, 12 Nov. 1896: Cab 8/1. See also the view of the Hong Kong General Chamber of Commerce expressed in Black to Chamberlain, 6 May 1898: CO129/283.

29. 'The Kun Fu Assistant Magistrate, with his office in present day Kowloon City, was responsible for the peace and order of 298 Punti villages and 194 Hakka villages': Peter L. Y. Ng, 'The 1819 Edition of the *Hsin-an Hsien-chih*: A Critical Examination with Translation and Notes', unpublished M.A. thesis, University of Hong Kong, 1961, p. 49. E. J. Eitel, *Europe in China* (Hong Kong: Kelly and Walsh, 1895), pp. 302–3, says that 'when the Colony became British, the headquarters of the Colonel in command of the Marine Constabulary stations of Taipang and Kowloon were removed to the citadel of Kowloon City.'

30. The civil authority who resided in the Walled City was the deputy magistrate under the district magistrate in Nam Tau, the main town in San On county. Stewart Lockhart, however, refers to the colonel commanding at Taipang as the Kowloon mandarin: report, 8 Oct. 1898: CP38, p. 45.

31. See, e.g., MacDonnell to Buckingham, no. 636, 11 Jan. 1869: CO129/136; MacDonnell to Granville, no. 701, 12 May 1869: CO129/137.

32. Stewart Lockhart, report, 8 Oct. 1898: CP38, p. 52. The concept of military officers exercising jurisdiction over civilians in China is a strange one, and it receives no support in the literature on Chinese local government.

33. Descriptive material on the Walled City is contained in the following sources: ibid., pp. 51–2; 'Kowloon, Old City' in *Old Hong Kong*; *Hong Kong Weekly Press*, vol. lix, 2 May 1904, pp. 338–9; Xavier to Stewart Lockhart, 25 Aug. 1898: vol. iii, *Stewart Lockhart's Papers*; Blake to Chamberlain, 3 Feb. 1899: JC9/3/3/3, *Chamberlain's Papers*; Jen Yu-wen, 'The Travelling Palace of Southern Sung in Kowloon' (1967) 7 *Journal of the Hong Kong Branch of the Royal Asiatic Society* 21; Walter Schofield, 'Defence Wall at Pass between Kowloon City and Kowloon Tsai' (1968) 8 *Journal of the Hong Kong Branch of the Royal Asiatic Society* 154; James Hayes, 'Old Ways of Life in Kowloon: The Cheung Sha Wan Villages' (1970) 7 *Journal of Oriental Studies* 153, 162; Hayes, review (1969) 9 *Journal of the Hong Kong Branch of the Royal Asiatic Society* 170. The general lawlessness of the region during the late Ch'ing, indicated by the fortifications, provided evidence for scattered references in the literature to various incidents involving the Walled City of Kowloon in the nineteenth century, but English sources are meagre. For further information, see W. P. Morgan, *Triad Societies in Hong Kong* (Hong Kong: Government Press, 1960), p. 62; Eitel, *Europe in China*, pp. 302–3; *China Mail*, 18 Apr. 1891; S. H. Peplow and M. Barker, *Hong Kong, Around and About* (Hong Kong: Ye Old Printerie, 2nd ed. 1931), p. 168. For material on Chinese walled cities generally, see G. William Skinner (ed.), *The City in Late Imperial China* (Stanford: Stanford University Press, 1977), especially the paper by Sen-dou Chang, pp. 75–100.

34. Geoffrey Robley Sayer, *Hong Kong: Birth, Adolescence and Coming of Age* (London, New York and Toronto: Oxford University Press, 1937), pp. 94–7.

35. See Jen, 'The Travelling Palace', p. 25.

36. There is a good deal of literature on this topic. A major secondary source is Stanley F. Wright, *China's Struggle for Tariff Autonomy: 1843–1938* (Shanghai: Kelly and Walsh, 1938); see also Wright, *Hart and the Chinese Customs* (Belfast: Wm. Mullan & Son, 1950). Reference might also be made to Endacott, *A History*,

pp. 189–94, and Alexander Michie, *The Englishman in China during the Victorian Era* (Edinburgh and London: William Blackwood and Sons, 1900), vol. ii, pp. 275–89. For printed primary sources see Chinese Imperial Maritime Customs, *Decennial Report 1892–1901* (Shanghai, 1906), vol. ii, pp. 202–31; James Russell, 'Memorandum on the "Hong Kong Blockade" for the Information of Governor Sir George Bowen', *Hong Kong Sessional Papers 1884*; 'Report of the Commissioners Appointed . . . to Enquire into the Circumstances Attending the Alleged Smuggling from Hong Kong into China of Opium and Other Goods', ibid.; 'Correspondence Relating to the Complaints of the Mercantile Community in Hong Kong against the Action of Chinese Revenue Cruisers in the Neighbourhood of the Colony', in *Correspondence, Dispatches, Reports, Returns, Memorials and Other Papers Respecting the Affairs of Hong Kong 1862–81* (Shannon: Irish University Press, 1971), pp. 373–5; 'Further Correspondence . . .', ibid., pp. 415–51. And see John King Fairbank, Katherine Frost Bruner, Elizabeth MacLeod Matheson (eds.), *The IG in Peking: Letters of Robert Hart, Chinese Maritime Customs 1868–1907* (Cambridge, Mass., and London: The Belknap Press of Harvard University Press, 1975) for various references in Hart's correspondence. These Hong Kong despatches are relevant: Egerton to Buckingham, no. 634, 9 Jan. 1869: CO129/136; Marsh to Kimberly, no. 238, 30 Oct. 1884: CO129/203: Bowen to Derby, no. 176, 16 May 1884; CO129/216; Cameron to Holland, no. 198, 27 May 1887: CO129/232.

37. 'Correspondence Relating to the Complaints of the Mercantile Community', p. 363.

38. Blake to Chamberlain, 18 Dec. 1899: JC9/3/4: *Chamberlain's Papers*.

39. See G. William des Voeux, *My Colonial Service* (London: John Murray, 1903), vol. ii, pp. 246–7, and various despatches and documents in the files: Botile to Commodore, Hong Kong, 19 May 1885: Adm 125/28, p. 105); Marsh to Stanhope, no. 369, 25 Nov. 1886: CO129/229; Hart, 'The Gap Light', 5 Aug. 1887, in Adm 125/35, pp. 26–32; other correspondence of 1887 contained in ibid., pp. 6, 14, 19–23, 33–40, 46; des Voeux to Holland, no. 12, 16 Jan. 1888: CO129/237; des Voeux to Knutsford, no. 187, 7 July 1888: CO129/238; Fleming to Knutsford, no. 321, 6 Sept. 1890: CO129/246; Digby Barker to Knutsford, no. 161, 22 May 1891: CO129/249; Digby Barker to Knutsford, no. 298, 9 Sept. 1891, no. 302, 11 Sept. 1891, and no. 364, 10 Nov. 1891: CO129/251; Robinson to Chamberlain, no. 15, 18 Jan. 1897: CO129/275.

40. S. Woodburn Kirby, *The War Against Japan* (London: HMSO, 1957), vol. i, p. 118.

41. 'Boundaries of the Colony of Hong Kong', report no. XVII: Cab 18/22A. See also Colonial Defence Committee, memorandum no. 85M, secret, 12 Nov. 1896: Cab 8/1, and memorandum no. 139M, secret, 28 Apr. 1898: Cab 8/2.

42. For general accounts of foreign imperialism in China during this period, see Langer, *The Diplomacy of Imperialism*; Paul Hibbert Clyde, *The Far East: A History of the Impact of the West on Eastern Asia* (New York: Prentice-Hall, 2nd ed. 1952); R. Stanley McCordock, *British Far Eastern Policy 1894–1900* (New York: Columbia University Press, 1931); Young, *British Policy in China*; Marilyn Blatt Young, *The Rhetoric of Empire: American China Policy 1895–1901* (Cambridge, Mass.: Harvard University Press, 1968), pp. 87–106; Philip Joseph, *Foreign Diplomacy in China 1894–1900* (London: George Allen and Unwin, 1928).

43. Unless the 1887 protocol signed at Lisbon, by which China confirmed the 'perpetual occupation and government of Macao and its dependencies by Portugal', is regarded as a loss of territory.

44. Lord Curzon's words, quoted by Schiffrin, *Sun Yat-sen*, p. 132.

45. 5/67/74, *Chamberlain's Papers*.

46. See Bertie to Salisbury, 28 Dec. 1897: FE/97/3, FO800/162 (*Bertie's Papers*); Cecil Smith to Bertie, confidential, 22 Dec. 1897: FE/97/2, ibid. Bertie had previously suggested: 'The acquisition of additional territory at Hong Kong except for a wrong done to us by China would afford France an excuse for taking something. Would it not be sufficient to give instructions to the authorities at Hong Kong to resist by force the landing of any Foreign Naval or Military Force, or any attempt by the Chinese to put up earthworks or place guns on it [the Kowloon promontory]? On the outbreak of hostilities we can take what we want without compensation.' Quoted by Wehrle, *Britain, China, and the Antimissionary Riots*, p. 104.

47. John E. Schrecker, *Imperialism and Chinese Nationalism* (Cambridge, Mass.: Harvard University Press, 1971), p. 35.

48. See G. P. Gooch and Harold Temperley (eds.), *British Documents on the Origins of the War, 1898–1914*, vol. i, *The End of British Isolation* (London: HMSO, 1927), pp. 19, 23–4.

49. Salisbury to MacDonald, tel. (separate and secret), 25 Feb. 1898: FO17/1338, following MacDonald's secret telegram of the same date that Hart had informed him of Chinese readiness to lease Weihaiwei: FO17/1340.

50. Balfour (?) to MacDonald, tel. no. 55, secret, 7 Mar. 1898: FO17/1342.

51. MacDonald to Salisbury, tel. no. 171, 10 Mar. 1898: FO17/1340.

52. Balfour (?) to MacDonald, tel. no. 67, 11 Mar. 1898: FO17/1342; Salisbury to MacDonald, tel. no. 68, 12 Mar. 1898: ibid.

53. Balfour to MacDonald, tel. no. 99, 22 Mar. 1898: FO17/1338.

54. Balfour to MacDonald, tel. no. 104, 23 Mar. 1898: ibid.

55. MacDonald to Salisbury, tel. no. 108, 30 Mar. 1898: FO17/1340.

56. Balfour to MacDonald, tel. no. 123, 30 Mar. 1898: FO17/1338.

57. For the acquisition of Weihaiwei, compare the account by Young, *British Policy*, pp. 69–75; see also Jen Sun E-tu, 'The Lease of Wei-hai Wei' (1950) 19 *Pacific Historical Review* 277.

58. Gooch and Temperley, *British Documents*, vol. i, p. 30.

Notes for Chapter 2

1. Brenan to Robinson, 7 Dec. 1897, enclosed in Robinson to Chamberlain, 15 Dec. 1897: CO537/34.

2. MacDonald to Salisbury, no. 46, 17 Mar. 1898: FO17/1333.

3. Salisbury to MacDonald, no. 15, 26 Jan. 1898: FO17/1332.

4. Salisbury to MacDonald, tel. no. 23, 25 Jan. 1898: FO17/1342. Compare Salisbury to MacDonald, tel. no. 76, 31 Dec. 1897: ibid.

5. MacDonald to Salisbury, tel. no. 85 (paraphrase), 17 Mar. 1898: FO17/1343.

6. Balfour to MacDonald, tel. no. 83, 21 Mar. 1898: FO17/1342.

7. Balfour to MacDonald, tel. no. 88, 19 Mar. 1898, and Bertie to MacDonald, tel. no. 87, 19 Mar. 1898: ibid.

8. Balfour to MacDonald, tel. no. 95, 22 Mar. 1898: ibid.

9. MacDonald to Salisbury, tel. no. 95, 22 Mar. 1898: FO17/1340.

10. Balfour to MacDonald, tel. no. 96, 22 Mar. 1898: FO17/1338.

11. Balfour to MacDonald, tel. no. 102, 23 Mar. 1898: ibid.

12. Bertie to MacDonald, tel. no. 113, 28 Mar. 1898: ibid.

13. MacDonald to Salisbury, tel. no. 114, 3 Apr. 1898: FO17/1340.

14. Balfour to MacDonald, tel. no. 129, 4 Apr. 1898: FO17/1338.

15. 'Record Book': FO233/44, p. 161.

16. MacDonald to Salisbury, tel. no. 122, 4 Apr. 1898: FO17/1340.

17. Balfour (?) to MacDonald, tel. no. 147, 13 Apr. 1898: FO17/1338.

18. 'Record Book': FO233/44, pp. 175–8.

19. MacDonald to Salisbury, tel. no. 135, 25 Apr. 1898: FO17/1340.

20. MacDonald to Salisbury, no. 102, 27 May 1898, in CO129/287.

21. In any case, the Colonial Office was unimpressed by that idea, Lucas minuting that it would be 'better to ask at once for all we want': on FO to CO, 25 Apr. 1898, transmitting MacDonald to Salisbury, tel. no. 135 of the same date: CO129/287.

22. Balfour to MacDonald, tel. no. 159, 16 Apr. 1898: FO17/1338.

23. MacDonald to Salisbury, tel. no. 140, 28 Apr. 1898: FO17/1340.

24. MacDonald to Salisbury, tel. no. 141, 29 Apr. 1898: ibid.; 'Record Book': FO233/44, pp. 186–90. A landing place on the west coast of the promontory for Chinese cruisers and passenger vessels from Canton was required, but no mention is made of it in the final convention (presumably the reservation of the Kowloon City pier was sufficient). The requested non-expropriation clause was accepted without demur.

25. Balfour to MacDonald, tel. no. 162, 28 Apr. 1898, and tel. no. 163, 30 Apr. 1898: FO17/1338; MacDonald to Salisbury, tel. no. 149, 4 May 1898: FO17/1340; minutes on Salisbury to MacDonald, tel. no. 183, 20 May 1898: FO17/1338.

26. Balfour to MacDonald, tel. no. 147, 13 Apr. 1898, and tel. no. 159, 26 Apr. 1898: FO17/1338.

27. Colonial Defence Committee, memorandum no. 139M, secret, 28 Apr. 1898: Cab 8/2.

28. MacGregor to CO, secret, 5 May 1898: CO129/286.

29. Admiralty to FO, secret, 11 May 1898, in ibid.

30. Buller to Admiralty, secret, 11 May 1898, enclosed in MacGregor to CO, secret, 13 May 1898: ibid.

31. See FO to CO, secret, 13 May 1898, and MacDonald to Salisbury, tel. no. 166, 15 May 1898, in CO129/287; MacDonald to Salisbury, tel. no. 149, 4 May 1898: FO17/1340.

32. Salisbury to MacDonald, tel. no. 183, 20 May 1898: FO17/1338.

33. 'Record Book': FO233/44, p. 211.

34. MacDonald to Salisbury, no. 102, 27 May 1898: FO17/1334.

35. 'Record Book': FO233/44, p. 181.

36. Though an additional agreement between Russia and China on 7 May 1898 provided that the administration and police of the city of Kinchow in Liaotung should be Chinese, the Chinese government surrendered all 'rights of sovereignty' in Kiaochow during the term of the lease, and Kwangchow Wan was to be governed and administered by France alone. See the terms of the actual treaties in John V. A. MacMurray (comp. and ed.), *Treaties and Agreements With and Concerning China 1894–1919* (New York: Oxford University Press, 1921), vol. i. The Walled City of Weihaiwei remained under Chinese jurisdiction, but as in the New Territories the arrangement was initially contested and subsequently criticized: see Colonial Office, confidential print, Eastern No. 75: CO882/6.

37. MacDonald to Salisbury, tel. no. 135, 25 Apr. 1898: FO17/1340.

38. On Balfour to Chamberlain, 25 Apr. 1898: CO129/287.

39. Balfour to MacDonald, tel. no. 159, 26 Apr. 1898: FO17/1338.

40. 'Record Book': FO233/44, p. 188.

41. MacDonald to Salisbury, tel. no. 140, 28 Apr. 1898: FO17/1340.

42. Balfour to MacDonald, tel. no. 162, 28 Apr. 1898: FO17/1338.

43. MacDonald to Salisbury, tel. no. 141, 29 Apr. 1898: FO17/1340.

44. MacDonald to Salisbury, no. 102, 27 May 1898: FO17/1334.

45. MacDonald to Salisbury, tel. no. 185, 26 May 1898, in CO129/287. See pp. 38–9, above.

46. Chamberlain to Salisbury, 6 June 1898: CO129/287.

47. Salisbury to Chamberlain, 9 June 1898: ibid.

48. Minute by Sir W. A. Baillie Hamilton on ibid. Stewart Lockhart 'was at first violently opposed' to Sir Cecil Smith's opinion that 'there will be no great difficulty in gradually eliminating the Chinese element', but is 'now inclined to take the same view': minute by Hamilton on Salisbury to Chamberlain, 10 June 1898: CO129/287.

49. Stewart Lockhart, report, 8 Oct. 1898: CP38, p. 52.

50. MacDonald to Bertie, private, 28 July 1898: FO17/1335.

51. MacDonald to Salisbury, no. 102, 27 May 1898: FO17/1334.

52. Enclosure in MacDonald to Salisbury, no. 130, 23 June 1898: FO17/1335.

53. See pp. 136–9, above.

54. See, e.g., Gray to Salisbury, 19 July 1898, enclosure in CP16, p. 10; Chatterton Wilcox to Sercombe Smith, 12 Aug. 1898, enclosure in CP26, p. 24; Chatterton Wilcox to Sercombe Smith, 2 Sept. 1898, enclosure in CP39, p. 65; Black to Chamberlain, no. 263, 16 Sept. 1898: CP40, p. 66.

55. Stewart Lockhart, report, 8 Oct. 1898: CP38, p. 51.

56. See Robinson to Ripon, secret, no. 23, 9 Nov. 1894: CO537/34; joint committee report no. XVII, 13 May 1895: Cab 18/22A; Colonial Defence Committee memorandum no. 85M, secret, 12 Nov. 1896: Cab 8/1; memorandum no. 139M, secret, 28 Apr. 1898: Cab 8/2.

57. See Cab 11/57.

58. For example, de Horsey to Seymour, no. 45, 25 Aug. 1898: Adm 125/87, pp. 146–7; director of military intelligence to Colonial Office, 21 Apr. 1899: CP124, p. 131; minutes on ibid.: CO129/296; Colonial Defence Committee, printed remarks no. 218R, 22 June 1899: Cab 9/2.

59. See Blake to Chamberlain, confidential, 13 June 1898: CO129/283.

60. *Hong Kong Weekly Press*, vol. xlvii, 18 June 1898, p. 482.

61. MacDonald to Salisbury, no. 102, 27 May 1898, in CO129/287.

62. Balfour to MacDonald, tel. no. 162, 28 Apr. 1898: FO17/1338.

63. FO to CO, secret, no. 48, 9 Dec. 1895: CO537/34.

64. Stewart Lockhart to Blake, 16 Mar. 1899, enclosure in CP102, p. 120.

65. MacDonald to Salisbury, tel. no. 140, 28 Apr. 1898: FO17/1340.

66. MacDonald to Salisbury, no. 7, 13 Jan. 1898: FO17/1333.

67. MacDonald to Salisbury, no. 102, 27 May 1898, in CO129/287.

68. Answer to a question by R. G. Webster, 14 June 1898, in FO17/1360. See also Major H. Bower, 'Notes on Affairs in China', written on 26 May when French designs had long been the subject of excited discussion: 'it is difficult to see whence

any attack the present garrison could not head off is likely to come. An extension of territory on the Kowloon side would however no doubt be advisable': enclosure in Intelligence Division to FO, 18 July 1898: FO17/1361.

69. Intelligence Division to FO, 21 Mar. 1898: FO17/1357; Admiralty to FO, 25 Mar. 1898: FO17/1358.

70. Hamilton to Stewart Lockhart, private, 27 Oct. 1899: vol. v, *Stewart Lockhart's Papers*.

71. A similar point is made by Wehrle, *Britain, China, and the Antimissionary Riots*, p. 104, in relation to the lease of Weihaiwei.

72. Minute of 28 Feb. 1899, enclosed in Bertie to CO, confidential, 26 Mar. 1900: CO521/1. This was said in relation to Weihaiwei, though no doubt the same policy was pursued when the New Territories negotiations began.

73. Immanuel C. Y. Hsü, *China's Entrance into the Family of Nations: The Diplomatic Phase, 1858-1880* (Cambridge, Mass.: Harvard University Press, 1960), pp. 111-12.

74. This accords with an explanation given in *Old Hong Kong*: the 'ancient Book of Law' (whatever that was) stated that an emperor who lost a city during his reign was unable to enter the royal temple, for shame prevented him from facing his ancestors' spirits. See 'Kowloon, Old City-2'. For further consideration of the relevance of Chinese culture to the convention, see my paper in R. P. Anand (ed.), *Cultural Factors in International Relations* (New Delhi: Abhinav Publications, 1981), pp. 113-28.

Notes for Chapter 3

1. *Hong Kong Weekly Press*, vol. xlix, 22 Apr. 1899, p. 322; see also 15 Apr. 1899, p. 300, for details of the proposed arrangements for the ceremony.

2. See various enclosures in Blake to Chamberlain, no. 107, 28 Apr. 1899: CP171, p. 164.

3. See Pollock to Navy League, London, 9 July 1898, in CO129/288.

4. See *China Mail*, 8 July 1898.

5. *Hong Kong Weekly Press*, vol. xlviii, 8 Oct. 1898, p. 284; see also Salisbury to MacDonald, tel. no. 212, 23 June 1898: FO17/1339.

6. *Hong Kong Weekly Press*, vol. xlviii, 17 Sept. 1898, p. 239.

7. ibid. (translated from *L'Echo de Chine*, a Shanghai newspaper). For Stewart Lockhart's own account, see 'Journal of Inspection through the Newly Leased Territory' and an undated letter from him to the acting colonial secretary in Hong Kong: vol. iii, *Stewart Lockhart's Papers*.

8. May to acting colonial secretary, 15 Oct. 1898, enclosure 3 in CP172, p. 193; cf. Stewart Lockhart to Chamberlain, confidential, 8 Oct. 1898: CP38, p. 42; 'Record Book': FO233/44, pp. 288, 309-10.

9. Black to Chamberlain, tel., 23 Apr. 1898: CO129/282.

10. See Chamberlain's circular to other colonies, 29 Apr. 1898, informing them that the six ships had left Hong Kong on 25 April: CO129/283.

11. MacDonald to Salisbury, tel. no. 185, 26 May 1898: FO17/1340.

12. Salisbury to MacDonald, tel. no. 202, 10 June 1898: FO17/1339. Lucas had

suggested on 6 June warning Stewart Lockhart 'that the date of taking over the territory is quite unsettled (Lord Salisbury thinks it might be as well to postpone in the hope of the war coming to an end) and the matter must remain strictly secret': minute on Clementi Smith to Lucas, 5 June 1898: CO129/287.

13. MacDonald to Salisbury, tel. no. 200, 13 June 1898: FO17/1341; Black to Chamberlain, confidential, 13 June 1898: CO129/283 (Macnaghten minuted: 'We have quite decided not to take over the new territory until any chance of the Americans using Mirs Bay as a Naval Base has passed away'); CO to FO, secret, 23 June 1898: ibid.

14. Tsungli Yamen to MacDonald, 29 May 1898, enclosure in CP19, p. 14; enclosure in MacDonald to Salisbury, no. 130, 23 June 1898: FO17/1335. See also Wright, *China's Struggle*, pp. 312–20, and Wright, *Hart and the Chinese Customs*, pp. 706–10.

15. Hart to MacDonald, 27 June 1898, enclosure in CP20, pp. 15–16; enclosure in MacDonald to Salisbury, no. 139, 4 July 1898: FO17/1335.

16. Black to Chamberlain, no. 221, 29 July 1898: CP25, p. 21; memorandum by Blake, 15 Sept. 1898: CP27, pp. 24–5; memorandum by Clementi Smith, 19 Sept. 1898: CP28, p. 26; Sercombe Smith to Lucas, private, 30 July 1898: CO129/284; Francis (China Association) to Salisbury, 14 Nov. 1898, enclosure in CP44, pp. 70–5; *Hong Kong Weekly Press*, vol. xlviii, 3 Sept. 1898, p. 190, and 9 Sept. 1898, p. 210.

17. Lucas to FO, confidential, 30 Nov. 1898: CP47, p. 79.

18. Telegram from Tsungli Yamen, 9 Mar. 1899, enclosure in CP75, p. 102; Wingfield to FO, 22 Mar. 1899: CP76, p. 102.

19. MacDonald to Salisbury, tel. no. 80 (paraphrase), 23 Mar. 1899, enclosure 2 in CP78, p. 104.

20. Salisbury to Bax-Ironside, tel. no. 63, 5 Apr. 1899, enclosure in CP86, p. 108.

21. Fairbank, Bruner and Matheson, *The IG in Peking*, vol. ii, p. 1202 (letter dated 15 Oct. 1899); see also p. 1197 (28 May 1899).

22. Lucas to FO, secret, 13 Apr. 1899: CP99, p. 115.

23. Black to Chamberlain, no. 191, 13 July 1898: CP15, p. 9.

24. This is apparent from the general correspondence, though there was usually a feud between old China hands and the Foreign Office: see Pelcovits, *Old China Hands*, p. 2, referring to the 'honeymoon' between the China Association and the Foreign Office in the period immediately following the Sino-Japanese war.

25. Stewart Lockhart, report, 8 Oct. 1898: CP38, p. 52. The Chinese ministers clearly meant the Walled City when demanding the reservation of jurisdiction in Kowloon City, but MacDonald originally seemed to believe that both the fort and the suburbs were referred to in the convention.

26. Bertie to CO, confidential, 10 Dec. 1898: CP52, p. 86.

27. Undated report by Ormsby, enclosure in CP34, pp. 32–3.

28. Stewart Lockhart, report, 8 Oct. 1898: CP38, p. 50; see also de Horsey's report, 25 Aug. 1898, in Adm 125/87, pp. 143–7.

29. Minutes on Stewart Lockhart, report, 8 Oct. 1898: CO129/289.

30. Lucas to FO, confidential, 30 Nov. 1898: CP47, p. 79.

31. Colonial Defence Committee memorandum no. 172M, secret, 19 Jan. 1899: Cab 8/2; Bertie to CO, confidential, 10 Dec. 1898, and enclosure: CP52, pp. 86–8; 'Record Book': FO233/44, pp. 480–4.

32. Blake to Chamberlain, no. 66, 17 Mar. 1899: CP102, pp. 117–22. Lucas

thought Stewart Lockhart's conversation with Wang 'most stately and reminded me of Gibbon': vol. xi, *Stewart Lockhart's Papers*.

33. Enclosed in Stewart Lockhart to Blake, no. 16, 20 Mar. 1899, enclosure in Blake to Chamberlain, no. 73, 24 Mar. 1899: CP125, p. 134.

34. This was a bamboo latticework fence some 8 feet high, constructed along the entire line and pierced by only six gates. The Kowloon commissioner of customs considered it manifestly impossible to build a fence along the new boundary: Chinese Imperial Maritime Customs, *Decennial Report, 1892–1901*, p. 203.

35. Lugard to Crewe, confidential, 2 Feb. 1910: CO129/365.

36. Minute on Black to Chamberlain, no. 242, 27 Aug. 1898: CO129/284. See also Black to Chamberlain, confidential, 13 June 1898: CO129/283; Black to Chamberlain, no. 242, 27 Aug. 1898: CP29, p. 27; *Hong Kong Weekly Press*, vol. xlviii, 15 Oct. 1898, p. 307.

37. T'an to Mansfield, 15 July 1898, enclosure in CP17, pp. 11–12; Tsungli Yamen to MacDonald, 10 Sept. 1898, enclosure in CP45, p. 76.

38. MacDonald to Tsungli Yamen, 20 Sept. 1898, enclosure in CP45, p. 77.

39. MacDonald to Salisbury, no. 193, 21 Sept. 1898: FO17/1336.

40. Minute on Black to Chamberlain, no. 209, 22 July 1898: CO129/284.

41. Sanderson to CO, 26 Sept. 1898: CP32, p. 30.

42. Lucas to FO, 29 June 1898: CP6, p. 5; Bertie to CO, 4 July 1898: CP10, p. 7; law officers to CO, 17 Oct. 1898: CP41, p. 68.

43. Lucas to FO, 26 Aug. 1898: CP21, p. 16; Sanderson to CO, 26 Sept. 1898: CP31, p. 29. See also Lucas to FO, 1 Oct. 1898: CP33, p. 31, and Sanderson to CO, 8 Oct. 1898: CP37, p. 33.

44. Sanderson to CO, 26 Sept. 1898: CP31, p. 29.

45. Draft proclamation communicated by Stewart Lockhart, 20 June 1898: CP1, p. 1.

46. Enclosure in Bertie to CO, confidential, 10 Dec. 1898: CP52, pp. 87–8; minute by Hamilton on same: CO129/287; Chamberlain to Blake, confidential, 23 Dec. 1898: CP55, p. 89.

47. Blake to Chamberlain, tel., 24 Dec. 1898: CP58, p. 90; Blake to Chamberlain, no. 345, 24 Dec. 1898: CP65, p. 98. The Colonial Office doubted if a few weeks more or less would make any difference: minute on above despatch: CO129/286.

48. Blake to Chamberlain, no. 66, 17 Mar. 1899: CP102, p. 118.

49. *Hong Kong Weekly Press*, vol. xlviii, 8 Oct. 1898, p. 284. See also 22 Oct. 1898, p. 328.

50. Enclosure 6 in Blake to Chamberlain, confidential, 28 Apr. 1899: CP172, p. 195.

51. ibid., various enclosures, pp. 193–6.

52. Blake to Chamberlain, tel. (paraphrase), 1 Apr. 1899: CP80, p. 105. See *Hong Kong Weekly Press*, vol. xlviii, 8 Apr. 1899, p. 276.

53. Blake to Chamberlain, no. 87, 7 Apr. 1899: CP140, p. 140; cf. Blake to Chamberlain, tel. (paraphrase), 3 Apr. 1899: CP82, p. 106.

54. *Hong Kong Weekly Press*, vol. 1, 2 Sept. 1899, p. 186. See also vol. xlix, 8 Apr. 1899, p. 274; 22 Apr. 1899, p. 324; and 29 Apr. 1899, pp. 345–6. Blake's justification of his trip is contained in Blake to Chamberlain, confidential, 7 Apr. 1899: CP158, p. 153.

55. May to Blake, 4 Apr. 1899, enclosure 4 in Blake to Chamberlain, no. 88, 7 Apr. 1899: CP141, p. 146. Other enclosures with this despatch provide much of the information in this and the next two paragraphs.

56. Blake to Chamberlain, no. 107, 28 Apr. 1899: CP171, p. 164.

57. Blake to Chamberlain, no. 88, 7 Apr. 1899: CP141, p. 141.

58. Blake to Chamberlain, confidential, 7 Apr. 1899: CP158, p. 153.

59. Enclosure 3 in Blake to Chamberlain, no. 93, 15 Apr. 1899: CP159, p. 158.

60. T'an to Mansfield, 10 Apr. 1899, enclosure 1 in Blake to Chamberlain, no. 93, 15 Apr. 1899: CP159, p. 156; Blake to Chamberlain, tel. (paraphrase), 11 Apr. 1899: CP94, p. 114; Chamberlain to Blake, tel. (paraphrase), 11 Apr. 1899: CP96, p. 114; Chamberlain to Blake, tel. (paraphrase), 13 Apr. 1899: CP98, p. 115; Lucas to FO, secret, 13 Apr. 1899: CP99, p. 115; Bax-Ironside to Salisbury, tel. (paraphrase), 14 Apr. 1899, enclosure 1 in CP101, p. 116.

61. See Blake to Chamberlain, no. 93, 15 Apr. 1899: CP159, p. 154; Powell to Seymour, 21 Apr. 1899, sub-enclosure 2 in CP190, p. 224; *Hong Kong Government Gazette 1899*, pp. 1376, 1406.

62. ibid., pp. 1909–10; *Hong Kong Weekly Press*, vol. xlix, 22 Apr. 1899, p. 324.

63. *Hong Kong Government Gazette 1899*, pp. 1475 ff; various enclosures in Blake to Chamberlain, no. 107, 28 Apr. 1898: CP171, pp. 164–89; Stewart Lockhart to Blake, confidential, 21 Apr. 1898, enclosure 9 in CP172, p. 197. And see a diary kept by Stewart Lockhart from 16 April to 12 July, 1899: vol. xxxvi, *Stewart Lockhart's Papers*.

64. It was at this time that the gates at Kat Hing Wai, the village at Kam Tin on the itinerary of most modern tourist buses, were blown down: see my account of their subsequent history in (1973) 13 *Journal of the Hong Kong Branch of the Royal Asiatic Society* 41.

65. See Chamberlain to Blake, tel. 17 Apr. 1899: CP110, p. 124; enclosures in FO to CO, confidential, 17 Apr. 1899: CP111, p. 125; Bax-Ironside to Salisbury, tel. (paraphrase), 20 Apr. 1899, enclosure in CP122, p. 129.

66. See Bax-Ironside to Salisbury, tel. (paraphrase), 30 Apr. 1899, enclosure in CP136, p. 139; Blake to Chamberlain, no. 87, 7 Apr. 1899: CP141, p. 141; Gascoigne to Blake, 20 Apr. 1899, enclosure 8 in CP172, p. 196; Pitzipios to Stewart Lockhart, 17 Apr. 1899, enclosure 19 in CP172, p. 205; Mansfield to Bax-Ironside, no. 18, 20 Apr. 1899, enclosure in CP219, p. 305.

67. Blake to Chamberlain, tel. (paraphrase), 20 Apr. 1899: CP118, p. 128; Bax-Ironside to Salisbury, tel. (paraphrase), 30 Apr. 1899, enclosure in CP136, p. 139.

68. Frederick Wakeman, Jr., *Strangers at the Gate: Social Disorder in China, 1839–1861* (Berkeley and Los Angeles: University of California Press, 1966), pp. 22–8. Wakeman distinguishes between two types of *t'uan-lien*: those organized on government request or authority, and those ('genuine *t'uan-lien*') organized by local leaders on their own behalf. The latter type is often referred to as 'local corps', but James Hayes suggests this term for both forms of *t'uan-lien*: review (1969) 9 *Journal of the Hong Kong Branch of the Royal Asiatic Society* 170, 172. That is how it is used here; it is in fact difficult to distinguish between the two classes when considering their participation in the April disturbances. It may be that properly authorized *t'uan-lien* forces were utilized in a 'genuine *t'uan-lien*' scheme.

69. Blake to Chamberlain, no. 87, 7 Apr. 1899: CP141, p. 142; Bax-Ironside to Salisbury, confidential, 12 May 1899, enclosure in CP219, p. 301.

70. Stewart Lockhart to Blake, 24 Apr. 1899, enclosure 26 in CP171, pp. 184–5, 189.

71. For an account of the main lineage groups in the New Territories, see Hugh D. R. Baker, 'The Five Great Clans of the New Territories' (1966) 6 *Journal of the Hong Kong Branch of the Royal Asiatic Society* 25; see also Baker, 'Clan Organisation and its Role in Village Affairs', in *Aspects of Social Organisation in the New Territories*

(Hong Kong: Hong Kong Branch of the Royal Asiatic Society, 1964), pp. 4–9. For the Tang clan see Jack M. Potter, *Capitalism and the Chinese Peasant* (Berkeley and Los Angeles: University of California Press, 1968); for the Liu clan of Sheung Shui see Baker, *A Chinese Lineage Village* (London: Frank Cass, 1968); for the Man clan of San Tin and Tai Hang see James L. Watson, *Emigration and the Chinese Lineage* (Berkeley, Los Angeles, London: University of California Press, 1975).

72. See Maurice Freedman, *Chinese Lineage and Society* (London: Athlone Press, 1966), pp. 82–9.

73. See, generally, R. G. Groves, 'Militia, Market and Lineage: Chinese Resistance to the Occupation of Hong Kong's New Territories in 1899' (1969) 9 *Journal of the Hong Kong Branch of the Royal Asiatic Society* 31 ff.

74. See MacDonald to Salisbury, no. 165, 7 Aug. 1898: FO17/1335.

75. *Hong Kong Daily Press*, 19 May 1899.

Notes for Chapter 4

1. Stewart Lockhart to Blake, 30 Apr. 1899, enclosure 11 in CP204, p. 252.

2. Stewart Lockhart to Blake, 1 May 1899, enclosure 17 in CP204, pp. 258–9.

3. Blake to Chamberlain, confidential, 13 May 1899: CP186, p. 219.

4. Chamberlain to Blake, confidential, 25 July 1899: CP230, p. 309.

5. See entry for 4 May in Stewart Lockhart's diary: vol. xxxvi, *Stewart Lockhart's Papers*. See also Stewart Lockhart to Blake, 20 Apr. 1899, enclosure 13 in CP171, p. 174.

6. Blake to Stewart Lockhart, 5 May 1899, enclosure 21 in CP204, p. 271; Stewart Lockhart to Blake, 5 May 1899, enclosure 22 in CP204, pp. 272–3.

7. Blake to Stewart Lockhart, 26 Apr. 1899, enclosure 16 in CP172, p. 203; Stewart Lockhart to Blake, 24 Apr. 1899, enclosure 21 in CP171, p. 178.

8. Stewart Lockhart to Blake, 26 Apr. 1899, enclosure 5 in CP204, pp. 247–8; Stewart Lockhart to Blake, 24 Apr. 1899, enclosure 13 in CP172, pp. 200–1; Blake to Chamberlain, tel. (paraphrase), 28 June 1899: CP206, p. 286.

9. Stewart Lockhart to Blake, 22 Apr. 1899, enclosure 10 in CP172, pp. 197–8.

10. Blake to Stewart Lockhart, 23 Apr. 1899, enclosure 11 in CP172, p. 199. And see *China Mail*, 9 Aug. 1899: if the monetary levy 'were in the nature of a fine, why was it not paid into Court in the usual way? But if, as the natives allege, it was compensation to the murdered man's relatives, under what British law was it levied, and by whose authority?'

11. Blake to Stewart Lockhart, 26 Apr. 1899, enclosure 16 in CP172, p. 203; Stewart Lockhart to Blake, 26 Apr. 1899, enclosure 14 in CP172, pp. 201–2.

12. Entry for 25 April: vol. xxxvi, *Stewart Lockhart's Papers*.

13. The perpetrators of the murder, however, received their due reward. With the full co-operation of the viceroy and the district magistrate the fugitives were arrested, and two of them were tried, sentenced to death, and executed. See Stewart Lockhart to Blake, 22 Apr. 1899, enclosure 10 in CP172, p. 198; enclosures 38–42 (4–20 May 1899) in CP204, pp. 281–3; Blake to Chamberlain, tel., 10 July 1899: CP217, p. 299; Blake to Chamberlain, no. 212, 4 Aug. 1899: CP237, p. 331; *Hong Kong Weekly Press*, vol. 1, 5 Aug. 1899, p. 109. Blake later suggested that China pay compensation to the widow as a condition of withdrawal from Sham Chun, but it

was doubted whether the claim was justifiable as the murder had been committed after Great Britain had assumed authority in the New Territories: see Blake to Chamberlain, 26 May 1899: CO129/291, and minute thereon.

14. Lucas to FO, secret, 17 Apr. 1899: CP112, p. 126; director of military intelligence to CO, 21 Apr. 1899: CP124, p. 131; Blake to Hamilton, private, 22 Apr. 1899: CO129/291; Blake to Chamberlain, confidential, 28 Apr. 1899: CP172, p. 189; Bertram Cox to FO, secret, 26 Apr. 1899: CP129, p. 136; White to CO, 25 Apr. 1899: CP126, p. 134.

15. Bax-Ironside to Salisbury, tel. (paraphrase), 20 Apr. 1899, enclosure in CP122, p. 129; Salisbury to Bax-Ironside, confidential, tel., 26 Apr. 1899, enclosure in CP131, p. 137; Bertie to CO, confidential, 1 May 1899: CP136, p. 139.

16. Blake to Chamberlain, tel., 26 Apr. 1899: CP127, p. 135; Lucas to FO, secret, 27 Apr. 1899: CP130, p. 136; Bertie to CO, secret, 28 Apr. 1899: CP133, p. 138; Bax-Ironside to Salisbury, tel. (paraphrase), 7 May 1899, enclosure in CP142, p. 148; Blake to Chamberlain, confidential, no. 186, 13 May 1899: CP186, p. 219; Bax-Ironside to Salisbury, tel., 9 May 1899, enclosure in CP143, p. 149; Chamberlain to Blake, tel. (paraphrase), 14 May 1899: CP155, p. 153.

17. *Hong Kong Weekly Press*, vol. xliv, 20 May 1899, p. 414. See also *China Mail*, 17 May 1899.

18. Buckle to consul, Canton, no. 53, 18 May 1899, enclosure 43 in CP204, p. 283; T'an to Mansfield, 19 and 21 May 1899, enclosures 45 and 47 in CP204, pp. 284–5.

19. Groves, 'Militia, Market and Lineage', p. 39; see also Stewart Lockhart, report, 8 Oct. 1898: CP38, pp. 50, 57; Seymour to Admiralty, 5 June 1899, enclosure in CP232, p. 312.

20. Gascoigne to Blake, 18 May 1899, enclosure 3 in CP202, p. 242.

21. See 'Gambling' in *Old Hong Kong*.

22. The words used in Bax-Ironside to Salisbury, tel. (paraphrase), 7 May 1899, enclosure in CP142, p. 148.

23. Blake to Chamberlain, tel. (paraphrase), 10 May 1899: CP148, p. 150; Blake to Chamberlain, tel., 17 May 1899: CP162, p. 160; Gascoigne to Blake, 18 May 1899, enclosure 3 in CP202, p. 241. For accounts of the occupation of Sham Chun, see also enclosures 1 and 2 in CP202, pp. 238–41; Seymour to Admiralty, 5 June 1899, enclosure in CP232, pp. 312–13; *China Mail*, 18 May 1899; *Hong Kong Weekly Press*, vol. xliv, 20 May 1899, p. 414.

24. Blake to Chamberlain, confidential, 28 Apr. 1899: CP172, p. 190.

25. Blake to Chamberlain, tel. (paraphrase), 21 May 1899: CP163, p. 160; Blake to Chamberlain, tel. (paraphrase), 26 May 1899: CP168, p. 162; Gascoigne to Blake, 26 May 1899, enclosure 5 in CP202, p. 243; Bertie to CO, secret, 27 May 1899: CP173, p. 209; Lucas to FO, secret, 5 June 1899: CP182, p. 217.

26. Chamberlain to Blake, tel. (paraphrase), 13 June 1899: CP187, p. 220.

27. Blake to Chamberlain, tel., 18 June 1899: CP193, p. 235; Blake to Chamberlain, tel. (paraphrase), 24 June 1899: CP200, p. 237; Blake to Chamberlain, tel. (paraphrase), 28 June 1899: CP206, p. 286; Blake to Chamberlain, secret, 19 Aug. 1899: CO129/293; Blake to Chamberlain, confidential, 2 Oct. 1899: CP253, p. 345.

28. See appendix to Colonial Defence Committee, memorandum no. 198M, secret, 28 Oct. 1899: Cab 8/2.

29. Blake to Chamberlain, tel., 3 Nov. 1899: CO129/294.

30. Blake to Chamberlain, tel. (paraphrase), 6 July 1899: CP211, p. 289; and minutes thereon in CO129/292; Blake to Chamberlain, confidential, 20 July 1899: CP233, p. 314. The major obstacle to any form of civil administration was the cost:

see Hamilton's minute on Blake to Chamberlain, confidential, 21 Aug. 1899: CO129/292.

31. Schaub to Blake, 29 May 1899, enclosure 1 in Blake to Chamberlain, no. 129, 31 May 1899: CP208, pp. 287–8; Blake to Chamberlain, tel. (paraphrase), 31 May 1899: CP175, p. 210; Lucas to FO, secret, 31 May 1899: CP176, p. 210; Bertie to CO, confidential, 1 June 1899: CP178, p. 212, and minute thereon by Hamilton: CO129/295; Chamberlain to Blake, tel. (paraphrase), 2 June 1899: CP179, p. 212.

32. T'an to Mansfield, 4 and 5 June 1899, enclosures 1 and 2 in CP215, pp. 291–2; Blake to Chamberlain, confidential, 9 June 1899: CP216, p. 299. This second (though putative) resistance movement was organized by Tang *literati* of Pan Tin: see Groves, 'Militia, Market and Lineage', pp. 52–5.

33. O'Gorman to Gascoigne, 6 June 1899, enclosure 5 in CP215, p. 294; enclosures in Blake to Chamberlain, confidential, 20 July 1899: CP233, pp. 315–22; enclosures in Blake to Chamberlain, confidential, 31 Aug. 1899: CP253, pp. 345–54; enclosures in Blake to Chamberlain, confidential, 17 Aug. 1899 and no. 256, 7 Sept. 1899: CO129/293; enclosures in Blake to Chamberlain, confidential, 8 Dec. 1899: CP288, pp. 377–80.

34. Blake to Chamberlain, confidential, 8 Dec. 1899: CP288, p. 377.

35. Bertie to CO, confidential, 4 Oct. 1899: CP254, p. 355; Lucas to FO, confidential, 9 Oct. 1899: CP255, p. 355; Chamberlain to Blake, tel., 2 Nov. 1899: CP270, pp. 365–6; Gascoigne to Blake, 13 Nov. 1899, enclosure 5 in CP288, p. 377.

36. Wehrle, *Britain, China, and the Antimissionary Riots*, p. 108.

37. Chamberlain to Blake, tel. (paraphrase), 13 June 1899: CP187, p. 220.

38. Colonial Defence Committee, printed remarks no. 218R, 22 June 1899: Cab 9/2; WO to CO, secret, 25 July 1899: CO129/296; Knox to CO, secret, 23 Sept. 1899: CP261, p. 361; Bertie to CO, confidential, 24 Oct. 1899: CP264, p. 363. CO129/295; Lucas to FO, confidential, 9 Oct. 1899: CP255, p. 356; Bertie to CO, confidential, 17 Oct. 1899: CP259, p. 360; Bertram Cox to FO, confidential, 21 Oct. 1899: CP261, p. 361; Bertie to CO, confidential, 24 Oct. 1899: CP264, p. 363.

39. Claude Severn, officer administering the government in Hong Kong, noted the expense of maintenance, the insignificance of the Chinese contribution, and the expensive repairs and reconditioning then required for the Gap Rock lighthouse. He suggested Gap Rock's inclusion in the lease, or at least a far larger contribution by the Chinese government towards the maintenance cost: Severn to Harcourt, confidential, 8 May 1912: CO129/390. London was doubtful, and Sir Francis May, on becoming governor, only wanted the 1888 arrangement reconsidered if cession of the rock was to be sought: May to Harcourt, confidential, 21 Oct. 1912: CO129/392. Sir John Jordan in Peking thought that there was no possibility of the Chinese government entertaining such a suggestion, and the matter was dropped: FO to CO, 25 Oct. 1912: CO129/396. Gap Rock has therefore remained part of China.

40. Blake to Chamberlain, tel., 17 June 1899: CP192, p. 234; Lucas to FO, 21 June 1899: CP194, p. 235; Salisbury to Bax-Ironside, tel. (paraphrase), 23 June 1899, enclosure in CP196, p. 236; Blake to Chamberlain, tel. (paraphrase), 24 June 1899: CP200, p. 237; Bertie to CO, confidential, 24 June 1899: CP201, p. 238; Lucas to FO, secret, 5 July 1899: CP210, p. 289.

41. Bax-Ironside to Salisbury, confidential, 6 July 1899, enclosure in CP238, p. 332; Lucas to FO, secret, 13 Sept. 1899: CP240, p. 334; Villiers to CO, secret, 18 Sept. 1899: CP245, p. 341; Bertie to CO, confidential, 4 Oct. 1899: CP254, p. 355; Lucas to FO, confidential, 9 Oct. 1899: CP255, p. 355; Bertie to CO, confidential, 17 Oct. 1899: CP259, p. 360; Lo Feng-lu to Salisbury, confidential, 17 Oct. 1899, enclosure in CP267, p. 364.

42. Bertram Cox to FO, confidential, 21 Oct. 1899: CP261, p. 361.

43. Schaub to Rowcroft, 1 July 1899, enclosure 6 in CP233, p. 317.

44. Enclosure in Blake to Chamberlain, confidential, 28 Dec. 1899: CP295, p. 384.

45. Lucas to FO, confidential, 13 Sept. 1899: CP239, p. 334.

46. Blake to Chamberlain, no. 145, 14 June 1899: CP223, p. 307; Bertie to CO, 13 Oct. 1899: CP256, p. 357; Chamberlain to Blake, no. 251, 31 Oct. 1899: CP268, p. 365; Lucas to FO, 17 Feb. 1900: CP300, p. 387; Bertie to CO, 3 Mar. 1900: CP304, pp. 392–3.

47. Chamberlain to Blake, no. 178, 8 June 1900: CP311, p. 396.

48. Bertie to CO, confidential, 17 Oct. 1899: CP259, p. 360.

49. Tsungli Yamen to Bax-Ironside, 21 May 1899, enclosure in CP231, p. 311.

50. Blake to Chamberlain, tel. (paraphrase), 30 May 1899: CP174, p. 209.

51. FO to Lo Feng-lu, 30 May 1899, enclosure in CP177, p. 212.

52. Lucas to FO, confidential, 9 Oct. 1899: CP255, p. 356.

53. MacDonald to Salisbury, no. 2, 5 Jan. 1900, enclosure 2 in CP303, p. 389.

54. Memorandum by vice-consul, Canton, 18 Aug. 1933: FO371/17133, p. 167. See also Salisbury to Chamberlain, 27 Apr. 1900: CO129/302; Endacott, *History*, pp. 167–8.

55. See appendix 3.

56. H. H. J. Gompertz, 'Report on the Land Court for 1900': *Hong Kong Government Sessional Papers 1900*, p. 371.

57. Stewart Lockhart to Blake, 24 Apr. 1899, enclosure 26 in CP171, p. 189.

58. Stewart Lockhart to Blake, 29 Apr. 1899, enclosure 13 in CP204, pp. 254–5.

59. Blake to Chamberlain, no. 107, 28 Apr. 1899: CP171, p. 168.

60. Stewart Lockhart to Blake, 24 Apr. 1899, enclosure 26 in CP171, p. 189.

61. Statement by Chau Kwan-nam, 22 Apr. 1899, enclosure 17 in CP204, p. 262.

62. Geoffrey Robley Sayer, *Hong Kong 1862–1919: Years of Discretion* (Hong Kong: Hong Kong University Press, 1975), p. 83.

63. See *Universal Gazette* (Shanghai), 19 May 1899, quoted in *China Mail*, 26 May 1899; *Hong Kong Weekly Press*, vol. xlix, 22 Apr. 1899, p. 323.

64. See note 61, above.

65. *China Mail*, 9 Aug. 1899.

66. Attachment to May to acting colonial secretary, 15 Oct. 1898, enclosure 3 in CP172, pp. 193–4.

67. T. C. Cheng, 'Chinese Unofficial Members of the Legislative and Executive Councils in Hong Kong up to 1941' (1969) 9 *Journal of the Hong Kong Branch of the Royal Asiatic Society* 7, 14, 19.

68. Report by Ho Tung in October 1898, enclosure 6 in CP172, pp. 195–6.

69. Blake to Chamberlain, confidential, 28 Apr. 1899: CP172, p. 190; *Hong Kong Government Gazette 1899*, p. 1376; 'Translations of Miscellaneous Chinese Documents', p. 6, and 'Papers regarding the New Territory, Hong Kong', no. 42, pp. 7–8: vol. iii, *Stewart Lockhart's Papers*.

70. Stewart Lockhart to Blake, 30 Apr. 1899, enclosure 14 in CP204, p. 256. Compare Blake's comments in Blake to Stewart Lockhart, 26 Apr. 1899, enclosure 15 in CP172, p. 202.

71. No reliable information on this man has been discovered. A Mr Li Sing was the prime mover in a plan to establish a new town between Lai Chi Kok and Sham

Shui Po: *China Mail*, 30 Oct. 1895, but it may not be the same man. Ho Tung had named a Mr Lai Hing as the head of the land company for whom Ng Lo-sam and Tang Yung-shen worked: note 68, above.

72. Stewart Lockhart to Blake, 30 Apr. 1899 and 1 May 1899, enclosures 14 and 15 in CP204, pp. 256–7.

73. Stewart Lockhart to Blake, 3 May 1899, enclosure 16 in CP204, p. 258.

74. See Stewart Lockhart's memorandum on Whitehead's protest against the Summoning of Chinese Ordinance: *Hong Kong Government Sessional Papers 1900*, p. 123.

75. Endacott, *History*, p. 265.

76. T'an to Mansfield, 23 Apr. 1899, enclosure 30 in CP204, pp. 276–8; Schiffrin, *Sun Yat-sen*, pp. 215–16; note 68, above; *Hong Kong Government Gazette 1899*, p. 1376.

77. Minute by Lucas regarding the answer to a question in parliament, April 1899: CO129/295; Bax-Ironside to Salisbury, confidential, 30 Apr. 1899, enclosure in CP191, p. 233.

78. Stewart Lockhart to Blake, 1 May 1899, enclosure 17 in CP204, p. 258. Compare Blake to Chamberlain, no. 88, 7 Apr. 1899: CP141, p. 143.

79. This situation arose from the very common perpetual lease system of land tenure. Powerful and well-established lineage groups laid claim to land which they did not themselves till; they often collected a 'tax' which, in some cases, seems to have been a function delegated by the district magistrate. In other cases, however, the tax was either fraudulent or represented a genuine rent paid by the tenant. See memorandum by Gompertz, 9 Jan. 1904, enclosure in May to Lyttelton, no. 221, 20 May 1904: CO129/322. See also J. T. Kamm, 'Taxlordism' (1977) 7 *Journal of the Hong Kong Branch of the Royal Asiatic Society* 68, and pp. 95–6, above.

80. Groves, 'Militia, Market and Lineage', p. 57.

81. Enclosure 6 in CP172, p. 195.

82. See note 61, above. Compare *Hong Kong Government Gazette 1899*, p. 1366.

83. Wakeman, *Strangers at the Gate*, p. 113. A further suggestion as to the motive for the resistance movement is perhaps worth a brief mention. It was said that the British take-over would mean the imposition of a tax on the manufacture of salt and the prohibition of salt smuggling; all those involved in the salt industry were therefore determined to fight for their economic existence: *Hong Kong Weekly Press*, vol. xlix, 20 May 1899, p. 327. But it was in the rice-growing areas (Yuen Long, Kam Tin, Ha Tsuen, Ping Shan) that organization for resistance began, and protection of the salt business is not mentioned in the captured documents or statements of ringleaders.

Notes for Chapter 5

1. See pp. 8, 54–5, above.

2. Stewart Lockhart, report, 8 Oct. 1898: CP38, pp. 46–9.

3. See minutes on Stewart Lockhart's report referred to in the previous note: CO129/289.

4. Chamberlain to Blake, confidential, 6 Jan. 1899: CP62, p. 92.

5. See note 3, above.

6. See appendix 2.

7. See appendix 5.

8. The Hong Kong Extension Exemption Ordinance (no. 10 of 1899). See W. Meigh Goodman, 'Memorandum on Some Legal Aspects of the Hong Kong Extension' (Dec. 1898): CP51, pp. 81-4.

9. The text is in MacMurray, *Treaties and Agreements*, vol. i, pp. 152-3.

10. Minute by Sir Robert G. W. Herbert on Bertie to CO, confidential, 13 Dec. 1899: CO521/1.

11. Report by the law officers, 22 Feb. 1899: FO834/69.

12. Bertie to CO, confidential, 22 Oct. 1900: CO521/1. 'I want to warn you that for political reasons it was considered desirable not to treat the leased territory at [Weihaiwei] as the leased territory at Hong Kong, but to treat it more on the lines of a Protectorate': Lucas to Stewart Lockhart, private, 30 Jan. 1902: vol. xi, *Stewart Lockhart's Papers*.

13. See R. F. Johnston, *Lion and Dragon in Northern China* (London: John Murray, 1910), p. 428.

14. See pp. 177-84, above.

15. See, generally, D. M. Emrys Evans, 'Common Law in a Chinese Setting— the Kernel or the Nut?' (1971) 1 HKLJ 9; Evans, 'The New Law of Succession in Hong Kong' (1973) 3 HKLJ 7. Chinese law was retained primarily in the area of family law (marriage, succession, adoption, and legitimacy). These aspects are now governed by a package of statutes enacted in the early 1970s.

16. cap. 97, LHK 1964 ed.

17. Strickland committee, *Chinese Law and Custom in Hong Kong* (Hong Kong: Government Printer, 1953), p. 7.

18. *Tang Kai-chung* v. *Tang Chik-shang* [1970] HKLR 276.

19. The problems associated with the identification and application of customary law need not be considered here. Useful sources of information and opinion include H. McAleavy, 'Chinese Law in Hong Kong: The Choice of Sources', in J. N. D. Anderson (ed.), *Changing Law in Developing Countries* (London: George Allen and Unwin, 1963), pp. 258-69; E. S. Haydon, 'The Choice of Chinese Customary Law in Hong Kong' (1962) 11 *International and Comparative Law Quarterly* 231; Haydon, 'Chinese Customary Law in Hong Kong's New Territories' (unpublished MS, undated but 1962); *Wong Kam-ying* v. *Man Chi-tai* [1967] HKLR 201, 211.

20. *Hong Kong Government Sessional Papers 1900*, p. 280.

21. See 'Memorandum on Land', ibid., pp. 266-9; Bruce Shepherd, 'Memorandum of Work Done in the Land Office, Hong Kong, in respect of the New Territories for the Year 1899', ibid., pp. 277-9; Stewart Lockhart, 'Report on the New Territory During the First Year of British Administration', ibid., pp. 253-7; H. H. J. Gompertz, 'Some Notes on Land Tenure in the New Territory', *Hong Kong Government Gazette 1901*, pp. 1395-400; memorandum by Gompertz, 9 Jan. 1904, enclosure in May to Lyttelton, no. 221, 20 May 1904: CO129/322. See also H. G. H. Nelson, 'British Land Administration in the New Territories of Hong Kong, and its Effects on Chinese Social Organisation' (unpublished paper presented at the conference of the London-Cornell project for East and Southeast Asian studies, August 1969).

22. Stewart Lockhart to Fiddian, private, 15 May 1900: CO129/298.

23. See enclosure in Blake to Chamberlain, no. 126, 30 Mar. 1900: ibid.

24. Whitehead to Chamberlain, 24 Mar. 1900: CO129/303.

25. Emphasis in original; see note 23, above.

26. See the report by Gompertz on the work of the Land Court up to 31 December 1901, in *Hong Kong Government Gazette 1901*, p. 702.

27. Memorandum by Cecil Clementi, 23 Feb. 1904, enclosure in May to Lyttelton, no. 221, 20 May 1904: CO129/322.

28. See note 79, chapter 4, above.

29. ibid.

30. See note 27, above.

31. May to Lyttelton, no. 221, 20 May 1904: CO129/322.

32. Memorandum by Gompertz on the ownership of Tsing Yi: *Hong Kong Government Gazette 1901*, pp. 1403-4.

33. Potter, *Capitalism and the Chinese Peasant*, p. 100.

34. Messer to May, 18 Feb. 1905: *Hong Kong Government Gazette 1905*, p. 411. Gompertz implied that the Kam Tin branch of the Tang lineage were 'responsible for the collection of the tax over half of what is now the New Territory': see note 28, above.

35. See Blake to Chamberlain, no. 289, 17 June 1903: CO129/317; Blake to Chamberlain, confidential, 20 Aug. 1903: CO129/318; minute by crown solicitor, enclosure in May to Lyttelton, no. 10, 9 Jan. 1904: CO129/322.

36. See minutes on May to Elgin, no. 125, 13 May 1907: CO129/340.

37. Report by Gompertz on the work of the Land Court in 1903, enclosure in May to Lyttelton, no. 58, 18 Feb. 1904; minute by crown solicitor enclosed in May to Lyttelton, no. 140, 29 Mar. 1904: CO129/322.

38. Report by Shepherd on the work of the Land Office in 1899: *Hong Kong Government Sessional Papers 1900*, p. 279.

39. Minute by Goodman enclosed in Blake to Chamberlain, no. 192, 21 May 1901: CO129/305.

40. Chamberlain to Blake, 4 July 1901: ibid.

41. Initially, by the Foreshores and Seabed Ordinance (no. 21 of 1901). See Geoffrey Marston, 'Colonial Enactments Relating to the Legal Status of Offshore Submerged Lands' (1976) 50 *Australian Law Journal* 402. The Colonial Office was displeased with alternative arrangements and insisted that compensation be given: see minutes on Blake to Chamberlain, no. 462, 2 Oct. 1903: CO129/318.

42. Petitioners to Lyttelton, 8 Aug. 1905: CO129/338.

43. Nathan to Elgin, no. 263, 23 Oct. 1906: CO129/335.

44. Enclosure 2 in ibid.

45. Chamberlain to Blake, confidential, 6 Jan. 1899: CP62, p. 96.

46. New Territories (Renewable Crown Leases) Ordinance (cap. 152, LHK 1969 ed.), s. 4(3) (a) and (b). It may be that the Executive Council refrained from increasing crown rent because of the promise made in 1906: see *LegCo Proc 1969*, p. 232. Not all land in the New Territories, however, was dealt with by cap. 152; the leases of all other lots were renewed under the Crown Leases Ordinance (no. 75 of 1973; cap. 40, LHK 1973 ed.), and a re-assessed rent is now being paid. For the discussion leading to a reduction in the proposed new crown rents see *LegCo Proc 1971-72*, pp. 725-64, 782. See also *LegCo Proc 1972-73*, pp. 609-12.

47. Nathan to Lyttelton, no. 178, 13 July 1905: CO129/329.

48. *Hong Kong Hansard 1899*, p. 35.

49. Memoranda, enclosures 1 and 2 in Clementi to Amery, secret, 27 Feb. 1929, in FO371/13949, pp. 357-9, 360-4.

50. Ashton-Gwatkin to CO, 25 Apr. 1929, in ibid., p. 366.

51. Enclosure in Beckett to FO, confidential, 8 Aug. 1928: FO371/13235, pp. 61–2; Mounsey to CO, 8 Sept. 1928: ibid., pp. 66–8.

52. See Stewart Lockhart, 'Report on the New Territory during the First Year of British Administration', *Hong Kong Government Sessional Papers 1900*, p. 252.

53. Stubbs to Amery, no. 304, 5 Aug. 1925: CO129/489, p. 11; see also G. N. Orme, 'Report on the New Territories, 1899–1912', *Hong Kong Government Sessional Papers 1912*, p. 155.

54. *Pong Wai-ting* v. *Attorney-General of Hong Kong* (1925) 20 HKLR 22.

55. See pp. 172–3, above.

56. Stubbs to Amery, no. 304, 5 Aug. 1925: CO129/489, pp. 8–9.

57. Clementi to Amery, no. 387, 1 Sept. 1926: CO129/494, p. 36.

58. ibid., p. 27.

59. ibid.

60. Stubbs to Amery, no. 304, 5 Aug. 1925: CO129/489, p. 10.

61. Amery to Clementi, confidential, 12 Feb. 1927: CO129/494, p. 18.

62. See pp. 173–4, above.

Notes for Chapter 6

1. See J. R. V. Prescott, *The Geography of Frontiers and Boundaries* (London: Hutchinson, 1965), p. 20; A. O. Cukwurah, *The Settlement of Boundary Disputes in International Law* (Manchester: Manchester University Press, 1967), pp. 16–85; Peter Lyon, 'Regional Organisations and Frontier Disputes', in Evan Luard (ed.), *The International Regulation of Frontier Disputes* (London: Thames and Hudson, 1970), pp. 111–13; Surya P. Sharma, *International Boundary Disputes and International Law* (Bombay: N. M. Tripathi, 1976), pp. 29–37.

2. Minute on Lugard to Crewe, confidential, 2 Feb. 1910: CO129/365.

3. Blake to Chamberlain, no. 282, date uncertain but September or October 1899, and enclosures: CO129/294.

4. Law officers to CO, 1 Jan. 1900: CP286, p. 376.

5. On law officers to CO, 1 Jan. 1900: CO129/302.

6. MacGregor to CO, 13 Feb. 1900: CP298, p. 386.

7. Lucas to FO, 23 Feb. 1900: CP301, p. 388; Bertie to CO, 27 Feb. 1900: CP302, p. 388.

8. Bertie to CO, 11 Jan. 1900: CP290, p. 381; Lucas to FO, 26 Jan. 1900: CP293, p. 383.

9. See *Ch'ing Mo Tui Wai Chiao She T'iao Yo Chi* (Taipei: Kuo Feng, 1963), pp. 408–11 (privately translated).

10. See Marston, 'Colonial Enactments', pp. 404–5. For a discussion of the colony's territorial waters, see pp. 120–2, above.

11. See James Hayes, 'The San On Map of Mgr Volonteri [*sic*]' (1970) 10 *Journal of the Hong Kong Branch of the Royal Asiatic Society* 193; Ronald C. Y. Ng, 'The San On Map of Mgr Volonteri' (1969) 9 *Journal of the Hong Kong Branch of the Royal Asiatic Society* 141.

12. Enclosure 1 in Blake to Chamberlain, no. 53, 10 Mar. 1899: CP93, p. 113.

13. Gascoigne to Chamberlain, no. 266, 6 June 1900: CO129/299.

14. See enclosure 3 in CP159, p. 158.

15. Minute on Gascoigne to Chamberlain, no. 303, 22 June 1900: CO129/299.

16. CO to FO, 18 Aug. 1900: CO129/299.

17. FO to CO, 15 Oct. 1900: CO129/302.

18. CO to director of military intelligence, 12 Nov. 1900: CO129/302.

19. Blake to Chamberlain, confidential, 18 July 1901: CO129/305.

20. See the opinion regarding the national status of inhabitants: law officers to CO, 27 Sept. 1899: CP252, p. 344.

21. Bertie to CO, 10 Jan. 1902: CO129/314.

22. The disagreement concerning territorial extent is principally a disagreement concerning the effect of *Keyn*'s case (1876) 2 Ex D 63. Cases illustrating opposing views are *Secretary of State for India* v. *Chelikani Rama Rao* (1916) 85 LJ PC 222 and *New South Wales* v. *The Commonwealth* (1975) 8 ALR 1.

23. Marston, 'Colonial Enactments', pp. 407–8.

24. Quoted in D. P. O'Connell and Ann Riordan, *Opinions on Imperial Constitutional Law* (Sydney, Melbourne, Brisbane: Law Book Co., 1971), p. 218.

25. Lugard to Crewe, confidential, 2 Feb. 1910: CO129/365. The quoted inscription is contained in Lugard's despatch, but it differs from the actual inscription as transcribed in December 1972 from the southern face of the northern stone, which reads as follows:

1902

This stone is in longitude 113° 52′E fixed by Lieut & Com^r F M Leake RN & the officers of HMS Bramble.

From here the boundary line extends due north until it meets the parallel of the southern extremity of the Nam-Tau Peninsula. Southward the boundary follows the western shore of Lantao Island.

26. Minute on May to Crewe, confidential, 8 Oct. 1910: CO129/369.

27. Minute on Lugard to Crewe, confidential, 2 Feb. 1910: CO129/365.

28. CO to FO, 28 May 1910, in CO129/365.

29. FO to CO, 11 June 1910: CO129/372. See also Crewe to May, confidential, 16 June 1910: CO129/372.

30. Enclosure in FO to CO, 17 Oct. 1910: CO129/373.

31. May to Crewe, confidential, 8 Oct. 1910: CO129/369.

32. Severn to Harcourt, tel., confidential, 7 May 1912: CO129/390.

33. FO to CO, 29 Jan. 1919: CO129/457.

34. Brenan to Cushenden, 30 Aug. 1928, in CO129/507.

35. Minute on Clementi to Amery, confidential, 23 Jan. 1929: CO129/515 (62811).

36. Barnes to CO, confidential, 28 Dec. 1935: CO129/558 (53711).

37. Cowell to Admiralty, confidential, 13 Feb. 1936: ibid.

38. See pp. 147–8, 181–2, above.

39. See FO371/20977, pp. 47–55.

40. United States Department of State, 'International Boundary Study: China—Hong Kong' (Washington: intelligence bulletin no. 13, April 1964), p. 1. For material on China's claim to a twelve-mile territorial sea, see Cohen and Chiu, *People's China and International Law*, pp. 470–97, 528–58.

41. US Department of State, 'International Boundary Study', p. 3.

42. *Hong Kong's Border with China* (no author, no publisher, no date, no pagination; probably published by the Hong Kong government in early 1968).

43. *Annual Report 1948*, p. 2.

44. See 'Exchange of Notes between the Government of the Chinese Republic and His Majesty's Government in the United Kingdom... for the Prevention of Smuggling between Hong Kong and Chinese Ports' (12 Jan. 1948), reproduced in Yin Ching-chen, *Treaties and Agreements between the Republic of China and Other Powers, 1929–1954* (Washington: Sino-American Publishing Service, 1957). Pursuant to this agreement the Hong Kong legislature enacted the Smuggling into China (Control) Ordinance (no. 51 of 1948; now cap. 242, LHK 1964 ed.).

45. *Hong Kong's Border with China*.

46. See T. G. Cooper, *Colony in Conflict* (Hong Kong: Swindon, 1970), pp. 186–213; *Annual Report 1967*, pp. 12–13; Cohen and Chiu, *People's China and International Law*, pp. 809–10.

47. Cukwurah, *The Settlement of Boundary Disputes*, p. 48.

48. Hazel Fox, 'Arbitration', in Luard, *The International Regulation of Frontier Disputes*, pp. 182–3.

49. Interpretation Ordinance (no. 2 of 1950).

50. Interpretation and General Clauses Ordinance (no. 31 of 1966; cap. 1, LHK 1975 ed.), second schedule.

51. See p. 110, above.

52. *Oyekan* v. *Adele* [1957] 2 All ER 785, 789. See chap. 10, note 36, below.

53. Appendix 2.

54. Either because it represents an acquisition of territory or because it is in exercise of a prerogative power to determine sea boundaries. For a critical examination of the latter power, see W. R. Edeson, 'The Prerogative of the Crown to Delimit Britain's Maritime Boundary' (1973) 89 *Law Quarterly Review* 364.

Notes for Chapter 7

1. *South China Morning Post*, 24 Apr. 1975.

2. See pp. 17–19, 36–8, 72–3, 81–2, above.

3. See appendix 3.

4. *Hong Kong Weekly Press*, vol. lix, 2 May 1904, pp. 338–9.

5. Stubbs to Amery, 26 June 1925: CO129/488.

6. Peplow and Barker, *Hong Kong, Around and About*, p. 10.

7. The 1901 census report states that there were 5,088 people in Kowloon City and 12,155 in nearby villages, out of 102,254 people in all of Kowloon south of the range: *Hong Kong Government Gazette 1901*, p. 1701. In 1911 the 'Kowloon City district' population numbered 6,325, the police inspector in charge reporting that 'nearly all Chinese, who acquire a certain amount of education, try to leave the place in order to seek their fortunes elsewhere': *Hong Kong Government Sessional Papers 1911*, pp. 103(4) and (39). The 1921 figures showed an increase of 2,181, 'partly accounted for by the presence of workmen engaged on the various works of improvement now in progress': *Hong Kong Government Sessional Papers 1921*, pp. 155, 173. By 1931 the district contained 22,634 people: *Hong Kong Government Sessional Papers 1931*, p. 104.

8. *Hong Kong Government Sessional Papers 1921*, p. 155.

9. T. R. Tregear and L. Berry, *The Development of Hong Kong and Kowloon as Told in Maps* (Hong Kong: University of Hong Kong Press, 1959), p. 19.

10. Peel to Cunliffe-Lister, confidential, 9 Jan. 1934, enclosure in Cowell to FO, 26 Feb. 1934: FO371/18140, pp. 184–6. See, especially, the enclosed plans for redevelopment of the Walled City, which included an open space 120 ft. wide on three sides. These plans were never carried out.

11. Orde to CO, 9 Mar. 1934: ibid., pp. 193–6. See also Ingram to FO, tel. no. 214, 23 Mar. 1934: ibid., p. 198, and Peel to Cunliffe-Lister, tel. no. 82, 2 June 1934, in ibid., p. 211.

12. Peel to Cunliffe-Lister, tel. no. 98, 6 July 1934, and no. 103, 16 July 1934: CO129/546 (33744); FO to Cadogan, tel. no. 473, 27 July 1934: FO371/18140, pp. 227–8; Peel to Cunliffe-Lister, tel. no. 112, 9 Aug. 1934: ibid., p. 241.

13. Wai Chiao Pu to Cadogan, 7 Sept. 1934: ibid., pp. 258–61.

14. Peel to Cadogan, confidential, no. 32, 1 Oct. 1934, in ibid., pp. 269–71; Cadogan to FO, tel. no. 659, 20 Oct. 1934: ibid., pp. 264–5.

15. Randall to Cadogan, tel. no. 364, 23 Oct. 1934: ibid., p. 266; 'Notes on Questions . . . Kowloon City Evictions' (7 Dec. 1934): FO371/19308, p. 398.

16. Smith to MacDonald, tel. no. 172, 18 July 1935, in FO371/19334, p. 20.

17. Cadogan to FO, tel. no. 647, 3 July 1935: ibid., p. 11.

18. MacDonald to Smith, tel. no. 126, 9 Aug. 1935, in ibid., p. 27.

19. Caldecott to Ormsby-Gore, tel. no. 54, 31 Mar. 1937, in FO371/20990, p. 27; see also p. 30.

20. Knatchbull-Hugessen to Caldecott, tel. no. 130, 3 May 1937, in ibid., pp. 39–40.

21. Smith to Ormsby-Gore, confidential, 23 June 1937, in ibid., p. 73.

22. Lai Chun-wai (comp.), *Centenary History of Hong Kong* (Hong Kong: Nam Chun Pin Yick Publishing House, undated but probably prepared in 1941 and published in 1948; in Chinese, privately translated), p. 87.

23. *Hong Kong Telegraph*, 6 Dec. 1947; *South China Morning Post*, 7 Dec. 1947.

24. According to the *South China Morning Post*, 17 Dec. 1947, a magistrate had made, the day before, an order for eviction and demolition and removal of material from the Walled City.

25. See Lai Chun-wai, *Centenary History*, pp. 98–101; *South China Morning Post* and *Hong Kong Telegraph*, 6 Dec. 1947, 12–14, 16 and 17 Jan. 1948.

26. *Hong Kong Telegraph*, 19 and 28 Jan. 1948.

27. At p. 3. And see 'Report of the Commissioner of Police for the Year 1947/48', p. 16.

28. Alexander Grantham, *Via Ports: From Hong Kong to Hong Kong* (Hong Kong: University of Hong Kong Press, 1965), p. 132.

29. *Re Wong Hon* [1959] HKLR 601. See pp. 169–70, above.

30. *Survey of China Mainland Press*, no. 2903, 22 Jan. 1963, pp. 26–7; the full text is in Cohen and Chiu, *People's China and International Law*, pp. 377–9.

31. Quoted by P. H. M. Jones, *Golden Guide to Hong Kong and Macau* (Hong Kong: Far Eastern Economic Review, 1969), p. 256.

32. Simon Head notes: 'Peking was clearly unaware of the Government's plans to resettle all those displaced and to help those carrying on trades to continue them in their new surroundings. Moreover, the Chinese Government had not consulted the poorer tenants in the Walled City before making its protests—and they were only too

happy to be resettled': *Far Eastern Economic Review*, 20 Feb. 1969, p. 333. See, generally, *South China Morning Post*, 18, 19, 22, and 23 Jan. 1963; *South China Sunday Post Herald*, 20 Jan. 1963.

33. *Hsinhua News Agency*, 29 July 1967, p. 3 (capitals added). The headmaster had failed to appear on a charge of assault and obstruction, and a warrant had been issued for his arrest: *South China Morning Post*, 25 July 1967.

34. *South China Morning Post*, 24 June 1970.

35. *Golden Guide*, p. 259.

36. For further speculations on this theme see Peter Wesley-Smith, 'The Walled City of Kowloon and its Law Today', in Marjorie Topley (ed.), *Hong Kong: The Interaction of Traditions and Life in the Towns* (Hong Kong: Hong Kong Branch of the Royal Asiatic Society, 1975), pp. 119–29.

37. Frank Leeming, *Street Studies in Hong Kong* (Hong Kong: Oxford University Press, 1977), p. 156.

38. See *South China Morning Post*, 27, 28, and 30 Dec. 1972, 30 Jan. 1973; *Sunday Post-Herald*, 7 Jan. 1973.

39. cap. 301, LHK 1974 ed.

40. See *South China Morning Post*, 9–11 June 1975; *Hong Kong Standard*, 3 July 1975; *Star*, 9 July 1975.

41. See, for example, *South China Morning Post*, 17 and 24 Jan. 1973, 17 Mar. 1973, 8 Nov. 1974, 9 Feb. 1975; *Sunday Post-Herald*, 20 May 1973; *Hong Kong Standard*, 24 Aug. 1973, 16 Sept. 1973, 11 Nov. 1973, 3 and 4 Dec. 1974.

42. *China Mail*, 18 Jan. 1973.

43. See all Hong Kong English-language newspapers of 13 June 1974.

44. HL Deb, 11 June 1974, vol. 352, col. 471.

45. ibid., col. 475.

46. *South China Morning Post*, 9 Apr. 1978.

Notes for Chapter 8

1. See pp. 48–51, above.

2. See memorandum by Blake, 22 Feb. 1902, enclosure in Blake to Chamberlain, 6 Mar. 1902: CO129/315.

3. The Arms and Ammunition Ordinance (no. 9 of 1900).

4. See Wright, *China's Struggle*, p. 317.

5. See Chinese Imperial Maritime Customs, *Decennial Report*, pp. 203–5.

6. See Lugard to Harcourt, confidential, 11 Feb. 1911: CO129/375.

7. See Clementi to Passfield, secret, 1 Aug. 1929: CO129/517 (62847).

8. Memorandum by A. H. Harris, 14 Jan. 1910, enclosure in Lugard to Crewe, confidential, 28 Apr. 1910; minute by Robinson on May to Crewe, confidential, 4 May 1910; Fiddes to FO, immediate, 17 June 1910; Campbell to CO, 29 June 1910: CO129/365.

9. Lampson to FO, no. 1587, 31 Oct. 1930, in CO129/531 (82755).

10. See Yin, *Treaties and Agreements*, pp. 393–9, 424–5, and p. 117, above.

11. For details of these arrangements, see Fleming to Knutsford, no. 228, 11 July 1890 and no. 293, 15 Aug. 1890: CO129/245; Sanderson to CO, confidential, 2 Sept.

1890: CO129/248; Nathan to Lyttelton, no. 364, 10 Oct. 1904: CO129/324; Lugard to Harcourt, confidential, 13 Mar. 1911, and minutes thereon: CO129/376; a memorandum prepared by the Foreign Office, 1 Oct. 1927, and MacKillop to Caine, 26 Aug. 1929: CO129/518 (62882). For a copy of the Chinese telegraph convention of 1896, see *Hertslet's China Treaties* (London: HMSO, 1908), vol. ii, pp. 1140–8.

12. Enclosure 1 in Nathan to Lyttelton, no. 364, 10 Oct. 1904: CO129/324.

13. See Lyttelton to Nathan, tel., 21 Nov. 1904: CO489/8.

14. Nathan to Lyttelton, no. 364, 10 Oct. 1904: CO129/324.

15. Lugard to Crewe, confidential, 3 Sept. 1908: CO129/348.

16. ibid.

17. Jordan to Grey, no. 575, 21 Dec. 1908, enclosure in Campbell to CO, 27 Jan. 1909: CO129/360.

18. Lugard to Crewe, confidential, 12 May 1909: CO129/356.

19. See May to Harcourt, confidential, 14 Nov. 1912: CO129/393.

20. The 1883–4 agreements then expired and were not renewed by the Chinese government: see Ingram to FO, no. 70, 17 Jan. 1930, in CO129/524 (72802).

21. Minute on Campbell to CO, 5 Sept. 1911: CO129/384.

22. See Chinese Imperial Maritime Customs, *Decennial Report*, pp. 213–14.

23. Minute by Robinson on May to Crewe, confidential, 9 June 1910: CO129/367; Clive Parry (ed.), *A British Digest of International Law Compiled Principally from the Archives of the Foreign Office: Phase One, 1860–1914* (London: Stevens, 1967), vol. v, pp. 149, 393–5.

24. See memorandum by Sir J. Walsham, enclosure in Sanderson to CO, 16 June 1892: CO129/257.

25. Memorandum, 17 July 1899, enclosure 2 in Blake to Chamberlain, no. 196, 21 July 1899: CP234, p. 323.

26. Law officers to CO, 27 Sept. 1899: CP252, p. 344; Parry, *British Digest of International Law*, vol. v, p. 404.

27. Yuan to Jamieson, 8 Nov. 1909, enclosure 2 in Jamieson to Jordan, no. 118, 29 Dec. 1909, in CO129/371.

28. Jordan to Grey, 19 Jan. 1910, in ibid.

29. Campbell to CO, 25 Jan. 1910: ibid.

30. Lugard to Harcourt, confidential, 16 Oct. 1911: CO129/380; Parry, *British Digest of International Law*, vol. v, p. 404.

31. Campbell to CO, 25 May 1910: CO129/372.

32. Minute by Robinson on May to Crewe, confidential, 9 June 1910: CO129/367. Compare the situation of a fugitive born in the New Territories who commits a crime in China and escapes to Hong Kong: p. 176, above.

33. Satow to CO, no. 410, 29 Nov. 1905, in CO129/336.

34. Minute referred to in ibid.

35. See Lugard to Harcourt, confidential, 16 Oct. 1911, its enclosures and minutes thereon: CO129/380.

36. See Tsai Chu-tung, 'The Chinese Nationality Law, 1909' (1910) IV *American Journal of International Law* 404–11 and supplement, p. 160.

37. The whole issue can be followed in this correspondence: May to Crewe, confidential, 9 June 1910: CO129/367; Campbell to CO, 5 Apr. 1911: CO129/383; Campbell to CO, 16 Sept. 1911: CO129/384; FO to CO, 27 Oct. 1911: CO129/385;

Lugard to Harcourt, confidential, 23 Nov. 1911: CO129/381; FO to CO, 29 June 1912: CO129/395; May to Harcourt, confidential, 14 Jan. 1913: CO129/399. See also the following files: CO129/501 (30014); CO129/507 (52710); CO129/523 (72770); CO129/543 (13798); CO323/1057 (62894/61127); CO825/18 (34025). And see Cohen and Chiu, *People's China and International Law*, pp. 746-9.

38. See the British Nationality Act 1981. Clive Parry, *Nationality and Citizen-ship Laws of the Commonwealth and of the Republic of Ireland* (London: Stevens, 1957), pp. 152 and 230, says that the territorial limits of Hong Kong, for the purposes of nationality, probably include the New Territories.

39. See D. P. O'Connell, *International Law* (London: Stevens, 2nd ed. 1970), vol. ii, pp. 743-6.

40. See pp. 47-8, above.

41. See, for instance, Ching-lin Hsia, *Studies in Chinese Diplomatic History* (Shanghai: Commercial Press, 1926), pp. 110-13, and Harold Scott Quigley, 'The Shantung Question in International Law' (1921) 6 *Chinese Social and Political Science Review* 71, 84-5.

42. Fitzmaurice, 'Position of Leased Territory in China during War', enclosure in Orde to Moore, 29 Sept. 1937: CO129/564 (53852).

43. See a further memorandum by Fitzmaurice in FO371/20977, p. 51.

44. Moore to Orde, 11 Oct. 1937: CO129/564 (53852).

45. Orde to Moore, 22 Oct. 1937: ibid. The neutrality question is further discussed at pp. 181-2, above.

Notes for Chapter 9

1. See Mary C. Wright (ed.), *China in Revolution: The First Phase, 1900-1913* (New Haven: Yale University Press, 1968), pp. 1-30; Schrecker, *Imperialism and Chinese Nationalism*, pp. 43-58, 250-8.

2. See Mrs Archibald Little, *Li Hung-chang: His Life and Times* (London, Paris, New York and Melbourne: Cassell, 1903), p. 304.

3. *China in Revolution*, p. 7.

4. Chow Tse-tung, *The May Fourth Movement* (Cambridge, Mass.: Harvard University Press, 1965), pp. 19-40.

5. ibid., p. 86; Wesley R. Fishel, *The End of Extraterritoriality in China* (New York: Octagon Books, 1974; first published in 1952), p. 36; Clive John Christie, 'The Problem of China in British Foreign Policy, 1917-1921', unpublished Ph.D. thesis, University of Cambridge, 1971, pp. 80-2.

6. Jordan to FO, tel. no. 63, 1 Feb. 1919: FO608/209.

7. See ibid., p. 292; John K. Fairbank, Edwin O. Reischauer and Albert M. Craig, *East Asia: The Modern Transformation* (London: Allen and Unwin, 1965), p. 655.

8. Christie, 'The Problem of China', p. 87.

9. Jordan to FO, tel. (paraphrase), no. 46, 23 Jan. 1919: FO608/209, pp. 341-2.

10. Minute dated 21 Jan. 1919: ibid., p. 340; see also note 8, above; Tilley to CO, 23 Feb. 1919: FO608/209, p. 353; CO to FO, 31 Jan. 1919: ibid., p. 343.

11. See Choate to Salisbury, 15 Nov. 1899, and reply, in CO129/295.

12. FO608/209, p. 325. See, generally, Young, *The Rhetoric of Empire*, chap. 6,

and Mingchien Joshua Bau, *The Open Door Doctrine in relation to China* (New York: Macmillan, 1923).

13. Quoted by Robert T. Pollard, *China's Foreign Relations, 1917–1931* (New York: Macmillan, 1933), p. 68.

14. See minute by Ronald Macleay on the Chinese memorandum of April 1919, in FO608/209, p. 313. Macleay submitted that 'we are not called upon to . . . give any promise of support'.

15. ibid., pp. 321–2; Pollard, *China's Foreign Relations*, pp. 73–5.

16. Fishel, *The End of Extraterritoriality*, p. 40; Ian H. Nish, *Alliance in Decline: A Study in Anglo-Japanese Relations 1908–23* (London: Athlone Press, 1972), pp. 272–4.

17. This is a favourite subject for historians, who have analysed and continue to analyse the conference from many different angles. See the bibliographical references in Robert H. Van Meter, Jr., 'The Washington Conference of 1921–1922: A New Look' (1977) 46 *Pacific Historical Review* 603.

18. W. N. Medlicott, *British Foreign Policy Since Versailles, 1919–1963* (London: Methuen, 1968), p. 20.

19. Barbara W. Tuchman, *Stilwell and the American Experience in China, 1911–1945* (New York: Macmillan, 1971), p. 84.

20. Chow, *The May Fourth Movement*, p. 86; Pollard, *China's Foreign Relations*, pp. 206–9; Raymond Leslie Buell, *The Washington Conference* (New York and London: Appleton, 1922), pp. 259–60.

21. Wellesley to CO, 22 Aug. 1921: CO537/747.

22. On ibid.

23. Grindle to FO, secret, 15 Sept. 1921: CO537/747; FO371/6645, pp. 50–6. The Standing Defence Sub-Committee of the Committee of Imperial Defence considered the question on 13 October 1921 and was generally opposed to the idea of abandoning the leased territory. The War Office was especially concerned at any suggestion of rendition. See ibid., pp. 63–72.

24. See Yamato Ichihashi, *The Washington Conference and After: A Historical Survey* (Stanford: Stanford University Press, 1928), pp. 160–6; Westel W. Willoughby, *Foreign Rights and Interests in China* (Baltimore: Johns Hopkins Press, 1927), vol. i, pp. 483–90; Mingchien Joshua Bau, *The Foreign Relations of China: A History and a Survey* (New York, Chicago, London and Edinburgh: Fleming H. Revell Co., 2nd ed. 1922), pp. 479–82.

25. Buell, *The Washington Conference*, p. 266.

26. Wm. Roger Louis, *British Strategy in the Far East 1919–1939* (Oxford: Clarendon Press, 1971), p. 106.

27. Christie, 'The Problem of China', p. 212.

28. See minutes of 12th meeting, 3 Dec. 1921: Cab 30/14, pp. 108–10, and Westel W. Willoughby, *China at the Conference: A Report* (Baltimore: Johns Hopkins Press, 1922), chap. 14.

29. Minutes of 13th meeting, 7 Dec. 1921: Cab 30/14, pp. 152–5.

30. Lugard to Crewe, secret, 26 May 1909: CO129/355.

31. Buell, *The Washington Conference*, p. 269.

32. Fishel, *The End of Extraterritoriality*, p. 52.

33. Johnston to Teichman, 25 Jan. 1930, in FO371/114697, p. 266.

34. Hungdah Chiu, 'Comparison of the Nationalist and Communist Chinese Views of Unequal Treaties', in Jerome Allen Cohen (ed.), *China's Practice of Interna-*

tional Law: Some Case Studies (Cambridge, Mass.: Harvard University Press, 1972), pp. 244–50.

35. See May to Lyttelton, confidential, 17 June 1904: CO129/323; Lugard to Crewe, secret, 26 May 1909: CO129/355; Severn to Harcourt, confidential, tel., 7 May 1912: CO129/390.

36. See minute in FO371/15484. Ten years later he suggested offering terms for an honourable agreement ceding the New Territories in perpetuity: 'The Future of Hong Kong' (1936) V *United Empire* XXVII, 22, at p. 24.

37. Clementi to Amery, secret, 19 Jan. 1926: CO129/491.

38. Clementi to Amery, tel., 19 Jan. 1927, in FO371/12399, p. 135; see also Clementi to Amery, secret, 27 Nov. 1926, in FO371/12469, p. 164 et seq.

39. Lampson to FO, tel. no. 145, 21 Jan. 1927: FO371/12399, p. 134.

40. Amery to Clementi, tel., 18 Feb. 1927, in FO371/12469, p. 168; minute on Clementi to Amery, tel., 19 Jan. 1927, in FO371/12399, p. 132. In December 1926 Walter Ellis of the Colonial Office minuted: 'I hope it may be possible to obtain from the new Government of China when established a cession of the New Territories in substitution for our present lease, in return for any concessions we may take regarding tariffs and extraterritoriality': on Clementi to Amery, no. 387, 1 Sept. 1926: CO129/494, p. 5. See also CO129/503 (30055).

41. Clementi to Amery, secret, personal, 26 Mar. 1927, in FO371/12498, p. 244.

42. See ibid., pp. 252–3, and memorandum by Sir W. Peel, enclosure in Shuckburgh to Wellesley, confidential, private, 31 Aug. 1927: FO371/15484, p. 514.

43. Enclosure in Beckett to FO, confidential, 8 Aug. 1928: FO371/13235, pp. 62–3.

44. On Clementi to Amery, secret, 27 Feb. 1929: CO129/513 (62723).

45. Mounsey to CO, 8 Sept. 1928, in FO371/13235, p. 68.

46. Memorandum by G. W. Swire, enclosure in Swire to Orde, 27 Jan. 1930: FO371/14724, p. 63.

47. FO to Lampson, tel., 2 July 1929: FO371/13899, pp. 65–7.

48. Johnston to Teichman, 25 Jan. 1930, in FO371/14697, p. 266.

49. Enclosure in Ellis to Orde, private, 14 Apr. 1930: ibid., p. 270.

50. See Gent to FO, 24 July 1929: FO371/13949.

51. Minute on Beckett to FO, confidential, 8 Aug. 1928: FO371/13235, p. 54.

52. Minute on Swire to Orde, private, 27 Jan. 1930: FO371/14724, p. 56.

53. See minutes on the following correspondence: Lampson to FO, tel. no. 543, 27 Aug. 1930: FO371/14684, p. 173; Ellis to Orde, 6 Oct. 1930: FO371/14685, pp. 634–5.

54. See minute by MacKillop on Ellis to FO, confidential, 12 Sept. 1930: ibid., pp. 602–3.

55. Lampson to FO, no. 1587, 31 Oct. 1930, in CO129/531 (82755). Lampson also noted that the governor, Peel, had rejected the idea of allowing China to run a preventive service of her own in the colony's waters, as the encouragement this would give to the irredentist tendencies of the southern Chinese was a real danger.

56. Minute on Grindle to Wellesley, confidential, 9 Jan. 1931: FO371/15484, p. 493.

57. Minute on Peel's memorandum, enclosure in Shuckburgh to Wellesley, confidential, private, 31 Aug. 1931: ibid., p. 514.

58. Orde to Lampson, no. 47, 20 Jan. 1932: FO371/16196, p. 4.

59. Minute by Pratt on Lampson to FO, confidential, 5 Nov. 1931: ibid., p. 1.

60. See FO371/17133, pp. 120–35.

61. Northcote to Ormsby-Gore, secret, 13 Apr. 1938, enclosure in Gent to FO, secret, 6 May 1938: FO371/22159, p. 133.

62. Northcote to MacDonald, secret, personal, 4 Aug. 1938, in FO371/22157, p. 165; see also Northcote to MacDonald, secret, 8 June 1938, in ibid., pp. 154–5.

63. See Cab 23/94, p. 142; FO371/22159, pp. 171–8. One minute commented, apparently on the Cabinet decision: 'I am very sceptical as to whether pusillanimity, tempered with hypocrisy, pays as a policy in the long run': on CO to FO, secret, 24 Aug. 1938: ibid., p. 163.

64. Minute by Brenan on Banks to FO, secret, [?] Oct. 1938: ibid., p. 201.

65. See minutes in Cab 23/94, p. 104.

66. Memorandum in FO371/14724, p. 119.

67. Sir John T. Pratt, War and Politics in China (New York: Books for Libraries Press, 1971; first published in 1943 by Jonathan Cape Ltd.), pp. 118–19.

68. See, generally, Evan Luard, Britain and China (London: Chatto and Windus, 1962), pp. 42–52. Nicholas R. Clifford, Retreat from China: British Policy in the Far East 1937–1941 (London: Longmans, 1967) is a useful overview, though there is no discussion of HMG's policy towards Hong Kong and the rendition question.

69. See MacDougall to Sabine, confidential, personal, 30 Dec. 1942: FO371/35824 (964).

70. Pratt to Clarke, private, 26 Dec. 1942: FO371/35905, referred to in Chan Lau Kit-ching, 'The Hong Kong Question During the Pacific War (1941–45)' (1973) II Journal of Imperial and Commonwealth History 56, at p. 68.

71. Compare Paskin to Clarke, confidential, 27 Aug. 1943: FO371/35824 (964).

72. Soong to Seymour, 11 Jan. 1943: ibid.

73. Chan, 'The Hong Kong Question', pp. 68–9; and see pp. 65–8 for a most useful discussion of the return of the New Territories alone, as opposed to return of the whole colony which Dr Chan's article is primarily about.

74. Wm. Roger Louis, Imperialism at Bay 1941–1945: The United States and the Decolonization of the British Empire (Oxford: Clarendon Press, 1977), pp. 7, 280 n, 438, 456.

75. ibid., p. 433.

76. (New York: Macmillan, 1947), p. 143, quoted by Chiu, 'Comparison of the Nationalist and Communist Chinese Views', p. 252.

77. Chan, 'The Hong Kong Question', pp. 71–3; Luard, Britain and China, pp. 181–2. The ceremonial surrender of the Japanese in Hong Kong was postponed because Chiang Kai-shek protested that Hong Kong lay within the Chinese war zone: G. B. Endacott, Hong Kong Eclipse (Hong Kong: Oxford University Press, 1978), pp. 232–3.

78. Chiu, 'Comparison of the Nationalist and Communist Chinese Views', pp. 254–5. See also Chen Chieh (China's vice-minister for foreign affairs), 'A Historical Review of China's Treaties' (1936) II The China Quarterly (Shanghai) 29.

79. 'A Comment on the Statement of the Communist Party of the USA' (8 Mar. 1963) in Cohen and Chiu, People's China and International Law, p. 380.

80. 'Khrushchev Group Turns World Youth Forum into Anti-China Forum' (25 Sept. 1964) in ibid., p. 382.

81. 'Hong Kong is Chinese Territory' (20 Aug. 1967) in ibid., p. 383.

82. ibid., p. 384.

83. China Mail, 9 Oct. 1895.

Notes for Chapter 10

1. Ralph A. Norem, *Kiaochow Leased Territory* (Berkeley: University of California Press, 1936), p. 86.

2. See pp. 54–5, 89–90, above.

3. Chamberlain to Blake, confidential, 6 Jan. 1899: CP62, p. 95.

4. Sanderson to CO, 26 Sept. 1898: CP32, p. 30. See p. 55, above.

5. Law officers to CO, 17 Oct. 1898: CP41, p. 68.

6. Lucas to FO, 29 June 1898: CP6, p. 5.

7. See appendix 2.

8. Memorandum, enclosure 2 in Clementi to Amery, secret, 27 Feb. 1929, in FO371/13949, pp. 363–4.

9. See p. 151, above.

10. Minute enclosed in Blake to Chamberlain, no. 196, 21 July 1899: CP234, p. 324.

11. See *Hong Kong Weekly Press*, vol. 1, 5 Aug. 1899, pp. 102, 109; Blake to Chamberlain, tel., 10 July 1899: CP217, p. 300.

12. Minute by Goodman, enclosure in Blake to Chamberlain, no. 192, 21 May 1901: CO129/305. See pp. 97–8, above.

13. Law officers to CO, 27 Sept. 1899: CP252, p. 344.

14. Law officers to CO, 1 Jan. 1900: CP286, pp. 375–6.

15. Memorandum, enclosure in Clementi to Amery, secret, 27 Feb. 1929, in FO371/13949, pp. 361–2.

16. Ellis to FO, 3 May 1929: FO371/13949, p. 369.

17. Memorandum by F. H. May, 6 July 1916, enclosure in May to Bonar Law, confidential, 23 Aug. 1916: CO129/434.

18. T'an to Mansfield, 15 July 1898, enclosure in Blake to Chamberlain, no. 209, 22 July 1898: CP17, p. 12. In the Yamen's letter to MacDonald of 10 Sept. 1898 it is added: 'If this [land tax] is all levied by Great Britain, then a rent must be calculated, the amount of which need not be considered now': enclosure in Bertie to CO, 21 Nov. 1898: CP45, p. 76. The 'rent' referred to here is apparently based on the Shanghai system where all landowners paid ground rent to the Chinese government.

19. '. . . but he did not attempt to uphold this argument': see 'Record Book': FO233/44, p. 301.

20. See vol. ii, *Stewart Lockhart's Papers*. Compare p. 55, above.

21. Yuan to Jamieson, 8 Nov. 1909, enclosure in Jamieson to Jordan, no. 118, 29 Dec. 1909, in CO129/371. See p. 144, above.

22. Yuan to Jamieson, 27 Dec. 1909, enclosure in FO to CO, 25 Jan. 1910: CO129/370.

23. See enclosure in Nathan to Lyttelton, no. 364, 10 Oct. 1904: CO129/324.

24. See note 17, above.

25. 'Extract from Canton Intelligence Report for Half Year ended 30th September, 1937' in CO129/564 (53852). Regulations made under the Prospecting and Mining Ordinance (no. 7 of 1906) established a licensing system for prospectors in the New Territories: see Nathan to Elgin, no. 31, 5 Feb. 1906: CO129/333; Nathan to Elgin, no. 206, 14 Aug. 1906: CO129/335.

26. Blake to Chamberlain, no. 87, 7 Apr. 1899: CP140, p. 141.

27. Chiu, 'Comparison of the Nationalist and Communist Chinese Views', pp. 254–5.

28. See Hsin Wu, 'A Criticism of Bourgeois International Law on the Question of State Territory' (1960) in Cohen and Chiu, *People's China and International Law*, pp. 322–6.

29. Salisbury to Lo, 30 May 1899, enclosure in Bertie to CO, confidential, 1 June 1899: CP177, p. 212.

30. See pp. 37, 51, above.

31. Cowell to FO, 26 Feb. 1934: FO371/18140, p. 189.

32. On Widdows to CO, secret, 16 May 1934, and Barnes to CO, confidential [date uncertain], in ibid., pp. 218–20.

33. Orde to CO, 9 Mar. 1934, in ibid., pp. 193–6.

34. *South China Morning Post*, 14 Jan. 1948.

35. [1959] HKLR 601.

36. There is an undisputed prerogative power to acquire territory outside Her Majesty's dominions. The various ways of acquiring such territory are usually listed as follows: treaty, capitulation, grant, usage, sufferance, and other lawful means (see Sir Kenneth Roberts-Wray, *Commonwealth and Colonial Law* (London: Stevens, 1966), p. 112, citing the preamble to the Foreign Jurisdiction Act 1890). In the case of the Walled City of Kowloon it could be contended that the treaty was the effective method, though that is contradicted by the argument presented in this chapter. Sufferance would not suffice, since China has never admitted that HMG 'acquired' the Walled City, though usage probably would. But it is not necessary to debate such issues as far as municipal law is concerned: 'other lawful means' includes the mere claim by the crown to have extended sovereignty over the territory concerned. This is so because the courts are not prepared to challenge such a claim, on the ground that it is an act of sovereign power (an 'act of state') which the courts are not competent to dispute. The claim may be made by order in council (*Sobhuza II* v. *Miller* [1926] AC 518, 525: 'This method of peacefully extending British dominion may well be as little generally understood as it is, where it can operate, in law unquestionable'), local ordinance (*Oyekan* v. *Adele* [1957] 2 All ER 785, 789: 'Their Lordships regard that recital [in an ordinance] as an authoritative statement by the British Crown of the effect of the treaty'), executive certificate, or simply by acts inconsistent with the lack of authority (ibid., p. 788: 'the courts of law look, not to the treaty, but to the conduct of the British Crown'). Once the claim is made, all that the courts can do is determine its extent (*Salaman* v. *Secretary of State for India* [1906] 1 KB 613, 639). There is no doubt that the *Re Wong Hon* decision is correct. See also *Nyali Ltd.* v. *Attorney-General* [1956] 1 QB 1, 15, *Post Office* v. *Estuary Radio Ltd.* [1968] 2 QB 740, 753, *Calder* v. *Attorney-General of British Columbia* (1969) 8 DLR (3d) 59, 74–82, *Milirrpum* v. *Nabalco Pty Ltd.* [1972–3] ALR 65, 141–6, and *New South Wales* v. *Commonwealth* (1975) 8 ALR 1, 28.

37. [1959] HKLR 601, 612.

38. ibid., p. 613.

39. ibid. In *Re Tse Lai-chiu, Deceased* [1969] HKLR 159, 179, Hogan CJ held that the *contemporanea expositio* maxim did not apply to the interpretation of Hong Kong ordinances since none was old enough.

40. *South China Morning Post*, 3 July 1975.

41. The Peace Preservation Ordinance was not repealed until 1967. The Banishment and Conditional Pardons Ordinance was repealed by the Deportation Ordinance 1912, which in section 4 empowered the governor in council to issue a deportation order against any person who was not, *in the opinion of the governor in council*,

a natural born or naturalized subject of Her Majesty.

42. See pp. 142–6, above.

43. cap. 115, LHK 1971 ed.

44. See pp. 92–5, above.

45. Enclosure in Stubbs to Amery, no. 304, 5 Aug. 1925: CO129/489.

46. Minute on ibid.

47. Amery to Clementi, no. 430, 26 Nov. 1925: CO129/489.

48. ibid.

49. Clementi to Amery, no. 387, 1 Sept. 1926: CO129/494, pp. 24–6.

50. Amery to Clementi, confidential, 12 Feb. 1927: ibid., pp. 15–16.

51. Clementi's paraphrase, in Clementi to Amery, no. 387, 1 Sept. 1926: ibid., p. 25.

52. See two booklets published by the New Territories Heung Yee Kuk: *Striving for Justifiable Rights for the People of the New Territories* (no date but probably 1974 or 1975), and *The New Territories Community of Hong Kong under Colonial Administration* (1977).

53. Cowell to CO, 26 Feb. 1934: FO371/18140, pp. 183–4. See also minute by Cowell on Lampson to FO, tel. no. 862, 8 Aug. 1933, in CO129/544 (13832); compare minute by Bader on Peel to Cunliffe-Lister, confidential, 9 Jan. 1934: CO129/546 (33744).

54. Luke T. Lee, *China and International Agreements: A Study of Compliance* (Durham, NC: Rule of Law Press, 1969), p. 38 n, notes that Peking, with reference to the New Territories boundary, has averred that a boundary within Chinese territory cannot be closed. Yet the boundary has in fact been closed, by both Hong Kong and Peking, for many years. The 'road from Kowloon to Hsinan' is discussed and illustrated in Hugh Baker, *Ancestral Images: A Hong Kong Album* (Hong Kong: South China Morning Post, 1979), pp. 29–32.

55. See R. D. Ormsby, 'Memorandum on Work Done by the Public Works Department in the New Territory during the year 1889', *Hong Kong Government Sessional Papers 1900*, p. 284, and his memorandum on the work done the following year: *Hong Kong Government Gazette 1901*, p. 1406.

56. Tregear and Barry, *The Development of Hong Kong and Kowloon*, pp. 17–19; *Hong Kong Government Sessional Papers 1921*, p. 155; Brian James Hudson, 'Land Reclamation in Hong Kong', unpublished Ph.D. thesis, University of Hong Kong, 1971. And see the map enclosed in Stubbs to Amery, no. 304, 5 Aug. 1925: CO129/489.

57. See *South China Morning Post* and *Hong Kong Standard*, 30 Jan. 1975.

58. MacDonald to Salisbury, no. 102, 27 May 1898, in CO129/287.

59. See Percy Horace Kent, *Railway Enterprise in China: An Account of its Origin and Development* (London: Edward Arnold, 1907), pp. 93, 173–5, 287–97; E-tu Zen Sun, *Chinese Railways and British Interests 1898–1911* (New York: Columbia University Press, 1954), pp. 9, 42–5, 73–89.

60. See p. 12, above.

61. Reproduced in LHK, 1964 ed.

62. See an undated and unsigned memorandum on the subject in vol. xxiv, *Stewart Lockhart's Papers*.

63. See p. 144, above.

64. Memorandum enclosed in Lugard to Harcourt, no. 318, 7 Sept. 1911: CO129/379.

65. See note 58, above.

66. See pp. 147-8, above.

67. For a general review of the literature, especially the German contributions, see Norem, *Kiaochow Leased Territory*, pp. 56-75. Chinese contributions include Hsia, *Studies in Chinese Diplomatic History*, pp. 98-120; Wen-sze King, 'The Lease Conventions between China and the Foreign Powers' (1916) 1 *Chinese Social and Political Science Review* 24-36; M. T. Z. Tyau, 'Diplomatic Relations between China and the Powers Since, and Concerning, the European War' (1917) 2 *Chinese Social and Political Science Review* 6-67; Tyau, *The Legal Obligations Arising out of Treaty Relations between China and Other States* (Taipei: Ch'eng-Wen, 1966; originally published in 1917), pp. 66-86; Leon Yang, *Les Territoires a Bail en Chine* (Paris: Presses Universitaires de France, 1929). For American views, see Quigley, 'The Shantung Question', pp. 71-90; Willoughby, *Foreign Rights and Interests in China*; C. Walter Young, *The International Status of Kwantung Leased Territory* (Baltimore: Johns Hopkins Press, 1931). An exception to the general lack of interest shown by British international lawyers is T. J. Lawrence, *War and Neutrality in the Far East* (London: Macmillan, 1904). See also the brief article by Sakutaro Tachi, 'Legal Aspects of Leased Territories' (1932) 1 *Contemporary Japan* 23.

68. See, for example, D. W. Greig, *International Law* (London: Butterworths, 1970), p. 144; J. G. Starke, *An Introduction to International Law* (London: Butterworths, 6th ed. 1967), p. 156; Ian Brownlie, *Principles of Public International Law* (Oxford: Clarendon Press, 1966), p. 104.

69. *International Law*, vol. i, p. 329.

70. *Kiaochow Leased Territory*, pp. 72-4, 81-6.

71. O'Connell, *International Law*, vol. i, p. 83.

72. *Kiaochow Leased Territory*, pp. 80-2.

73. Moore to Orde, 11 Oct. 1937: CO129/564 (53852).

74. See p. 91, above.

75. Hersch Lauterpacht, *Private Law Sources and Analogies of International Law* (London: Longmans, Green, 1927), pp. 181, 190.

76. *Kiaochow Leased Territory*, pp. 74-5, 84.

77. On Ellis to FO, 3 May 1929: FO371/13949, p. 367.

78. Parry, *British Digest of International Law*, vol. v, p. 152.

79. See, generally, Lord McNair, *The Law of Treaties* (Oxford: Clarendon Press, 1961).

80. See O'Connell, *International Law*, vol. i, pp. 253-64.

81. Roberts-Wray, *Commonwealth and Colonial Law*, pp. 26-7.

82. Joseph Lazar, 'The Status of the Leasehold in International Law', unpublished Ph.D. thesis, University of Minnesota, 1965. See Walter Wheeler Cook (ed.), *Fundamental Legal Conceptions as Applied in Judicial Reasoning and Other Legal Essays by Wesley Newcombe Hohfeld* (New Haven: Yale University Press, 1923).

83. See *United States Foreign Relations, 1900*, pp. 387 ff, quoted by Norem, *Kiaochow Leased Territory*, pp. 62-4, and Lazar, 'The Status of the Leasehold', pp. 154-5; *United States v. Smith* (1925-26) 3 *Annual Digest of Public International Law Cases* 118-19. The Chinese view is well expressed by Vi Kyuin Wellington Koo, *The Status of Aliens in China* (New York: 1912), pp. 252-64; see especially his summary of the Japanese argument in 1899: p. 255.

84. See pp. 146-8, above.

85. See note 42, chapter 8, above.

86. See p. 48, above.

87. Lassa F. L. Oppenheim, *International Law* (London: Longmans, 4th ed. 1926), vol. i, p. 364; Sir Mark F. Lindley, *The Acquisition and Government of Backward Territory in International Law* (London: Longmans, Green, 1926), pp. 243–4; John Westlake, *International Law* (Cambridge: Cambridge University Press, 2nd ed. 1910–13), part i, pp. 135–6.

88. See note 42, chapter 8, above.

89. *Secretary of State for India* v. *Sardar Rustam Khan* [1941] AC 356, 368. See Roberts-Wray, *Commonwealth and Colonial Law*, p. 27 n.

90. Britain could, however, if necessary rely on the Foreign Jurisdiction Act 1890 as justifying exercise by the crown of powers equivalent to those which could be exercised in ceded territory. See *Sardar Rustam Khan* [1941] AC 356, 368. In discussing the law of, and relating to, a 'composite colony' Roberts-Wray, *Commonwealth and Colonial Law*, p. 110, writes: 'where two or more tracts of land acquired by different means have been fused for the purposes of government, the nature of one area may determine the character of the whole'. The only authority for this tentative proposition is a case where a ceded colony was absorbed by a settled colony, and Roberts-Wray's arguments against the converse amalgamation would apply equally to a composite of ceded and leased territories. Roberts-Wray does not rely on this 'absorption' idea in relation to Hong Kong.

91. See (1927) 21 *Proceedings of the American Society of International Law* 87–99; Anthony Lester, 'Bizerta and the Unequal Treaty Theory' (1962) 11 *International and Comparative Law Quarterly* 847; Ingrid Detter, 'The Problem of Unequal Treaties' (1966) 15 *International and Comparative Law Quarterly* 1069. For discussions of Chinese attitudes towards unequal treaties, see Tseng Yu-hao, *The Termination of Unequal Treaties in International Law* (Shanghai: Commercial Press, 1933); Hungdah Chiu, *The People's Republic and the Law of Treaties* (Cambridge, Mass.: Harvard University Press, 1972), pp. 70–1, 96–9; Chiu, 'Comparison of the Nationalist and Communist Chinese Views'; James Chieh Hsiung, *Law and Policy in China's Foreign Relations: A Study of Attitudes and Practice* (New York and London: Columbia University Press, 1972), pp. 251–4; Cohen and Chiu, *People's China and International Law*, chap. 12 and pp. 1116–29, 1244–45, 1314; Lung-fong Chen, *State Succession Relating to Unequal Treaties* (Hamden, Connecticut: Archon Books, 1974).

92. See Herbert W. Briggs, 'Unilateral Denunciation of Treaties: The Vienna Convention and the International Court of Justice' (1974) 68 *American Journal of International Law* 51; Franciszek Przetacznik, 'The Validity of Treaties Concluded Under Coercion' (1975) 15 *Indian Journal of International Law* 173.

93. See, for instance, Tyau, *Legal Obligations*, p. 210; Hsia, *Studies in Chinese Diplomatic History*, pp. 114–16. The use made of the doctrine by the People's Republic is summarized by Hsiung, *Law and Policy*, p. 248. For general discussions, see Oliver J. Lissitzyn, 'Treaties and Changed Circumstances (Rebus Sic Stantibus)' (1967) 61 *American Journal of International Law* 895; S. A. Tiewul, 'Fisheries Jurisdiction Cases (1973) and the Ghost of Rebus Sic Stantibus' (1973) 6 *New York University Journal of International Law and Politics* 455; William L. Scheffler, 'The Politicization and Death of Rebus Sic Stantibus' (1974) 2 *Syracuse Journal of International Law and Commerce* 67; H. F. Koeck, '"Changed Circumstances" Clause after the United Nations Conference on the Law of Treaties (1968–69)' (1974) 4 *Georgia Journal of International and Comparative Law* 93; Akos Toth, 'The Doctrine of Rebus Sic Stantibus in International Law' [1974] *Juridical Review* 56, 147, 263.

94. See p. 152, above.

95. Briggs, 'Unilateral Denunciation of Treaties', pp. 64–8.

96. See 'Peking MCC Requisitions Foreign Barracks in City' (1950) in Cohen and Chiu, *People's China and International Law*, pp. 1054–5, and 'A Comment on the Statement of the Communist Party of the USA' (1963), ibid., p. 380.

97. ibid., pp. 1122–9.

98. ibid., pp. 453, 1427, 1434, 1445.

99. 'Report on the Question of the Boundary Line between China and Burma...' (1957), in ibid., p. 427; see also p. 431.

100. ibid., pp. 1127–8.

101. 'Statement of the Government of the People's Republic of China, May 24, 1969', in ibid., p. 461.

102. From an article quoted by Chiu, 'Comparison of the Nationalist and Communist Chinese Views', p. 259.

103. Wang Yao-t'ien, in Cohen and Chiu, *People's China and International Law*, p. 1119.

104. See note 102, above.

105. See 'China Protests against British Attempts to Demolish Premises in Kowloon City' (1963) in Cohen and Chiu, *People's China and International Law*, pp. 377–9.

106. ibid., p. 384.

107. Norman Miners, *The Government and Politics of Hong Kong* (Hong Kong: Oxford University Press, 1975), p. 26.

108. *South China Morning Post*, 2 Sept. 1975.

109. Albert H. Putney, 'The Termination of Unequal Treaties' (1927) 21 *Proceedings of the American Society of International Law* 87, 90.

Notes for Epilogue

1. The best general assessment of the value of Hong Kong to Britain and China and of the various factors likely to determine the colony's future is Miners, *The Government and Politics of Hong Kong* (2nd ed. 1977), part 1. See also Miners' paper 'Can the Colony of Hong Kong Survive 1997? (1979) *Asia Pacific Community*, No. 6, pp. 100–14. Other comments are included in P. B. Harris, 'The International Future of Hong Kong' (1972) 48 *International Affairs* 60; Nigel Cameron, *Hong Kong: The Cultured Pearl* (Hong Kong: Oxford University Press, 1978), postscript; William F. Beazer, *The Commercial Future of Hong Kong* (New York, London: Praeger, 1978), pp. 124–56; Dick Wilson, 'New Thoughts on the Future of Hong Kong' (1977) 8 *Pacific Community* 588.

2. Appendix 2.

3. Compare *Nyali Ltd.* v. *Attorney-General* [1956] 1 QB 1, 22, per Morris LJ.

4. It is possible that, in law, Britain could merely ignore 1997 and, after that date, rely on the Interpretation and General Clauses Ordinance (see pp. 120–2, above) or on governmental behaviour as an authoritative declaration as to the territory claimed by the crown (see chap. 10, note 36, above). It would be a foolhardy commentator who sought to predict how the courts would react, for we have here advanced into the mists of constitutional theory. The matter is likely to remain

hypothetical, for such a 'solution' to the problem of 1997 would not be politically satisfactory: Hong Kong's security will have to be based on firmer grounds than the opinion of a government legal adviser.

5. So it seemed, at least, towards the end of 1978. But from the perspective of late 1979 (when page proofs were being read), negotiation of a new agreement for the extended lease of the New Territories by Great Britain appeared much less unlikely. The political climate in China at the close of the 1970s had undergone astonishingly rapid change. In its issue of 2 Nov. 1979 the *Far Eastern Economic Review*, pp. 16–17, urged the British government to initiate discussions designed to maintain the territorial integrity of Hong Kong well beyond 1997.

6. After this sentence was written the Chinese vice-premier Teng Hsiao-ping asked the governor of Hong Kong to tell investors in the colony to 'put their hearts at ease': *South China Morning Post*, 7 April 1979.

BIBLIOGRAPHY

I. Official Records from the
Public Record Office, London

COLONIAL OFFICE

CO129: original correspondence, Hong Kong
This series is the basic source for this study. It contains despatches and telegrams from the governor of Hong Kong, and correspondence from other offices in London and from individuals. It often includes the draft of replies. Minutes by Colonial Office staff on incoming correspondence and the occasional memorandum are also bound in these volumes.

Some use was made of brief notes prepared by G. B. Endacott on selected volumes from CO129/199–313.

CO537: original correspondence (supplementary), Colonies (general)
The most useful records for this study are contained in vol. 34, which collects together most of the early material on the proposed extension of Hong Kong's boundaries. Vol. 747 contains Colonial Office files relating to the Washington conference.

CO882: confidential prints
There are several useful prints included in this series, but by far the most valuable for this work is in vol. 5: 'Hong Kong. Correspondence (20 June 1898, to 20 August 1900) respecting the Extension of the Boundaries of the Colony' (Eastern No. 66), abbreviated in the notes to 'CP' and the serial number of the despatch or telegram referred to.

CO349: register of correspondence, Hong Kong
Useful for a quick survey and for the occasional summary of an item marked with the dreaded 'destroyed under statute'.

CO489: correspondence, Hong Kong, register of out-letters

CO323: general correspondence, warrants, commissions, etc.

CO521: register of correspondence, Weihaiwei

FOREIGN OFFICE
FO17: general correspondence, China
The basic source for communications between the British minister in Peking and the Foreign Office from 1897 to 1898.

FO371: political correspondence, China
The FO17 series stops in 1906 and is continued here.

FO233/44: 'Record Book of Interviews with Yamen, June 1897–November 1899'

FO608: correspondence and papers of the British delegation to the peace congress, 1919–1920

CABINET
Cab 7:   Colonial Defence Committee, minutes etc.
Cab 8:   Colonial Defence Committee, memoranda
Cab 9:   Colonial Defence Committee, remarks
Cab 11: Colonial Defence Committee, defence schemes
Cab 18: Committee of Imperial Defence, miscellaneous volumes
Cab 23: Cabinet minutes, December 1916–December 1922
Cab 30: papers relating to the Washington conference, 1921–1922

ADMIRALTY
Adm 125: correspondence, China

II. Private Papers

Search was made of the papers of Lord Lansdowne and Sir T. Sanderson, 1898–1905, and of Sir John Ardagh, 1896–1901, in the Public Record Office, London (FO800/115 and PRO30/40 respectively) but they contain nothing useful to my purposes in this work. The same is true of Sir Frederick Lugard's papers and those of Sir Matthew Nathan at Rhodes House Library, Oxford.

The following three sets of papers do contain small amounts of relevant material:

Salisbury's Papers (Christ Church Library, Oxford)
Chamberlain's Papers (University Library, Birmingham)
Bertie's Papers (Public Record Office, London: FO800/159–62 for the 1899–1919 period)

Stewart Lockhart's Papers (National Library of Scotland, Edinburgh) are of more immediate relevance to this study than those of Salisbury, Chamberlain or Bertie, and more material of interest was found. The papers are not yet, however, thoroughly catalogued, and there are many more in the possession of Stewart Lockhart's daughter. I did not attempt to gain access to these.

I searched in vain for the papers of Sir Henry Blake, but they do not appear in any well-known collection and perhaps do not exist. I also attempted, unsuccessfully, to track down the papers of Sir Cecil Clementi.

III. Official Papers

Apart from the confidential prints mentioned above, use was made of the various reports contained in the *Hong Kong Government Gazette* and *Sessional Papers*, especially from 1899 to 1912. These are of considerable value to local historians, though most can also be found in the CO129 series. Some original correspondence has also been printed in Hong Kong.

'Despatches and other Papers relating to the Extension of the Colony of Hong Kong' *Gazette 1899* 1347. Most of these can be found in the confidential print Eastern No. 66, but there are a few useful documents not included there.

'English Translation of the Proclamations issued by the Magistrate of the San On District and the Viceroy of Canton regarding the New Territory' *Gazette 1899* 1559. Reproduced as appendix 6.

'Extracts from Papers relating to the Extension of the Colony of Hong Kong' *Gazette 1899* 531. This contains part of Stewart Lockhart's report and other documents also in Eastern No. 66.

'Further Papers relating to the Military Operations in connection with the Disturbances on the taking over of the New Territory' *Gazette 1899* 1473.

GOMPERTZ, H. H. J., 'Report on the Ownership of Ts'ing I (Chung Hue) Island' *Gazette 1901* 1403.

—— 'Report on the Work of the Land Court for the seven months ending December 31st, 1900' *Gazette 1901* 1400.

—— 'Report on the Work of the Land Court up to the 31st December, 1901' *Gazette 1902* 700.

—— 'Some Notes on Land Tenure in the New Territory' *Gazette 1901* 1395.

ORME, G. N., 'Report on the New Territories, 1899–1912' *Sessional Papers 1912* 43.

ORMSBY, R. D., 'Memorandum on Work Done by the Public Works Department in the New Territory during the Year 1899' *Gazette 1900* 283.

—— 'Work Done by the Public Works Department in the New Territory, during the Year 1900' *Gazette 1901* 1406.

'Proclamation issued under Her Majesty's Order in Council, dated the 20th day of October, 1898' *Gazette 1899* 522. Reproduced as appendix 5.

RUSSELL, JAMES, 'Memorandum on the "Hong Kong Blockade" for the Information of Governor Sir George Bowen' *Sessional Papers 1884* (1).

SHEPHERD, BRUCE, 'Memorandum of Work Done in the Land Office, Hong Kong, in respect of the New Territories for the Year 1899' *Sessional Papers 1900* 277.

STEWART LOCKHART, J. H., 'Memorandum on Land' *Sessional Papers 1900* 266. Since this is attached to one of Stewart Lockhart's reports it is assumed that he was the author, but it is possible that it was written by one of the officers specializing in land administration.

—— 'Report on the New Territory during the First Year of British Administration' *Sessional Papers 1900* 252.

—— 'Report on the New Territory for the Year 1900' *Gazette 1901* 1389.

—— 'Report on the New Territory for the Year 1901' *Gazette 1902* 696.

—— 'Report on the New Territory since the Inauguration of British Rule' *Gazette 1900* 635.

The following printed sources were also consulted:

British Parliamentary Papers:
China, No. 1 (1898), *Correspondence respecting the Affairs of China.*
China, No. 1 (1899), *Correspondence respecting the Affairs of China.*
China, Imperial Maritime Customs, *Decennial Report 1892–1901* (Shanghai, 1906).
Correspondence, Dispatches, Reports, Returns, Memorials and Other Papers respecting the Affairs of Hong Kong 1862–81 (Shannon: Irish University Press, 1971).

GOOCH, G. P., AND TEMPERLEY, HAROLD (eds.), *British Documents on the Origins of the War, 1898–1914* Vol. i: *The End of British Isolation* (London: HMSO, 1927).

Hertslet's China Treaties Vol. ii (London: HMSO, 1908).

Hong Kong Government [?], *Hong Kong's Border with China* (probably published in early 1968).

Hong Kong Government Printer, *A Gazetteer of Place Names in Hong Kong, Kowloon and the New Territories* (Hong Kong. No date but 1960).

Hong Kong Hansard, Proceedings of the Legislative Council. Consulted regarding the lease and occupation of the New Territories.

MACMURRAY, JOHN V. A. (comp. and ed.), *Treaties and Agreements With and Concerning China, 1894–1919* Vol. i: *Manchu Period (1894–1911)* (New York: Fertig, 1971. First published by Oxford University Press in 1921).

PARRY, CLIVE (ed.), *A British Digest of International Law compiled principally from the Archives of the Foreign Office. Phase One, 1860–1914* 10 vols. (London: Stevens and Sons, 1967).

Strickland committee, *Chinese Law and Custom in Hong Kong* (Hong Kong: Government Printer, 1953).

YIN CHING-CHEN (comp. and ed.), *Treaties and Agreements between the Republic of China and Other Powers, 1929–1954* (Washington: Sino-American Publishing Service, 1957).

IV. Newspapers

A systematic study of all available Hong Kong newspapers from 1895 to 1910 was undertaken, with spot checks for the later years (especially relating to incidents concerning the Walled City). Some assistance was gained from a collection of extracts from the *China Mail* available in the Department of History, University of Hong Kong. The newspapers referred to are listed below. The most useful of these for the period of the acquisition and occupation of the New Territories is the *Hong Kong Weekly Press*, which reprinted material from the *Hong Kong Daily Press* and is indexed.

China Mail
Hong Kong Daily Press
Hong Kong Standard
Hong Kong Telegraph
Hong Kong Weekly Press

South China Morning Post
South China Morning Post and Hong Kong Telegraph
South China Sunday Post-Herald
I also consulted *Hsinhua News Agency* and *Survey of China Mainland Press* reports in relation to the Walled City.

V. Books, Articles, and Theses

In presenting a 'select' bibliography the choice will always be to some extent arbitrary, and works will be omitted which some readers would prefer to see listed. Included below is every secondary source mentioned in the notes. Many items are comparatively insignificant but appear for the sake of comprehensiveness.

ARLINGTON, L. C., *Through the Dragon's Eyes* (London: Constable, 1931).

AYERS, WILLIAM, *Chang Chih-tung and Educational Reform in China* (Cambridge, Mass.: Harvard University Press, 1971).

BAKER, HUGH D. R., *A Chinese Lineage Village* (London: Frank Cass, 1968).

—— *Ancestral Images: A Hong Kong Album* (Hong Kong: South China Morning Post, 1979).

—— 'Clan Organisation and its Role in Village Affairs', in *Aspects of Social Organisation in the New Territories* (Hong Kong: Hong Kong Branch of the Royal Asiatic Society, 1964).

—— 'The Five Great Clans of the New Territories' (1966) 6 *Journal of the Hong Kong Branch of the Royal Asiatic Society* 25.

BAU, MINGCHIEN JOSHUA, *The Foreign Relations of China: A History and a Survey*, 2nd ed. (New York, Chicago, London, Edinburgh: Fleming H. Revell Co., 1922).

—— *The Open Door Doctrine in relation to China* (New York: Macmillan, 1923).

BEAZER, WILLIAM F., *The Commercial Future of Hong Kong* (New York, London: Praeger, 1978).

BRIGGS, HERBERT W., 'Unilateral Denunciation of Treaties: The Vienna Convention and the International Court of Justice' (1974) 68 *American Journal of International Law* 51.

BROWNLIE, IAN, *Principles of Public International Law* (Oxford: Clarendon Press, 1966).

BUELL, RAYMOND LESLIE, *The Washington Conference* (New York and London: Appleton, 1922).

CAMERON, NIGEL, *Hong Kong: The Cultured Pearl* (Hong Kong: Oxford University Press, 1978).

CHAN LAU KIT-CHING, 'The Hong Kong Question During the Pacific War (1941–45)' (1973) II *Journal of Imperial and Commonwealth History* 56.

CHEN, LUNG-FONG, *State Succession Relating to Unequal Treaties* (Hamden, Connecticut: Archon Books, 1974).

CHEN CHIEH, 'A Historical Review of China's Treaties' (1936) II *The China Quarterly* (Shanghai) 29.

CHENG, T. C., 'Chinese Unofficial Members of the Legislative and Executive Councils in Hong Kong up to 1941' (1969) 9 *Journal of the Hong Kong Branch of the Royal Asiatic Society* 7.

CHIANG KAI-SHEK, *China's Destiny* (New York: Macmillan, 1947).

CHIU, HUNGDAH, 'Comparison of the Nationalist and Communist Chinese Views of Unequal Treaties', in Cohen, Jerome Allen (ed.), *China's Practice of International Law: Some Case Studies* (Cambridge, Mass.: Harvard University Press, 1972).

—— *The People's Republic and the Law of Treaties* (Cambridge, Mass.: Harvard University Press, 1972).

CHOW TSE-TUNG, *The May Fourth Movement* (Cambridge, Mass.: Harvard University Press, 1965).

CHRISTIE, CLIVE JOHN, 'The Problem of China in British Foreign Policy, 1917–1921', Unpublished Ph.D. thesis, University of Cambridge, 1971.

CLEMENTI, CECIL, 'The Future of Hong Kong' (1936) V *United Empire* XXVII 22.

CLIFFORD, NICHOLAS R., *Retreat from China: British Policy in the Far East 1937–1941* (London: Longmans, 1967).

CLYDE, PAUL HIBBERT, *The Far East: A History of the Impact of the West on Eastern Asia*, 2nd ed. (New York: Prentice-Hall, 1952).

COHEN, JEROME A., AND CHIU, HUNGDAH, *People's China and International Law: A Documentary Study* (Princeton, New Jersey: Princeton University Press, 1974).

COOK, WALTER WHEELER (ed.), *Fundamental Legal Conceptions as Applied in Judicial Reasoning and Other Legal Essays by Wesley Newcombe Hohfeld* (New Haven: Yale University Press, 1923).

COOPER, T. G., *Colony in Conflict* (Hong Kong: Swindon, 1970).

CUKWURAH, A. O., *The Settlement of Boundary Disputes in International Law* (Manchester: Manchester University Press, 1967).

DETTER, INGRID, 'The Problem of Unequal Treaties' (1966) 15 *International and Comparative Law Quarterly* 1069.

DUGDALE, BLANCHE E. C., *Arthur James Balfour* (London: Hutchinson, 1936).

EDESON, W. R., 'The Prerogative of the Crown to Delimit Britain's Maritime Boundary' (1973) 89 *Law Quarterly Review* 364.

EITEL, E. J., *Europe in China* (Hong Kong: Kelly and Walsh, 1895).

ENDACOTT, G. B., *A History of Hong Kong*, 2nd ed. (Hong Kong, London, New York: Oxford University Press, 1973).

―― *Hong Kong Eclipse* (Hong Kong: Oxford University Press, 1978).

EVANS, D. M. EMRYS, 'Common Law in a Chinese Setting—the Kernel or the Nut?' (1971) 1 HKLJ 9.

―― 'The New Law of Succession in Hong Kong' (1973) 3 HKLJ 7.

FAIRBANK, JOHN KING, BRUNER, KATHERINE F., AND MATHESON, ELIZABETH MACLEOD (eds.), *The IG in Peking: Letters of Robert Hart, Chinese Maritime Customs 1868–1907* (Cambridge, Mass., and London: The Belknap Press of Harvard University Press, 1975).

FAIRBANK, JOHN K., REISCHAUER, EDWIN O., AND CRAIG, ALBERT M., *East Asia: The Modern Transformation* (London: Allen and Unwin, 1965).

FISHEL, WESLEY R., *The End of Extraterritoriality in China* (New York: Octagon Books, 1974; first published in 1952).

FOX, HAZEL, 'Arbitration', in Luard, Evan (ed.), *The International Regulation of Frontier Disputes* (London: Thames and Hudson, 1970).

FRASER, PETER, *Joseph Chamberlain: Radicalism and Empire, 1868–1914* (London: Cassell, 1966).

FREEDMAN, MAURICE, *Chinese Lineage and Society* (London: Athlone Press, 1966).

GRANTHAM, ALEXANDER, *Via Ports: From Hong Kong to Hong Kong* (Hong Kong: University of Hong Kong Press, 1965).

GREIG, D. W., *International Law* (London: Butterworths, 1970).

GROVES, R. G., 'Militia, Market and Lineage: Chinese Resistance to the Occupation of Hong Kong's New Territories in 1899' (1969) 9 *Journal of the Hong Kong Branch of the Royal Asiatic Society* 31.

HAN SU-YIN, *The Crippled Tree* (London: Panther Books, 1972).

HARRIS, FRANK, *My Life and Loves* (Corgi Books, 1966).

HARRIS, P. B., 'The International Future of Hong Kong' (1972) 48

International Affairs 60.

HAYDON, E. S., 'Chinese Customary Law in Hong Kong's New Territories', Unpublished MS, undated but 1962.

——— 'The Choice of Chinese Customary Law in Hong Kong' (1962) 11 *International and Comparative Law Quarterly* 231.

HAYES, JAMES, 'Old Ways of Life in Kowloon: The Cheung Sha Wan Villages' (1970) 7 *Journal of Oriental Studies* 153.

———*The Hong Kong Region 1850–1911* (Hamden: Archon Books, 1977).

——— 'The San On Map of Mgr Volontieri' (1970) 10 *Journal of the Hong Kong Branch of the Royal Asiatic Society* 193.

HSIA, CHING-LIN, *Studies in Chinese Diplomatic History* (Shanghai: Commercial Press, 1926).

HSIUNG, JAMES CHIEH, *Law and Policy in China's Foreign Relations: A Study of Attitudes and Practice* (New York and London: Columbia University Press, 1972).

HSÜ, IMMANUEL C. Y., *China's Entrance into the Family of Nations: The Diplomatic Phase, 1858–1880* (Cambridge, Mass.: Harvard University Press, 1960).

HYAM, RONALD, *Elgin and Churchill at the Colonial Office, 1905– 1908: The Watershed of the Empire-Commonwealth* (London, Melbourne, Toronto: Macmillan, 1968).

ICHIHASHI, YAMATO, *The Washington Conference and After: A Historical Survey* (Stanford: Stanford University Press, 1928).

JEN SUN E-TU, 'The Lease of Wei-hai Wei' (1950) 19 *Pacific Historical Review* 277. (See also entry under ZEN SUN E-TU, below.)

JEN YU-WEN, 'The Travelling Palace of Southern Sung in Kowloon' (1967) 7 *Journal of the Hong Kong Branch of the Royal Asiatic Society* 21.

JOHNSTON, R. F., *Lion and Dragon in Northern China* (London: John Murray, 1910).

JONES, P. H. M., *Golden Guide to Hong Kong and Macau* (Hong Kong: Far Eastern Economic Review, 1969).

JOSEPH, PHILIP, *Foreign Diplomacy in China 1894–1900* (London: George Allen and Unwin, 1928).

JUDD, DENIS, *Balfour and the British Empire: A Study in Imperial Evolution, 1874–1932* (London, Melbourne, Toronto: Macmillan, 1968).

KAMM, J. T., 'Taxlordism' (1977) 7 *Journal of the Hong Kong Branch of the Royal Asiatic Society* 68.

KENT, PERCY HORACE, *Railway Enterprise in China: An Account of its Origin and Development* (London: Edward Arnold, 1907).

KING, WEN-SZE, 'The Lease Conventions between China and the Foreign Powers' (1916) 1 *Chinese Social and Political Science Review* 24.

KIRBY, S. WOODBURN, *The War Against Japan* (London: HMSO, 1957).

KOECK, H. F., ' "Changed Circumstance" Clause after the United Nations Conference on the Law of Treaties (1968–69)' (1974) 4 *Georgia Journal of International and Comparative Law* 93.

KOO, VI KYUIN WELLINGTON, *The Status of Aliens in China* (New York, 1912).

KUBICEK, ROBERT V., *The Administration of Imperialism: Joseph Chamberlain at the Colonial Office* (Durham, NC: Duke University Press, 1969).

LAI CHUN-WAI (comp.), *Centenary History of Hong Kong* (Hong Kong: Nam Chun Pin Yick Publishing House, undated but probably prepared in 1941 and published in 1948; in Chinese, privately translated).

LANGER, WILLIAM L., *The Diplomacy of Imperialism 1890–1902* 2nd ed. (New York: Alfred A. Knopf, 1960).

LAUTERPACHT, HERSCH, *Private Law Sources and Analogies of International Law* (London: Longmans, Green, 1927).

LAWRENCE, T. J., *War and Neutrality in the Far East* (London: Macmillan, 1904).

LAZAR, JOSEPH, 'The Status of the Leasehold in International Law', Unpublished Ph.D. thesis, University of Minnesota, 1965.

LEE, LUKE T., *China and International Agreements: A Study of Compliance* (Durham, NC: Rule of Law Press, 1969).

LEEMING, FRANK, *Street Studies in Hong Kong* (Hong Kong: Oxford University Press, 1977).

LESTER, ANTHONY, 'Bizerta and the Unequal Treaty Theory' (1962) 11 *International and Comparative Law Quarterly* 847.

LETHBRIDGE, H. J., *Hong Kong: Stability and Change* (Hong Kong: Oxford University Press, 1978).

LINDLEY, MARK F., *The Acquisition and Government of Backward Territory in International Law* (London: Longmans, Green, 1926).

LISSITZYN, OLIVER J., 'Treaties and Changed Circumstances (Rebus Sic Stantibus)' (1967) 61 *American Journal of International Law* 895.

LITTLE, MRS ARCHIBALD, *Li Hung-chang: His Life and Times* (London, Paris, New York and Melbourne: Cassell, 1903).

LO JUNG-PANG (ed.), *K'ang Yu-wei: A Biography and a Symposium* (Tucson: University of Arizona Press, 1967).

LOUIS, WM. ROGER, *British Strategy in the Far East 1919–1939* (Oxford: Clarendon, 1971).

—— *Imperialism at Bay 1941–1945: The United States and the Decolonization of the British Empire* (Oxford: Clarendon, 1977).

LUARD, EVAN, *Britain and China* (London: Chatto and Windus, 1962).

LYON, PETER, 'Regional Organisations and Frontier Disputes', in Luard, Evan (ed.), *The International Regulation of Frontier Disputes* (London: Thames and Hudson, 1970).

MARSTON, GEOFFREY, 'Colonial Enactments Relating to the Legal Status of Offshore Submerged Lands' (1976) 50 *Australian Law Journal* 402.

MCALEAVY, H., 'Chinese Law in Hong Kong: The Choice of Sources', in Anderson, J. N. D. (ed.), *Changing Law in Developing Countries* (London: George Allen and Unwin, 1963).

MCCORDOCK, R. STANLEY, *British Far Eastern Policy 1894–1900* (New York: Columbia University Press, 1931).

MCNAIR, LORD, *The Law of Treaties* (Oxford: Clarendon, 1961).

MEDLICOTT, W. N., *British Foreign Policy Since Versailles, 1919–1963* (London: Methuen, 1968).

MESNY, WILLIAM (ed.), *Mesny's Chinese Miscellany* (Shanghai, 1899).

MICHIE, ALEXANDER, *The Englishman in China during the Victorian Era* (Edinburgh and London: William Blackwood and Sons, 1900).

MINERS, NORMAN, *The Government and Politics of Hong Kong* (Hong Kong: Oxford University Press, 1975).

MORGAN, W. P., *Triad Societies in Hong Kong* (Hong Kong: Government Press, 1960).

NELSON, H. G. H., 'British Land Administration in the New Territories of Hong Kong, and its Effects on Chinese Social Organisation', Unpublished paper presented at the conference of the London-Cornell project for East and Southeast Asian Studies, August 1969.

NG, PETER L. Y., 'The 1819 Edition of the *Hsin-an Hsien-chih*: A Critical Examination with Translation and Notes', Unpublished M.A. thesis, University of Hong Kong, 1961.

NG, RONALD C. Y., 'The San On Map of Mgr Volonteri' (1969) 9 *Journal of the Hong Kong Branch of the Royal Asiatic Society* 141.

NISH, IAN H., *Alliance in Decline: A Study in Anglo-Japanese Relations 1908–23* (London: Athlone, 1972).

NOREM, RALPH A., *Kiaochow Leased Territory* (Berkeley: University of California Press, 1936).

NORTON KYSHE, JAMES WILLIAM, *The History of the Laws and Courts of Hong Kong* (London: Fisher Unwin, 1898).

O'CONNELL, D. P., *International Law*, 2nd ed. (London: Stevens, 1970).

O'CONNELL, D. P., AND RIORDAN, ANN, *Opinions on Imperial Constitutional Law* (Sydney, Melbourne, Brisbane: Law Book Co., 1971).

'OLD COLONIAL', *Old Hong Kong* (a series of articles published in the *South China Morning Post* between 17 June 1933 and 13 April 1935 and bound together in the Library of the University of Hong Kong).

OPPENHEIM, LASSA F. L., *International Law*, 4th ed. (London: Longmans, 1926).

PARRY, CLIVE, *Nationality and Citizenship Laws of the Commonwealth and of the Republic of Ireland* (London: Stevens, 1957).

PEARL, CYRIL, *Morrison of Peking* (London: Penguin, 1970).

PELCOVITS, NATHAN A., *Old China Hands and the Foreign Office* (New York: King's Crown Press, 1948).

PEPLOW, S. H., AND BARKER, M., *Hong Kong, Around and About*, 2nd ed. (Hong Kong: Ye Olde Printerie, 1931).

POLLARD, ROBERT T., *China's Foreign Relations, 1917–1931* (New York: Macmillan, 1933).

POTTER, JACK M., *Capitalism and the Chinese Peasant* (Berkeley and Los Angeles: University of California Press, 1968).

PRATT, JOHN T., *War and Politics in China* (New York: Books for Libraries Press, 1971; first published by Jonathan Cape Ltd in 1943).

PRESCOTT, J. R. V., *The Geography of Frontiers and Boundaries* (London: Hutchinson, 1965).

PRZETACZNIK, FRANCISZEK, 'The Validity of Treaties Concluded Under Coercion' (1975) 15 *Indian Journal of International Law* 173.

PUTNEY, ALBERT H., 'The Termination of Unequal Treaties' (1927) 21 *Proceedings of the American Society of International Law* 87.

QUIGLEY, HAROLD SCOTT, 'The Shantung Question in International Law' (1921) 6 *Chinese Social and Political Science Review* 71.

ROBERTS-WRAY, KENNETH, *Commonwealth and Colonial Law* (London: Stevens, 1966).

SAYER, GEOFFREY ROBLEY, *Hong Kong: Birth, Adolescence and Coming of Age* (London, New York, Toronto: Oxford University Press, 1937).

—— *Hong Kong: 1862–1919: Years of Discretion* (Hong Kong: Hong Kong University Press, 1975).

SCHEFFLER, WILLIAM L., 'The Politicization and Death of Rebus Sic Stantibus' (1974) 2 *Syracuse Journal of International Law and Commerce* 67.

SCHIFFRIN, HAROLD Z., *Sun Yat-sen and the Origins of the Chinese Revolution* (Berkeley, Los Angeles, London: University of California Press, 1970).

SCHOFIELD, WALTER, 'Defence Wall at Pass between Kowloon City and Kowloon Tsai' (1968) 8 *Journal of the Hong Kong Branch of the Royal Asiatic Society* 154.

SCHRECKER, JOHN E., *Imperialism and Chinese Nationalism: Germany in Shantung* (Cambridge, Mass.: Harvard University Press, 1971).

SHARMA, SURYA P., *International Boundary Disputes and International Law* (Bombay: N. M. Tripathi, 1976).

SKINNER, G. WILLIAM (ed.), *The City in Late Imperial China* (Stanford: Stanford University Press, 1977).

STARKE, J. G., *An Introduction to International Law*, 6th ed. (London: Butterworths, 1967).

TACHI, SAKUTARO, 'Legal Aspects of Leased Territories' (1932) 1 *Contemporary Japan* 23.

TIEWUL, S. A., 'Fisheries Jurisdiction Cases (1973) and the Ghost of Rebus Sic Stantibus' (1973) 6 *New York University Journal of International Law and Politics* 455.

TOTH, AKOS, 'The Doctrine of Rebus Sic Stantibus in International Law' [1974] *Juridical Review* 56, 147, 263.

TREGEAR, T. R. AND BERRY, L., *The Development of Hong Kong and Kowloon as Told in Maps* (Hong Kong: University of Hong Kong Press, 1959).

TSAI CHU-TUNG, 'The Chinese Nationality Law, 1909' (1910) IV *American Journal of International Law* 404.

TSENG YU-HAO, *The Termination of Unequal Treaties in International*

Law (Shanghai: Commercial Press, 1933).

TUCHMAN, BARBARA W., *The Proud Tower: A Portrait of the World Before the War: 1890–1914* (Bantam Books, 1967).

—— *Stilwell and the American Experience in China, 1911–1945* (New York: Macmillan, 1971).

TYAU, M. T. Z., 'Diplomatic Relations between China Since, and Concerning, the European War' (1917) 2 *Chinese Social and Political Science Review* 6.

—— *The Legal Obligations Arising out of Treaty Relations between China and Other States* (Taipei: Ch'eng-Wen, 1966; originally published in 1917).

TYLER, FERDINAND, *Pulling Strings in China* (London: Constable, 1929).

UNITED STATES DEPARTMENT OF STATE, 'International Boundary Study: China—Hong Kong' Washington: intelligence bulletin no. 13, April 1964.

VAN METER, JR., ROBERT H., 'The Washington Conference of 1921–1922: A New Look' (1977) 46 *Pacific Historical Review* 603.

DES VOEUX, G. WILLIAM, *My Colonial Service* (London: John Murray, 1903).

WAKEMAN, JR., FREDERICK, *Strangers at the Gate: Social Disorder in China, 1839–1861* (Berkeley and Los Angeles: University of California Press, 1966).

WATSON, JAMES L., *Emigration and the Chinese Lineage* (Berkeley, Los Angeles, London: University of California Press, 1975).

—— 'Hereditary Tenancy and Corporate Landlordism in Traditional China: A Case Study' (1977) 11 *Modern Asian Studies* 161.

WEHRLE, EDMUND S., *Britain, China, and the Antimissionary Riots 1891–1900* (Minneapolis: University of Minnesota Press, 1966).

WESLEY-SMITH, PETER, 'The Kam Tin Gates' (1973) 13 *Journal of the Hong Kong Branch of the Royal Asiatic Society* 41.

—— 'The Walled City of Kowloon and its Law Today' in Topley, Marjorie (ed.), *Hong Kong: The Interaction of Traditions and Life in the Towns* (Hong Kong: Hong Kong Branch of the Royal Asiatic Society, 1975).

WESTLAKE, JOHN, *International Law*, 2nd ed. (Cambridge: Cambridge University Press, 1910–1913).

WILLIAMSON, JAMES A., *A Short History of British Expansion: The Modern Empire and Commonwealth*, 5th ed. (London: Macmillan, 1964).

WILLOUGHBY, WESTEL W., *China at the Conference: A Report* (Baltimore: Johns Hopkins Press, 1922).

—— *Foreign Rights and Interests in China* (Baltimore: Johns Hopkins Press, 1927).

WILSON, DICK, 'New Thoughts on the Future of Hong Kong' (1977) 8 *Pacific Community* 588.

WRIGHT, MARY C. (ed.), *China in Revolution: The First Phase, 1900–1913* (New Haven: Yale University Press, 1968).

WRIGHT, STANLEY F., *China's Struggle for Tariff Autonomy: 1843–1938* (Shanghai: Kelly and Walsh, 1938).

—— *Hart and the Chinese Customs* (Belfast: Wm. Mullan & Son, 1950).

YANG, LEON, *Les Territoires a Bail en Chine* (Paris: Presses Universitaires de France, 1929).

YOUNG, C. WALTER, *The International Status of Kwantung Leased Territory* (Baltimore: Johns Hopkins Press, 1931).

YOUNG, L. K., *British Policy in China, 1895–1902* (Oxford: Clarendon Press, 1970).

YOUNG, MARILYN BLATT, *The Rhetoric of Empire: American China Policy 1895–1901* (Cambridge, Mass.: Harvard University Press, 1968).

ZEN SUN E-TU, *Chinese Railways and British Interests 1898–1911* (New York: Columbia University Press, 1954).

INDEX

at Tai Po Hui, 59, 60; policy of Hong Kong government towards, 69

GAMBLING, 117, 130; in Kowloon City, 17; Sham Chun and, 74
Gap Rock, 12, 13, 17, 33, 40, 44, 79, 220; construction of lighthouse on, 20-1; original proposal to acquire, 21; excluded from lease of New Territories, 39; further proposals for acquisition of, 39, 72, 78
Garvey, T. W., 128
Gascoigne, W. J., 62, 77; sends troops to Tai Po Hui, 60; and occupation of Sham Chun, 74; and map of New Territories, 108
Gent, G. E. J., 5, 115
Germany: imperialist activity in China, 21-8; disturbed Far Eastern balance of power, 152
Giers, Nikolai K., 27
Gindrinker's Line, 118
Gollan, Henry, 101
Gompertz, H. H. J., 95, 224
Goodman, William Meigh, 94; and 'the shell case', 98; and nationality issue, 143
Goronwy-Roberts, Lord, 133-4
Graham, Frederick, 5
Great Northern Telegraph Company of Copenhagen, 139
Green Island, 12
Grey, Edward, 112

HAMILTON, W. A. BAILLIE, 5, 6, 54-5, 89
Han Su-yin, 6
Hanihara, M., 154
Harding, A. H., 5
Harris, A. H., 138
Hart, Robert, 50, 211; proposals re customs in New Territories, 48-9
Hay, John, 151
Hayes, James, 217
Heung Yee Kuk, 103, 173-4

Hillier, H. M.: proposals for implementation of customs pledge, 49, 50; and IMC property in New Territories, 80
Ho Kai, 84
Ho Lap-pun, 96
Ho Tung, Robert, 58, 84, 86, 87, 222
Hohfeld, Wesley Newcombe, 181
Hong Kong: campaign for expansion of, 11-17; vulnerability of, 11, 12-16, 21, 154; advantages of expansion of, 14; motives for expansion of, 16-17
Hong Kong blockade: see Customs blockade of Hong Kong
Hong Kong Extension Exemption Ordinance, 91
Hong Kong Regiment, 77, 78; attend hoisting of flag at Tai Po, 45; action at Tai Po Hui, 62; action against alleged murderers of Tang Cheung-hing, 70
Hong Kong Volunteers: see Volunteers
Hoppo, 19
Hsu Ying-kuei, 1
Huang Hua, 163, 186
Huey Fong, 121
Hundred days of reform, 1, 149

IMPERIAL MARITIME CUSTOMS: proposed exclusion from Hong Kong, 14; office in Hong Kong, 20, 138; lighting programme, 20; discussion of, during negotiation of convention, 38-9; removal of customs houses, 38, 59, 61, 75, 136, 138; proposals for cooperation by Britain in New Territories, 48-50; temporary retention of customs houses, 62; property in New Territories surrendered without payment, 80-1; survey of northern boundary, 108; and three-mile limit, 112; and waters of Tai O harbour, 113; and alleged purpose of enclosing waters in leasehold,